MACROMEDIA® DIRECTOR® MX

Creating Powerful Multimedia

Prentice
Hall

Upper Saddle River, NJ 07458

Library of Congress Cataloging-in-Publication Data

Macromedia Director MX: Creating Powerful
    Multimedia/Against The Clock
    p. cm. — (Against The Clock Series)
ISBN 0-13-113288-1
1. Director (Computer File). 2. Multimedia systems.
    I. Against The Clock (Firm). II. Series.

VP/Publisher: Natalie E. Anderson
Executive Editor: Steven Elliot
Assistant Editor: Allison Williams
Senior Project Manager: Kristine Lombardi Frankel
Marketing Manager: Steven Rutberg
Marketing Assistant: Danielle Torio
Associate Director of Production and Manufacturing:
    Vincent Scelta
Manager, Production: Gail Steier De Acevedo
Production Project Manager: Lynne Breitfeller
Composition: Against The Clock, Inc.
Design Director: Maria Lange
Design Coordinator: Christopher Kossa
Cover Design: LaFortezza Design Group, Inc.
Cover Icon Design: James Braun
Sidebar Icon Design: Bill Morse
Printer/Binder: Press of Ohio

The fonts utilized in these training materials are the property of Against The Clock, Inc., and are supplied to the legitimate buyers of the Against The Clock training materials solely for use with the exercises and projects provided in the body of the materials. They may not be used for any other purpose, and under no circumstances may they be transferred to another individual, nor copied or distributed by any means whatsoever.

Against The Clock and the Against The Clock logo are trademarks of Against The Clock, Inc., registered in the United States and elsewhere. References to and instructional materials provided for any particular application program, operating system, hardware platform, or other commercially available product or products do not represent an endorsement of such product or products by Against The Clock, Inc. or Prentice Hall, Inc.

Macromedia Director, Flash, Generator, FreeHand, Dreamweaver, and Fireworks and are registered trademarks of Macromedia, Inc. PageMaker, Photoshop, Acrobat, Adobe Type Manager, Illustrator, InDesign, Premiere, After Effects and PostScript are trademarks of Adobe Systems Incorporated. Macintosh is a trademark of Apple Computer, Inc. QuarkXPress is a registered trademark of Quark, Inc. CorelDRAW!, Painter, and WordPerfect are trademarks of Corel Corporation. FrontPage, Publisher, PowerPoint, Word, Excel, Office, Microsoft, MS-DOS, and Windows are either registered trademarks or trademarks of Microsoft Corporation.

Other product and company names mentioned herein may be the trademarks of their respective owners.

Pearson Education LTD.
Pearson Education Australia PTY, Limited
Pearson Education Singapore, Pte. Ltd
Pearson Education North Asia Ltd
Pearson Education Canada, Ltd
Pearson Educación de Mexico, S.A. de C.V.
Pearson Education – Japan
Pearson Education Malaysia, Pte. Ltd
Pearson Education, Upper Saddle River, New Jersey

10 9 8 7 6 5 4 3 2 1

Prentice Hall

ISBN 0-13-113288-1

CONTENTS

Purpose

The Against The Clock series was developed specifically for those involved in the field of computer arts, and now — animation, video, and multimedia production. Many of our readers are already involved in the industry in advertising and printing, television production, multimedia, and in the world of Web design. Others are just now preparing for a career in these professions.

This series provides you with the necessary skills to work in these fast-paced, exciting, and rapidly expanding fields. While many people feel they can simply purchase a computer and the appropriate software, and begin designing and producing high-quality presentations, the real world of high-quality printed and Web communications requires a far more serious commitment.

The Series

The applications presented in the Against The Clock series stand out as the programs of choice in professional computer arts environments.

We use a modular design for the Against The Clock series, allowing you to mix and match the drawing, imaging, and page-layout applications that exactly suit your specific needs.

Titles available in the Against The Clock series include:

Macintosh: Basic Operations
Windows: Basic Operations
Adobe Illustrator: Introduction and Advanced Digital Illustration
Macromedia FreeHand: Digital Illustration
Adobe InDesign: Introduction and Advanced Electronic Mechanicals
Adobe PageMaker: Creating Electronic Documents
QuarkXPress: Introduction and Advanced Electronic Documents
Microsoft Publisher: Creating Electronic Mechanicals
Microsoft PowerPoint: Presentation Graphics with Impact
Microsoft FrontPage: Creating and Designing Web Pages
HTML & XHTML: Creating Web Pages
Procreate Painter: A Digital Approach to Natural Art Media
Adobe Photoshop: Introduction and Advanced Digital Images
Adobe Premiere: Digital Video Editing
Adobe After Effects: Motion Graphics and Visual Effects
Macromedia Director: Creating Powerful Multimedia
Macromedia Flash: Animating for the Web
Macromedia Dreamweaver: Creating Web Pages
Preflight and File Preparation
TrapWise and PressWise: Digital Trapping and Imposition

You will see a number of icons in the sidebars; each has a standard meaning. Pay close attention to the sidebar notes where you will find valuable comments that will help you throughout this book and in the everyday use of your computer. The standard icons are:

The Hand-on-mouse icon indicates a hands-on activity — either a short exercise or a complete project. The complete projects are located at the back of the book, in sequence from Project A through E.

The Pencil icon indicates a comment from an experienced operator or trainer. Whenever you see this icon, you'll find corresponding sidebar text that augments the subject being discussed at the time.

The Key icon is used to identify keyboard equivalents to menu or dialog box options. Using a key command is often faster than selecting a menu option with the mouse. Experienced operators often mix the use of keyboard equivalents and menu/dialog box selections to arrive at their optimum speed of execution.

The Caution icon indicates a potential problem or difficulty. For instance, a certain technique might lead to pages that prove difficult to output. In other cases, there might be something that a program cannot easily accomplish, so we present a workaround.

If you are a Windows user, be sure to refer to the corresponding text or images whenever you see this Windows icon. Although there isn't a great deal of difference between using these applications on a Macintosh and using them on a Windows-based system, there are certain instances where there's enough of a difference for us to comment.

For the Reader

On the Resource CD-ROM, you will find a collection of font and data files. These files, necessary to complete both the exercises and projects, may be found in the **RF_Director** folder on the Resource CD-ROM.

For the Trainer

The Trainer's materials, available online, include various testing and presentation materials in addition to the files that are supplied with this book.

- **Overhead presentation materials** are provided and follow along with the book. These presentations are prepared using Microsoft PowerPoint, and are provided in both native PowerPoint format and Acrobat Portable Document Format (PDF).

- **Extra free-form projects** are provided and may be used to extend the training session, or they may be used to test the reader's progress.

- **Test questions and answers** are included. These questions may be modified and/or reorganized.

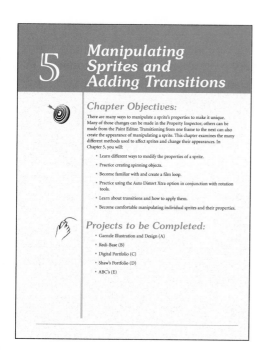

Chapter openers *provide the reader with specific objectives.*

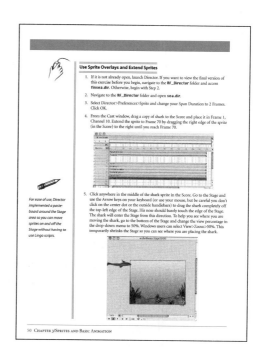

Sidebars and hands-on activities *supplement concepts presented throughout the book.*

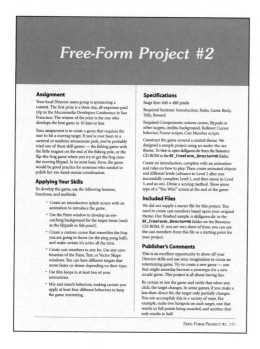

Free-form projects *allow readers to apply their new skills in real-world research and design projects.*

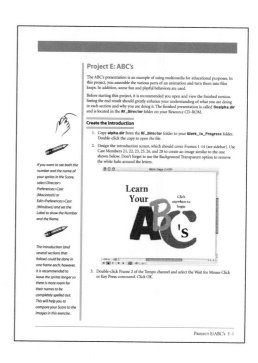

Step-by-step projects *result in finished artwork — with an emphasis on proper file-construction methods.*

In addition to explanatory text and illustrations, Against The Clock learning materials contain two primary building blocks: exercises and projects. Projects always result in a finished piece of work — digital imagery typically built from the ground up, utilizing photographic-quality images, vector artwork from illustration programs, and type elements from the library supplied on your Resource CD-ROM.

This book, *Macromedia Director: Creating Powerful Multimedia,* uses several step-by-step projects you will complete during your learning sessions. (There are also free-form project assignments immediately preceding the two reviews.) Images of the step-by-step projects you will complete while you read this book are displayed on the inside front and back covers. Here's are brief overviews of the projects:

Project A: Gaenzle Illustration and Design

Designed to provide a tour through a typical Director production, this project was specifically created to familiarize you with a working Director file. This particular production makes use of sound and various graphics and transitions. Even though you will not actually create this file, it is important to browse around and become familiar with the parts and pieces that were used to develop it.

Project B: Redi-Base

This project assumes the reader was hired by a client to create a presentation that could be used by sales representatives to market the Redi-Base product. Redi-Base will be featured and sampled at an upcoming food festival. While you create the production, you will work with keyframes and Director's timeline, and practice moving and extending sprites.

Project C: Digital Portfolio

One of the most important aspects of a designer's career path is the creation and compilation of a compelling portfolio of work. This portfolio kiosk, developed by Elizabeth Beecher, a student from Allentown Business School, displays some of her professional-quality artwork. In this project, you have the option to substitute your own work and develop a personal art portfolio.

Project D: Shaw's Portfolio

An interactive portfolio is the basis of this project. Although we provide images, video, and sound files, you can use you own components to complete the production. The specifications for the project call for various screens that display digital images of an artist's portfolio. The final production will have an introductory section and a main menu, followed by imagery that shows the artist's work.

Project E: ABC's

The ABC presentation is an example of using multimedia for educational purposes. This fanciful project is designed to provide practice assembling an interactive project with animations, and turning multiple sprites into film loops.

ACKNOWLEDGMENTS

I would like to thank the writers, illustrators, editors, and others who have worked long and hard to build the Against The Clock series. And special thanks to Dean Bagley, Production Manager, for his hard work and dedication to our team.

A big thank you to the dedicated teaching professionals whose comments and expertise contributed to the success of these products, including Matt Orsman of Wichita Area Technical College, and Kara Waxman of Against The Clock.

A special thanks to Michele Ebert of Allentown Business School for contributing the "Working with Lingo" chapter. And to Steve Skrzenski who created various projects and exercises throughout this book.

A big thanks to the Allentown Business School students including Elizabeth Beecher, Sally Behler, Nick Gathagan, Greg Gaenzle, and Chris Shaw for their project contributions.

Thanks to Laurel Cucchiara, copyeditor, and final link in the chain of production for her help in making sure we all said what we meant to say.

A big thanks to Kerry Reardon for her attention to detail.

— *Ellenn Behoriam, January 2003*

Our History

Against The Clock (ATC) was founded in 1990 as a part of Lanman Systems Group, one of the nation's leading systems integration and training firms. The company specialized in developing custom training materials for such clients as L.L. Bean, *The New England Journal of Medicine*, the Smithsonian, the National Education Association, *Air & Space Magazine*, Publishers Clearing House, the National Wildlife Society, Home Shopping Network, and many others. The integration firm was among the most highly respected in the graphic arts industry.

To a great degree, the success of Lanman Systems Group can be attributed to the thousands of pages of course materials developed at the company's demanding client sites. Throughout the rapid growth of Lanman Systems Group, founder and general manager Ellenn Behoriam developed the expertise necessary to manage technical experts, content providers, writers, editors, illustrators, designers, layout artists, proofreaders, and the rest of the chain of professionals required to develop structured and highly effective training materials.

Following the sale of the Lanman Companies to World Color, one of the nation's largest commercial printers, Ellenn embarked on a project to develop a new library of hands-on training materials engineered specifically for the professional graphic artist. A large part of this effort is finding and working with talented professional artists, authors, and educators from around the country.

The result is the ATC training library.

About the Author

Tara Gray attended Rochester Institute of Technology in the early 1990's where she received her B.F.A. in graphic design with a concentration in psychology. Later, she received an M.S. in electronic publishing with a concentration in interactive media design. After leaving Rochester Institute, Tara began her professional career working for two of the finest color printers in the country, World Color Press (Northeast Graphics) and Webcraft Technologies.

In addition to teaching in the Visual Communications Associate degree program at Allentown Business School, Tara also does freelance design work and authors books such as this title from ATC. Tara moonlights as a subject specialist evaluator for the Accreditation Council for Independent Colleges and Schools and the PA Department of Education evaluating multimedia, computer animation, video, and Web programs.

Getting Started

Platform

The Against The Clock (ATC) series is designed for both the Macintosh and Windows platforms. On the Macintosh, Director MX requires Mac OS X 10.1 or higher; on the Windows platform, it requires Windows 98 SE, Windows 2000, or Windows XP.

Prerequisites

This book is based on the assumption that you have a basic understanding of how to use your computer. This includes standard dialog boxes with OK and Cancel buttons. In most of the exercises, it is assumed you will click the OK button to change the values of a dialog box according to the instructions provided.

You should know how to use your mouse to point and click, as well as to drag items around the screen. You should be able to resize and arrange windows on your desktop to maximize your available workspace. You should know how to access pop-up menus, and understand how check boxes and radio buttons work. Lastly, you should know how to create, open, and save files. It is also helpful to have a firm understanding of how your operating system organizes files and folders, and how to navigate your way around them.

The CD-ROM and Initial Setup Considerations

Before you begin to use your Against The Clock book, you must set up your system so you have access to the various files and tools to complete your lessons.

Resource Files

This book comes complete with a collection of resource files, which are an integral part of the learning experience. They are used throughout the book to help you construct increasingly complex elements. These building blocks should be available for practice and study sessions to allow you to experience and complete the exercises and project assignments smoothly, spending a minimum amount of time looking for the various required components.

All the files you need to complete the exercises and projects in this book are located on your Resource CD-ROM, and contained in a folder named **RF_Director**. It's best to copy the entire folder onto your hard drive – if you have 450 megabytes or more of available space. If not, you can work directly from the Resource CD-ROM.

Work In Progress Folder

Before you begin to work on the exercises or projects in this book, you should create a folder called **Work_In_Progress**, either on your hard drive or on a removable disk. As you work through the steps in the exercises, you will be directed to save your work in this folder.

If your time is limited, you can stop at a logical point in an exercise or project, save the file, and later return to the point at which you stopped. In some cases, the exercises in this book build upon work you already completed; you will need to open a file from your **Work_In_Progress** folder and continue to work on the same file.

Locating Files

Files that you need to open are indicated by a different typeface (for example, "Open the file named **clouds.dir**"). The location of the file also appears in the special typeface (for example, "Open **chairs.dir** from your **Work_In_Progress** folder").

When you are directed to save a file with a specific name, the name appears in quotation marks (for example, "Save the file as "animation_practice.dir" to your **Work_In_Progress** folder").

In most cases, resource files are located in the **RF_Director** folder, while exercises and projects on which you continue to work are located in your **Work_In_Progress** folder. We repeat these directions frequently in the early chapters, and add reminders in sidebars in the later chapters. If a file is in a location other than these two folders, the path is indicated in the exercise or project (for example, "Open the file from the **Movies** folder, found inside your **RF_Director** folder").

File Naming Conventions

Files on the Resource CD-ROM are named according to the Against The Clock naming conventions to facilitate cross-platform compatibility. Words are separated by an underscore, and all file names include a lowercase three-letter extension you see as part of the file name.

When your Windows system is first configured, the views are normally set to a default that hides these extensions. This means you might have a dozen different files named "myfile," all of which could have been generated by different applications. This can become very confusing.

On a Windows-based system, you can change this view. Double-click My Computer (the icon on your desktop). From the View menu, select Folder Options. From Folder Options, select the View tab. Within the Files and Folders folder is a check box for Hide File Extensions for Known File Types. When this is unchecked, you can see the file extensions.

It's easier to know what you're looking at if file extensions are visible. While this is a personal choice, we strongly recommend viewing the file extensions. The native Director extension is .dir.

Fonts

You must install the ATC fonts from the Resource CD-ROM to ensure your exercises and projects work as described in the book. These fonts are provided on the Resource CD-ROM in the ATC Fonts folder. Specific instructions for installing fonts are provided in the documentation that came with your computer.

We strongly recommend you install a font-management utility program on your computer. Installing fonts at the system level can be cumbersome, and can significantly affect your computer's performance if you install too many fonts.

If you choose not to install the fonts, you will receive a warning message when you attempt to open a document containing the ATC typefaces.

Key Commands

There are three keys that are generally used as modifier keys — they don't do anything by themselves when pressed, but they either perform some action or type a special character when pressed with another key or keys.

We frequently note keyboard shortcuts that can be used in Director. A slash character indicates the key commands differ for Macintosh and Windows systems; the Macintosh commands are listed first, followed by the Windows commands. If you see the command "Command/Control-P", for example, Macintosh users would press the Command key and Windows users would press the Control key; both would then press the "P" key.

The Command/Control key is used with another key to perform a specific function. When combined with the "S" key, it saves your work. When combined with the "O" key, it opens a file; with the "P" key, it prints the file. In addition to these functions, which work with most Macintosh and Windows programs, the Command/Control key can be combined with other keys to control specific Director functions. At times, it is also used in combination with the Shift and/or Option/Alt keys.

The Option/Alt key, another modifier key, is often used in conjunction with other keys to access special typographic characters. On a Windows system, the Alt key is used with the number keys on the numeric keypad. For example, Alt-0149 produces a bullet (•) character. The Alt key can be confusing because not only do you use it to type special characters, you can also use it to control program and operating system functions. Pressing Alt-F4, for example, closes programs or windows, depending on which is active. On a Macintosh computer, the Option key is often used with a letter key to type a special character.

The Shift key is the third modifier key. While you're familiar with using this key to type uppercase letters and the symbols on the tops of the number keys, it's also used with Command/Control and Option/Alt in a number of contexts.

System Requirements for Director MX

Macintosh:

- PowerPC® processor (G3, G4, or G4 dual)
- Mac OS X version 10.1 or higher (10.2 recommended)
- 128 MB of RAM (192 MB recommended)
- 280 MB of available hard disk space
- Color monitor capable of 1024 × 768-pixel resolution, 16-bit color display
- CD-ROM drive

Windows:

- Intel® Pentium® III processor or higher; fully compliant alternative processor
- Windows 98 Second Edition, Windows 2000, Windows XP
- 128 MB of RAM (192 MB recommended)
- 280 MB of available hard disk space
- Color monitor capable of 1024 × 768-pixel resolution, 16-bit color display
- CD-ROM drive

Introduction

Macromedia Director has long been a powerhouse in the world of multimedia. Director was initially created in the 1980's as a two-dimensional animation program. It has evolved into an almost universal editor and layout tool for media of all types. With Director, you can turn text, images, sounds, digital videos, 3-D objects, 2-D and 3-D animations into complex multimedia experiences.

Director is commonly used to create educational CD-ROMs, games, instructional presentations, interactive encyclopedias, the interactive portions of DVDs and enhanced CDs, corporate presentations, and informational kiosks such as those found in your local music and book stores. It is a powerful program that places no limits on your creative vision.

For those of you who have used earlier versions of Director, you will be excited to see the new features of the product. Director MX sports an entirely new interface for the Macintosh, as it is now OS X-native. (The Windows version of the product is very similar to previous versions.) MX includes a limited version of the Control panel along the bottom edge of the Stage window to allow easy access to those options. Enhanced Flash integration is available for those who want to create pieces of their projects in Flash. New Lingo capabilities that allow Director to control 3D objects have been added.

One advantage that Director has over most competitive offerings is Lingo — a powerful built-in scripting language. With Lingo, you can write scripts for customized and advanced tasks that aren't available from the standard Director interface. The language is quite robust, and as a result, it can be a little intimidating; but you'll find that with a few simple commands, you can accomplish some very impressive results. Through many of the exercises provided in this book, you'll learn how to use Lingo to make your materials more intuitive and interesting.

Learning how to use Director can help you on your way to becoming a talented multi-media artist, but it is by no means the only skill you need to master. There are many other aspects of designing and developing a compelling multimedia project — creativity and imagination being two of the most important.

Like all design work, multimedia projects should be carefully planned before you code a single line of script or apply a single effect to an object. It is far easier to create a project according to plan than it is to take it apart, try to fix it, and figure out a way to put it back together again. A multimedia project consists of various elements that are all tied together — remove one of them and the rest (typically) do not work correctly. With a complex project, sometimes finding the problem is as difficult — or more so — than fixing it.

Many successful multimedia designers follow a basic list of tasks when approaching a new project or a major update to one that already exists. Here's a sample:

- Meet with the client to define the project's goals and target audience.
- Create thumbnail sketches and storyboards.
- Refine sketches and create a flowchart diagram of how a user will navigate through the project.
- Create detailed layouts, screen by screen, explaining exactly what will be on each screen and where the items will be placed.
- Create a prototype of the project.
- Present the prototype to the client for last-minute changes and additions.
- Create the final project.

When you follow these guidelines and stay in very close contact with your client, there is a good chance you can avoid costly mistakes that could prove impossible to repair.

Throughout the process, the basic elements of design must be applied. Good design sense can easily fall by the wayside when you get excited about Director and decide to include every possible video, sound, and special effect in a single project. Lack of grace, faulty alignment, and poor balance are clear indicators of a project prepared by a novice. Elegance, clarity, and proper use of color and balance are the hallmarks of experienced multimedia designers. As you read this book, we hope you learn how to apply these professional touches to your projects.

1 Getting Acquainted with Director

Chapter Objectives:

Macromedia Director MX has a unique, robust interface. In order to use Director to create meaningful presentations and animations, it is important for new users to become completely familiar with the interface. The first chapter of this book examines the main group of palettes and windows you use to create a multimedia presentation in Director. In Chapter 1, you will:

- Discover how to navigate through the Director interface.

- Become familiar with and use the Stage, Score, Cast, Playback Head, Control panel, Control bar and Property Inspector.

- Explore the differences between linking and embedding files.

- Learn to import and add cast members.

- Gain an understanding of some of Director's unique terminology.

- Launch the program and work through a full-length, hands-on project.

Projects to be Completed:

- Gaenzle Illustration and Design (A)

- Redi-Base (B)

- Digital Portfolio (C)

- Shaw's Portfolio (D)

- ABC's (E)

Getting Acquainted with Director

Director's interface may initially seem intimidating to new users because of its numerous palettes, windows, and dialog boxes. The logical setup of these components, however, makes it easy to remember where they are and how to access them. A theater metaphor is used for the names and actions of Director's most common palettes. For example, the blank area shown in the graphic below is called the *Stage*. The Stage is where your creations unfold. You can also control your movie (stop, play, rewind, fast-forward) from the Control bar along the bottom of the Stage.

The *Cast* is used to assemble your characters for display on the Stage. The Cast can contain video, images, text, sounds, and props. The Cast is similar to the backstage area of a theater — the place where the actors wait until they are needed.

Next is the *Score*. Here, you tell your cast members where to go, how to behave, and when to perform. It essentially contains the directions and cues for your actors.

Last, but certainly not least, is the *Property Inspector*. You can use it to change the properties, or attributes, of any aspect of your presentation, regardless of what type of media it is.

You cannot close a Director movie file without closing the Director program. The only exception to this rule is to select File>Open to open a new movie or another movie. This allows the current movie to close and the other movie to take its place.

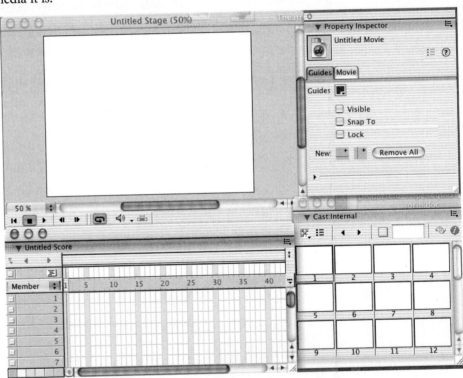

The Director interface. Clockwise from the top left are the Stage, Property Inspector, Cast, and Score.

The Stage

The blank expanse in the middle of your monitor is the Stage. As previously stated, your creations unfold here. When the curtain goes up, or you click the Play button, this is where the objects appear and interact.

Different Stage sizes are available for your movie. The general suggestions and information listed below will help you make decisions regarding Stage size.

You can select Window>Stage or press Command/Control-1 to access the Stage, but it is usually open as long as Director is running. The Stage size usually defaults to 320×240 pixels. This size is acceptable if you are going to create an interactive presentation for the Internet; however, it is a bit small for creating traditional multimedia. For such projects, it is recommended that you work at a minimum size of 640×480 pixels, which simulates the size of a 14-in. monitor. Until you have experience working in Director, this is also the maximum Stage size you should use. Anything larger could cause technical difficulties.

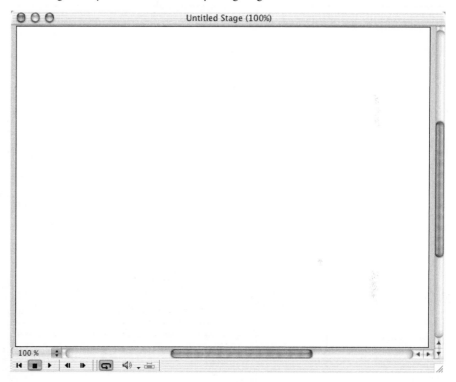

The Stage.

You can adjust the Stage size at any time by clicking on the Stage to make it active, and choosing a size from the Property Inspector (Window>Property Inspector). There are a few issues to consider when deciding to choose a Stage size larger than 640×480 pixels:

- Who is your audience?
- Will viewers use anything larger than 14-in. monitors?
- Will viewers use machines powerful enough to run the software?
- Will complex video, sound, and graphics displayed at larger sizes slow down your project?
- Do you know how to streamline your project if it slows to a crawl?

You don't have to rely on the items available in Director's interface to create your projects. Director also contains a powerful scripting language called Lingo. Lingo allows you to control Director in ways the interface doesn't allow. You will learn more about Lingo later in this book.

Once these questions are answered, you can safely increase the Stage size. For now, let's concentrate on Director's default settings.

The Stage can be moved around your monitor by dragging its Title bar. Moving the Stage may be necessary when you need to fit many of Director's palettes on the screen at one time.

You can add a color, or change the color and/or size of the Stage using the Property Inspector. Once you change the Stage color, the Stage remains that color for the entire movie unless you utilize Director's scripting language, called Lingo (in which case, you could change the Stage color of each frame). If you want more than one color, you have the option of creating various colored backgrounds in the Paint Editor. (We discuss the Paint Editor in Chapter 2.)

Property Inspector

In the Property Inspector, which can be accessed by pressing Command-Option-S (Macintosh) or Control-Alt-S (Windows), you find the customizable attributes for all of your cast members, sprites (discussed in Chapter 3), and the movie itself. You can click the appropriate tab at the top of the Property Inspector window to access these attributes.

The Property Inspector can be viewed in two different modes: the Graphic view (the one we will refer to throughout the book) and List view, which you can access by clicking on the icon to the left of the question mark at the top-right of the Property Inspector.

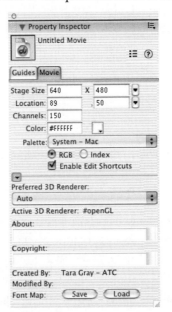 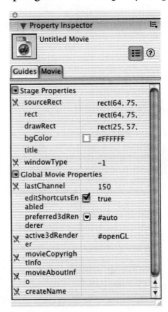

The Property Inspector shown in Graphic view (left) and List view (right).

The Movie and Guides tabs are always present because they relate to the movie itself. The other tabs display as needed. For instance, if you have a QuickTime video highlighted, the QuickTime tab appears in the Property Inspector. If the tab you are looking for is not displayed in the Property Inspector, you probably don't have the correct cast member or sprite highlighted to display that particular tab.

Getting Started

1. Double-click the Director icon to launch Director. The empty white box that appears in the center of your monitor is the Stage. If it does not automatically appear, you can access it from the Window menu. You can also use the keyboard shortcut, Command/Control-1 (the number 1).

2. Click on the Stage to make it active. Make certain the Property Inspector is open. If it is not, select Window>Property Inspector to open it.

3. At the top of the Property Inspector, click the Movie tab. Make certain your screen size is set to 640 × 480 pixels. If it is not, change the setting to 640 × 480.

4. Click the Color pop-up palette to the right of the Color hexadecimal field. In the Color palette that appears, select the color of your choice. Notice that the Stage color changes.

5. Select Director>Quit Director (Macintosh) or File>Exit (Windows) to close the movie and Director. Do not save your changes.

The Cast

You place actors and graphics on the Cast, as well as place, view, and store all of your backgrounds, sounds, videos, behaviors, scripts, images, and text. It can be displayed in List view or Thumbnail view. Many users prefer Thumbnail view because you can actually see the graphics, a feature not included in List view. Those who often use lists and do not need to view their graphics during development will probably prefer the List view. You can toggle between both views by clicking the second button from the left on the Cast window.

The second button from the left toggles between the Thumbnail and List views.

Each item occupies its own line in the list, or its own thumbnail slot, and is identified as a cast member. Additionally, you can easily assign names to cast members to better identify them. Naming your cast members is recommended, since it becomes difficult to stay organized when your projects become more intricate. To name a cast member, highlight it in the Cast, click the cursor in the Text window at the top, enter the name, and press Return/Enter to apply the new information.

The Cast window can be accessed from the Window menu. You can drag the bottom-right corner of the Cast window to adjust the Cast's width and height, making it flexible for monitors of all sizes. You can also collapse the window into a Title bar to increase your workspace. To do this, click the arrowhead in the top-left corner of the window.

In the thumbnail Cast, each type of cast member, such as text or video, appears with a small icon depicting its file type in the bottom-right corner of each thumbnail. In the list Cast, the icon itself is the first item you see on each line. For example, a cast member with a Paintbrush icon is a graphic and can be edited in Director's Paint Editor, whereas a cast member with an "A" icon is editable text and can be edited in Director's Text Editor.

A single cast member can, and frequently is, repeatedly used in a movie. The actual cast member located in the Cast slot/list is the source for the multiple versions you create. If you alter the original cast member in the Cast, it alters all the versions of the cast member you created throughout the movie.

The following images show the Cast in Thumbnail and List views, respectively. When the Cast is in List view, you can click the column headings to sort the cast members by name, number, script type, file type, or date modified. In the image below, the cast members are sorted by number – the number assigned to the cast member when it was imported or created.

Cast in Thumbnail view.

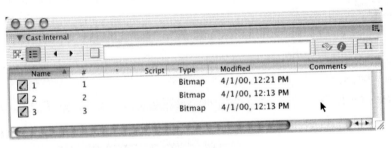

Cast in List view

Either type of Cast can be sorted by highlighting all cast members, selecting Modify>Sort, and then choosing a method to sort your Cast.

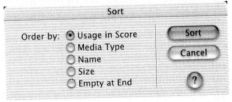

The Sort palette.

To provide a better understanding of your goal for this series of exercises, view the finished product before starting Step 1 below. To view the finished product, navigate to the **RF_Director** folder and open **finchap1.dir**. When you are ready, begin with Step 1.

Manipulate the Cast

1. Double-click the Director icon to launch the application.

2. Open **chap1.dir** in the **RF_Director** folder.

3. If it is not already open, select Cast from the Window menu to access the Cast.

4. Drag the lower-right corner of the window to resize the Cast window to the size you prefer. For this exercise, make sure the Cast is in Thumbnail view.

5. Click the picture of Cast Member 1 to highlight it.

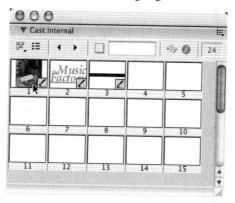

6. At the top of the Cast window, click inside the text field in the top center. There should be a 1 in the box. Type "Gift Image" (without quotation marks) and then press the Return/Enter key on your keyboard. The cast member's name is changed to Gift Image.

7. Rename Cast Member 2 to "Logo Text", and Cast Member 3 to "Address Text".

8. Select File>Save As. Change the name of the document to "practice.dir", and save it in your **Work_In_Progress** folder.

9. Keep this movie open for the next exercise.

If you need help setting up the Work_In_Progress folder, please refer to the Getting Started section of this book.

Cast Window Buttons

You can use the arrow buttons to the left of the Cast name field to navigate forward or backward through your Internal Cast window. The blue circle with the "i" is the Cast Member Properties button, and the shortcut to the Property Inspector. When you click the button, information on the currently selected cast member is displayed. The button to the left of the Cast Member Properties button is the Cast Member Script button, which we discuss later in the book.

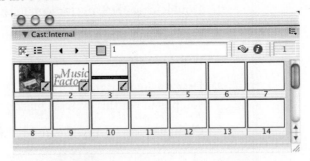

*The Cast Member Script and Cast Member Properties buttons
are to the right of the Cast name field.*

Use the Cast Window Buttons

1. Continue working in the open practice.dir from the previous exercise. Click the Gift Image cast member to select it.

2. Click the right arrow button (Next Cast Member button) at the top of the Cast window twice, and then click the left arrow button (Previous Cast Member button) twice to return to the first cast member (Gift Image). As you can see, you can use these arrow buttons to navigate through the Cast.

3. Click the Cast Member Properties button (looks like an exclamation point) at the top of the Cast window. Gift Image is a bitmap graphic, so the Property Inspector displays the bitmap properties of the cast member.

You can edit a Lingo script from the Script window. Each cast member can be scripted to perform various actions.

The keyboard shortcut to import cast members is Command/Control-R.

The Import dialog box for the Windows version looks a little different than the illustration shown. It doesn't have an Options button; however it does include Move Up and Move Down buttons, which are quite helpful during development.

4. Let's see what a Script window looks like. Click the Cast Member Script button (to the left of the Cast Member Properties button) at the top of the Cast:Internal window. The Script window appears.

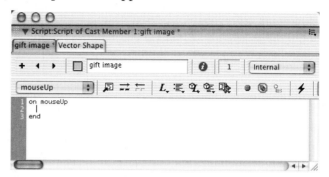

5. Click the red dot in the top-left corner of the Title bar (Macintosh), or click the "X" in the upper-right corner (Windows) to close the script window.

6. Save your changes and keep this file open for the next exercise.

Imported Cast Members

You can import cast members that were created in an external application into your multimedia project. Even though Director includes Paint and Vector Graphics windows that are suitable for creating basic graphics, Adobe Photoshop is currently the raster-based graphics creation program of choice for most designers.

There are currently three ways to import cast members:

- **Drag-and-Drop** (Macintosh only). You can click on a file, drag it from its current location on your hard drive, and drop it in the next open thumbnail slot or at the bottom of the list in your Cast.

- **File>Import**. You can select File>Import to display the Import Files window. Here, you can browse and select the files you need, click Add, and then click Import.

- **Lingo Scripts**. You can write custom Lingo scripts to import new cast members.

Director supports most common file formats currently used to save animations, images, sounds, videos, color palettes, Web images, and text files. For a current list of accepted file types, refer to the end of this chapter.

If you had not highlighted a specific empty slot in the Cast before importing the new file, the file would have been placed into the next available slot, rather than this specific slot. Director automatically assigned a name to the cast member. If the Cast had been in List view, you would not have been able to specify where the new file would go before you imported it. You would have had to rearrange your cast members afterward.

For now, we will use the File>Import method.

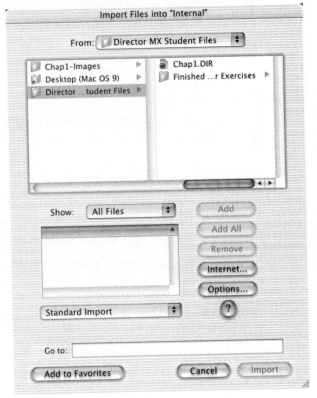

The Import dialog box.

Import Cast Members

1. With practice.dir still open, click Cast Slot 6 (your Cast should be in the Thumbnail view for this exercise). Select File>Import to display the Import Files window.

2. Select **violin.pct** from the **RF_Director** folder. Click the Add button to move the file into the bottom box.

3. Ensure the drop-down menu at the bottom displays Standard Import. Click the Import button. You might see a dialog box requesting information about color bit depth. You can use either 32- or 24-bit; however, 16-bit (if available) will, in most cases, produce smaller files without a noticeable loss of image quality.

4. The new file (named violin) is now in the cast member Slot 6.

5. Save your changes and keep this file open for the next exercise.

If you want to experiment with linking various files, change the drop-down menu in the Import Files window from Standard Import to Link to External File before importing. Make sure you set the option back to Standard Import when you are done.

Director automatically links files that are too large to embed; this keeps your movie at a manage-able size. Director typically links all video files and some larger sound files. Be sure to keep an eye on your Cast so you know which files are linked — it is easy to accidentally throw away linked files.

Cast members can be easily deleted if you happen to import one by mistake. To do so, simply highlight the cast member and press the Delete key.

Linked vs. Embedded Cast Members

In the previous exercise, you successfully imported and embedded a cast member. When you embed a file, you permanently paste an exact copy of the original file into Director. You don't need to keep the original file with the Director file.

You can also create a linked cast member. The original file of a linked cast member resides outside your Director project and is merely linked to the project. You must save all linked files in the same folder as your movie; if not, your movie will not work correctly. In the image below, notice the Paintbrush icon on the Clarinet cast member has a dog-eared top-right corner, indicating the file is linked, rather than embedded.

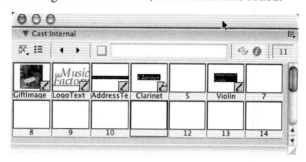

Clarinet is linked as per the dog-eared icon; the others are embedded.

You can manually link files rather than embed them. Expert developers pick and choose what they want to embed and what they want to link. For our purposes, you can embed everything except digital video files, which Director automatically links.

Manually Link a File

1. With practice.dir still open, select the Violin cast member if it is not already highlighted.

2. Select File>Import and import **clarinet.pct** as a linked file. To do this, change the Standard Import option to Link to External File in the Import dialog box. Click Add and then click Import. Director automatically places the file in cast member Slot 7.

3. Notice that you linked a small graphic icon that normally would not have been linked. Also note that it was put into cast member Slot 7. This is because the Violin graphic in Slot 6 was the last item you highlighted in your Cast, and the next open slot was Slot 7.

4. Highlight Slot 4 and then import the following images (be sure to reset the Import option to Standard Import): **fiddle.pct**, **flute.pct**, **guitar.pct**, and **oboe.pct**. If you correctly highlighted Slot 4 before importing, the images should have filled up Slots 4, 5, 8, and 9. If you incorrectly loaded them, press Command/Control-Z to undo this last step, and try it again.

5. Save your changes and keep this document open for the next exercise.

Creating Cast Members in Director

You can create a variety of cast members with Director. In the Window menu, you will find palettes and windows that provide the necessary tools to create paint graphics, vector graphics, and text.

Macintosh users can select Insert>Media Elements>Sound to access the Sound palette, which is capable of recording sound from an internal or external device, such as a CD player. This method of capturing sound requires less memory than most other methods.

With the exception of video and sound (for the Windows platform), you can produce a complete multimedia production in Director. In Chapter 2, you will learn how to utilize the Paint and Text Editors to create cast members with Director.

The Score

It might be helpful to think of the Score in musical terms. Your Cast holds all of your notes (cast members). The Score is where you combine the notes to form music. Until you compose your multimedia production, it is nothing more than a group of cast members waiting to be used, similar to notes waiting to be turned into music.

Director doesn't support internally capturing sound on the Windows platform.

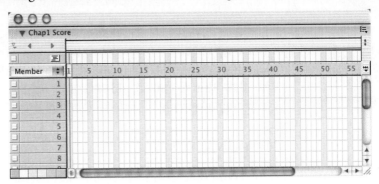

The Score.

Open the Score

1. Continue working in practice.dir. Select Score from the Window menu to access the Score window. If necessary, reposition the Cast and Score windows until they both fit on your screen.

2. Drag the bottom-right corner of the Score window until you are comfortable with the size of your working environment. It is advisable to keep your Score window relatively small and use the scroll bars along the bottom and right sides to navigate.

3. Select Save from the File menu to save your changes. Keep the file open for the next exercise.

Frames

There are several numbers across the top of the Score. These are called *frames*. Each column of cells is a frame. A movie starts at Frame 1 and continues across the frames until it is finished. A movie could consist of 50 or 5,000 frames, depending on the content.

You can add frames at any time by selecting Insert>Frames and indicating how many additional frames you need. Director inserts new frames immediately after the current frame. For example, if you are on Frame 1 and insert 10 new frames, they will be inserted between Frames 1 and 2. If you are on Frame 30, new frames will be inserted between Frames 30 and 31.

You can remove frames, but only one frame at a time. To do so, you can select Insert>Remove Frame to delete the currently active frame.

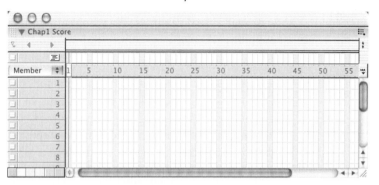

Frames are the numbers going across the top from left to right.

Place a Cast Member in the Score

1. Continue working in practice.dir. Drag the Gift Image cast member to the Stage. This graphic serves as the background for our movie. Notice the new object that is now displayed in the Score. If it doesn't start at Frame 1, drag it back to Frame 1. On the Stage, drag the image to the top-right corner so the top and right edges of the image are touching the top and right edges of the Stage.

*Once a cast member is placed in the Score, it is called a **sprite**. We'll discuss sprites in greater detail in Chapter 3.*

You can make a sprite occupy any number of frames by dragging it from either end.

2. The movie will be 50 frames long, so take the right side of the sprite (this is the correct term for a cast member you put into the Score) in the Score and drag (or Option/Alt-drag if the sprite only covers one frame) the sprite out to Frame 50. The sprite should now span Frames 1-50.

3. Save your changes and keep the document open for the next exercise.

Channels

The rows of the Score are called *channels*. They hold cast members. The numbered rows are called Visual channels. They hold anything that might show up on the Stage, including video, text, graphics, and images.

When you open a new movie, Director defaults to 150 available channels, but there are up to 1,000 available channels for any Director movie (except for educational versions of Director, which tend to limit your number of channels). To make more channels available, click the Movie tab in the Property Inspector and adjust the box labeled "150" to whatever number you need. Due to memory constraints, Macromedia recommends that you keep the number of channels to a minimum.

You can click the small square to the left of each channel number to turn off any channel you don't want to see. This is similar to turning on/off layers in Photoshop.

Channels in Director resemble layers in Photoshop in terms of the stacking order of your items. The only difference is that they are reversed in Director – the items nearest the top of the Score are the farthest back on the Stage. Your background should go in Channel 1 and subsequent items are placed in the next available channels as needed. The higher the number, the closer the item is to the top (front) of the Stage.

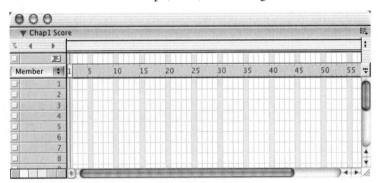

Channels are the numbers shown on the left side of the Score.

Place Cast Members in Different Channels

1. Continue working in practice.dir.

2. Drag the Logo Text cast member to Frame 1, Channel 2 (directly under the first sprite). When you drag cast members straight to the Score, they are placed in the exact center of the Stage. Place the logo text in the black area in the top-left corner of the Stage. Center it between the left edge of the Stage and the left edge of Gift Image.

   At this point, you see red text with a white background.

3. Highlight the Logo Text sprite in the Score by clicking in the middle of it — don't click the first or last frame. While the sprite is still highlighted, select Ink>Copy in the Property Inspector, and pull down the Ink Effects menu. Select Background Transparent. The white background disappears.

4. Extend the Logo Text sprite so it covers Frames 1-50 in Channel 2. (If you have difficulty, refer to Step 2 of the previous exercise). This ensures the logo text stays on the Stage throughout the entire 50 frames of the movie.

5. Save your changes and keep the movie open for the next exercise.

Playback Head

As you look at the Score, you notice a red rectangle with a vertical red line extending from the top and bottom. This is called the *Playback Head*. Notice the red rectangle is on top of a particular frame. Wherever the Playback Head is located, that particular frame is displayed on the Stage. Anything under that red line, from the top of the Score to the bottom, is visible.

You can drag the Playback Head right and left to see the progression of your movie, or you can drag it to a particular frame.

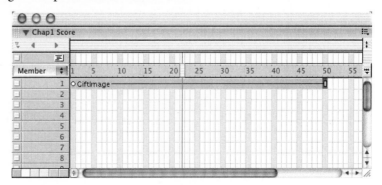

The Playback Head is the vertical red line that runs down through Frame 22.

Add Sprites to the Score

1. Continue working in practice.dir. Drag the Playback Head to Frame 1 if it is not already there.

2. Drag address text from the Cast to the Stage (do not drag it to the Score). Center address text in the black area across the bottom of the Stage. Notice that when you drag something directly to the Stage, you can place it anywhere you prefer. It is not automatically centered.

3. Your new sprite should be in Frame 1, Channel 3 of your Score. If it is not, drag it to the correct location. Extend this sprite to cover Frames 1-50.

4. Drag the Playback Head to Frame 4 or click Frame 4 and your Playback Head jumps to that location. This is where you want your next sprite to start when you drag it to the Stage.

5. Drag Violin to the Stage and place it under the line in the Music Factory logo. Make certain it is in Channel 4 in the Score and extends from Frame 4 to Frame 50.

6. Drag your Playback Head to Frame 10, and then drag a copy of Fiddle to the Stage. Place it, left aligned, under the word Violin. Make certain it is in Channel 5 and extends from Frame 10 to Frame 50.

7. Drag the Playback Head to Frame 16 or click Frame 16, Channel 6. This is where you want your next sprite to start when you drag it to the Stage.

8. Drag a copy of Guitar to the Stage and place it, left aligned, under the word Fiddle. Make certain it is in Channel 6 and extends from Frame 16 to Frame 50.

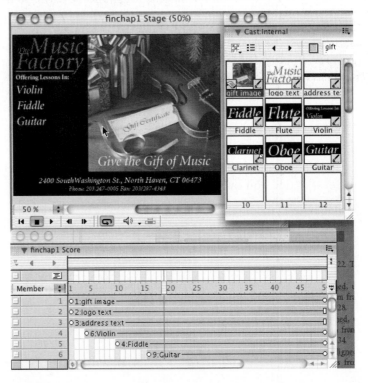

9. Drag the Playback Head to Frame 22 or click Frame 22. This is where you want your next sprite to start.

10. Drag a copy of Flute to the Stage and place it, left aligned, under the word Guitar. Make certain it is in Channel 7 and extends from Frame 22 to Frame 50.

11. Drag the Playback Head to Frame 28 or click on Frame 28.

12. Drag a copy of Oboe to the Stage and place it, left aligned, under the word Flute. Make certain it is in Channel 8 and extends from Frame 28 to Frame 50.

13. Drag the Playback Head to Frame 34 or click Frame 34.

14. Drag a copy of Clarinet to the Stage and place it, left aligned, under the word Oboe. Make certain it is in Channel 9 and extends from Frame 34 to Frame 50.

Feel free to go back to any of the sprites and readjust the spacing between them to make them all fit. Be careful to highlight the whole sprite in the Score before moving the sprite on the Stage; if you do not, it creates unwanted motion/animation. If this happens, delete the sprite and repeat the step.

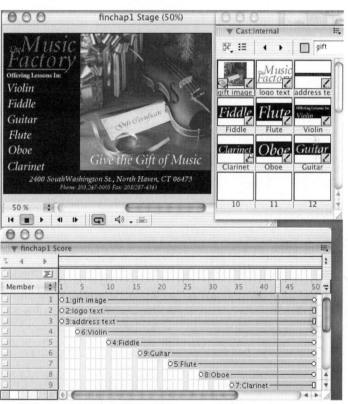

15. Save your changes and keep this file open for the next exercise.

Special Channels

There are various special channels that contain objects that are not graphic in nature. These might include sound files, color palettes, frame scripts, transitions, and Tempo changes. These channels are not numbered; rather, icons denote them. You will learn about these special channels one at a time as we use them in upcoming chapters. If these channels are hidden, you can click the button with the double arrow, located on the right edge of the Score directly above the frames, to view them.

Remember where the Special Channels Hide/Show button is located on the Score. Many new users forget where this button is located.

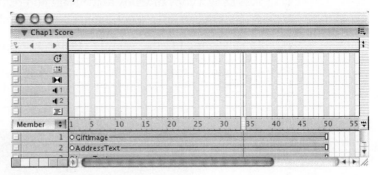

The special channels section includes anything above the frame numbers.

Control Panel

The Control panel is a small window that contains the buttons for controlling your movie, including Play, Stop and Rewind. The Control panel resembles the front of a VCR. You can access the Control panel from the Window menu.

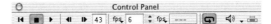

From left to right, the first three buttons are Rewind, Stop, and Play. Their functions are self-explanatory.

The next two buttons are Step-Forward and Step-Backward. These buttons allow you to step through the movie one frame at a time.

The box with the "43" in it displays the current frame number. In other words, the movie (Playback Head) was on Frame 43 when the image was captured.

The box with the "6" in it refers to the preferred frame rate of your movie. This is the speed at which your movie will run. It is currently set to 6 frames per second (fps). Director defaults to 15 fps, which is a good speed to show animation. Thirty fps is often used when video is incorporated in a Director project because video is typically shot at 29.9 frames per second. A setting of 30 fps allows video to sync up well with the frame rate of the Director movie. You can also change the value to Seconds Per Frame by selecting this option from the fps drop-down menu located to the left of the box.

The box with the three dashes in it shows the actual frame rate of the movie. As you play your Director movies, watch this box to see the speed at which the movie is running. The drop-down menu for this numeric box has four options: Frames Per Second, Seconds Per Frame, Running Total, and Estimated Total. If you choose either of the latter two options and play your movie, the numeric box will display the length of your presentation in seconds. This can be quite useful if your presentation must be a certain length. It cannot, however, account for different users if your movie is an interactive presentation — each person would undoubtedly spend a different amount of time in each area.

The button to the right of the actual frame rate box is the Loop button. This toggle button is set to loop in the previous image. This loop button causes your movie to continually repeat. Using this particular loop button does not permanently affect your movie; it is only temporary. If you want your movie to continually loop after it is turned into a finished projector or Shockwave movie, you must add a Lingo command.

The button that resembles a megaphone is the sound level. If there are sound waves streaming from the megaphone, your sound is turned on. If you drag down on the arrow, you can adjust the volume of the sound. You can also mute the sound if you prefer.

The last icon is the Play Selected Frames Only button. You can highlight several frames in your movie, click this button, and then click Play. Director will play only the frames you highlighted.

Control Bar

New to Director MX is the addition of a Control bar placed along the bottom of the Stage. Those of you who have used earlier versions of Director will recognize that the components of the Control bar are similar to those on the Control panel. Macromedia decided to put some of these controls across the bottom of the Stage where they are easy to access and always available.

Since they are the same icons as those shown in the Control panel, we won't define them again here. If you need to review these icons and their functions, please refer to the previous section for complete definitions.

Use the Control Bar and the Control Panel

1. With practice.dir still open, select Window>Control Panel to access the Control panel if it is not already open.

2. Click the Rewind button on the Control bar at the bottom of the Stage to rewind the movie.

3. Click the Play button on the Control bar to play the movie.

4. Click the Stop button on the Control bar to stop the movie.

5. Use the Control panel to finish this exercise. The movie is short, so let's loop it and try again. Click the Loop button.

6. Watch the frame rate in the Control panel. Do the numbers match? Does the actual speed match the preferred speed?

7. Select File>New>Movie to close the current movie. Save changes if prompted to do so.

Director must always have a file open for the application to continue to run. Closing the Stage window only makes the Stage disappear from view; it does not close the movie.

Toolbar

The Toolbar, which can be accessed from the Window menu, is a panel of shortcut controls. If you can spare the screen space, the Toolbar can make your workflow easier and more efficient. For example, you can click the Paintbrush button to go directly to the Paint window; click the "A" and a Text window opens. If you allow your cursor to linger on a button for a few seconds, the name of the tool becomes visible. The Toolbar can be turned on/off from the Window menu.

From left to right, the icons below are New Movie, New Cast, Open, Import, Save, Save All, Publish, Undo, Cut, Copy, Paste, Find Cast Member, Exchange Cast Member, Rewind, Stop, and Play.

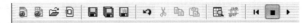

The left half of the Toolbar.

From left to right, the icons below are Stage, Cast, Score, Property Inspector, Library Palette, Paint, Vector Shape, Text, Shockwave 3D, Behavior Inspector, Script, and Message Window.

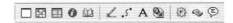

The right half of the Toolbar.

Maximizing Performance of Your Director Project

It is not always easy to keep Director running smoothly. To facilitate the success of future projects, follow the tips provided below. Implement them whenever possible to enhance your experiences with Director.

File Sizes

Keep all file sizes to a minimum. When you create images in any program, remember that vector-based images and graphic files are smaller than comparable raster-based images and graphic files. Most illustration programs are vector-based, including Adobe Illustrator and Macromedia FreeHand; Photoshop is raster-based. Director provides palettes for creating either type of image or graphic file.

Compressing any video or sound file helps to keep file sizes low. When you are ready to publish to the Web, Director offers JPEG compression for individual cast members or the whole movie. There is more on this topic in the "Preparation and Delivery" chapter at the end of this book.

Working from the Hard Drive

It is advisable to work from your hard drive, rather than a CD-ROM or any other removable medium. Working from the hard drive accomplishes two things:

- It reduces the risk of file corruption, which occurs quite easily with most removable media.
- The transfer rate is much faster from your hard drive than it is from removable media, so your movie will play much faster (and better) if you run it from your hard drive.

Memory Issues

If possible, close all other applications while you work in Director. Director requires a lot of RAM, so the fewer applications you have open, the better.

If you get any virtual memory errors while using Director, it probably means your hard drive is too full to continue. You can remove some old files you don't use anymore to resolve this problem.

Acceptable File Formats

The highlighted formats tend to be used most often in real-world projects, usually without any problems.

Type of File	Supported Formats
Animation/ Multimedia	Image BMP, GIF, JPEG, LRG (xRes), Photoshop 3.0 or later, MacPaint, PNG, TIFF, PICT, Targa
Multiple-image file	Windows only: FLC, FLI. Macintosh only: PICS, Scrapbook.
Sound	AIFF, WAV, MP3 Audio, Shockwave Audio, Sun AU, uncompressed and IMA compressed, RealAudio
Video	QuickTime 2, 3, 4, 5 & 6; AVI, RealVideo
Text	RTF, HTML, ASCII (text only), Lingo scripts
Palette	PAL, Photoshop CLUT
3D	.W3D, .OBJ

Chapter Summary

In this chapter, you learned the primary layout of Director's interface. You discovered how to correctly utilize and manipulate Director's main windows.

In addition, you learned some of Director's commonly used terminology, which will be of value in many different animation arenas. You also learned the difference between (and importance of) linking and embedding files.

Finally, you discovered how to work with and create a fully functional presentation. These are the basics that will prepare you to create Director movies.

Complete Project A: Gaenzle Illustration and Design

2 *Text and Graphics*

Chapter Objectives:

In order to create the meaningful presentations and animations discussed in Chapter 1, you must learn how to create your own cast members. This chapter examines the Paint and Text Editors — the primary editors used to create graphic and text cast members. Even if you intend to create your graphics in Adobe Photoshop and text in Microsoft Word, you still need to know how to use the tools in the Paint and Text Editors to manipulate your finished cast members. In Chapter 2, you will:

- Learn how to navigate through the new Editors window.

- Become familiar with and practice using many of the basic tools in the Paint Editor.

- Explore the Text Editor and Text Inspector.

- Learn how to create editable text and bitmap text, and discover the difference between the two formats.

- Gain an understanding of Ink effects and gradients.

Projects to be Completed:

- Gaenzle Illustration and Design (A)

- Redi-Base (B)

- Digital Portfolio (C)

- Shaw's Portfolio (D)

- ABC's (E)

Text and Graphics

Director MX includes an Editor window that contains all of the editors you need to modify media elements (graphics, text, QuickTime video, 3-D graphics, and more). Prior to Director MX, each of these editors was found on an individual palette. Now, they all reside in one window; you can click a specific tab to access the editor you want to use.

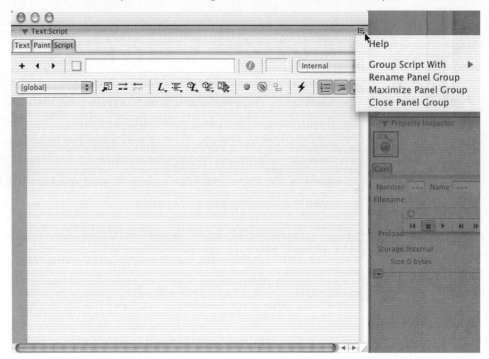

Your editors may not all show up in the Editor window the first time you open it. Director MX allows you to customize your Editor window, as well as have multiple Editor windows that contain different clusters of editors.

To add an editor to an existing group, you would open the new editor (it opens in a separate window). Then you would navigate to the drop-down menu on the top-right side of that window and choose Group With. Then, you would select one of the tabs in an existing editor group, and the editor would be added to that group.

Two of the most commonly used Director editors are the Paint and Text Editors. You can use these two editors to create cast members for Director projects. As you become experienced in Director, you will probably create your graphics, complex text treatments, and illustrations in other graphics applications (including Adobe Illustrator, Macromedia FreeHand, and Adobe Photoshop) and import them into Director.

Paint Editor

The Paint Editor is a bitmap-based image-creation window that is used for the following tasks:

- Creating bitmap graphics or text.
- Making adjustments to imported bitmap graphics.
- Rotating, skewing, and distorting any bitmap graphics currently in your Cast.

For those of you who have used Adobe Photoshop or an illustration program such as Illustrator or FreeHand, most of the tools in the Paint Editor will look familiar.

The top row of items in the Paint Editor is identical to the top row of items in the Cast. It contains a text field for naming your graphic, the Forward, Backward, and Next buttons, and the Cast Member Script and Cast Member Properties icons.

In this chapter, you will experiment with all the tools displayed on the left side of the window except the Registration tool and the Patterns box. You will work with those tools later in this book.

To find the keyboard shortcuts to any of the tools in this window, simply hover your cursor over a tool and a yellow tool tip pops up with the name of the tool and a letter in parentheses. The letter is the keyboard shortcut. For example, "Z" is the keyboard shortcut for the Magnifying Glass tool.

Filled Shape Tools

There are three filled shape tools: the Filled Rectangle, Filled Ellipse, and Filled Polygon tools. When creating these shapes, use the color in the Foreground Color box. You can choose a new color for a tool at any time.

The tools on the left are the filled shape tools.

Foreground and Background Color Boxes

Director provides two boxes for choosing colors. The box in the upper left is the Foreground Color box. The box in the bottom right is the Background Color box. If you click either box, the Color Picker pops up, which allows you to choose new colors.

The Foreground and Background Color boxes.

The steps listed in this exercise are the first steps you should take when you create any Director movie. Your Stage size, however, will typically be 640 x 480 pixels or larger, not necessarily the size listed here.

Work with Filled Shapes and Colors

1. If it is not already open, launch Director.

2. Director creates an untitled movie each time it is launched. If you currently have another Director movie open, select File>New>Movie (or press Command/Control-N) to open a new movie.

3. Select a Stage Color from the Property Inspector (under the Movie tab) and change your Stage Size to 512 × 342 pixels (for this exercise only).

4. If they are not already open, access the Stage and Cast windows. Close all other windows.

5. Select File>Save As and name your movie "graphics.dir". Save this file in your **Work_In_Progress** folder.

6. Open the Paint Editor from the Window menu or press Command/Control-5. Resize your Paint Editor as necessary so you can see all of its features.

7. Click the Foreground Color box and select a color from the palette that appears.

8. Click the Filled Rectangle tool and draw a rectangle on the canvas in the Paint Editor. Make certain the Ink Effects drop-down menu at the bottom of the Paint Editor is set to Normal. The rectangle automatically fills with the color identified in the Foreground Color box.

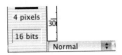

9. Click inside the text field at the top of the Paint Editor (the cast member Name field) and enter your own descriptive name for this cast member. Press Return/Enter. The rectangle becomes your first cast member.

10. Click the plus sign (+) at the top of the Paint Editor to display a new blank canvas. Notice that in the Cast, Cast Member 2 is now highlighted.

11. Save your changes and keep this document open for the next exercise.

Outlined Shape Tools

Director also offers three tools for outlined shapes — the Outlined Rectangle, Outlined Ellipse, and Outlined Polygon tools. When using the outlined shape tools, the outline color is the color found in the Foreground Color box.

The shapes on the right side are the outlined shape tools.

To change the thickness (weight) of an outline, you can select a different line width from the area under the Foreground Color box. You can double-click the last line-width option (the one that says "4 pixels") to make the line any width you prefer. A box appears, allowing you to customize the outline width.

Choose the width, measured in pixels, from the options above.

If you're using a filled shape tool to create a gradient, and you don't want an outline, you can select the top line width to set "no line." This action results in an object that has a gradient fill and no outline.

Paint Bucket Tool

The Paint Bucket tool works the same way in Director as it does in Adobe Photoshop and Adobe Illustrator. You can choose the color you want from the Foreground Color box. Then you can click the Paint Bucket icon, and click an existing object to fill it with the color you chose. If you don't have an existing object, you can draw an object using one of the drawing or painting tools in the Paint Editor, and then fill it with the color of your choice using the Paint Bucket tool.

The icon on the right that resembles a bucket is the Paint Bucket tool.

Eyedropper Tool

The Eyedropper tool is used to select colors in an image. Once selected, you can apply those colors to other images. To use the Eyedropper tool, you can open the Paint Editor; there must be an image in the window. You can select the Eyedropper tool from the Toolbar, and then hover the tool over a color you want to sample in the image. Then you can click that color with the Eyedropper tool. If you were to look at your Foreground Color box, you would see the color you sampled. It could then be used to fill shapes.

The icon on the left that resembles a medicine dropper is the Eyedropper tool.

If you want to create a square or circle, hold down the Shift key while you draw with either the Rectangle or Ellipse tools.

Create and Fill an Outlined Shape

1. Continue working in the open graphics.dir. Click the Outlined Ellipse tool in the Paint Editor. Hold down the Shift key while using the tool to draw a perfect circle.

2. Select a color for the fill of the circle from the Foreground Color box.

3. Select the Paint Bucket tool from the tools on the left, and then click inside the circle to fill it with the foreground color you selected.

4. Assign a name to the object (whatever name you prefer). Click the plus sign (+) in the upper-left corner of the Paint Editor to create an empty canvas for the next member in your Cast.

5. Keep the document open for the next exercise.

Gradients

A gradient blends the colors within an object from one color to another, or from black to white. To create a gradient, you must first select two colors. These choices, however, are not selected from the Foreground and Background Color boxes, but from two smaller boxes located side by side directly below the color boxes. The one on the left is the starting color; the one on the right is the ending color. When you click either box, color choices appear.

The starting color is the box on the left; the ending color is the box on the right.

If you click between the two gradient color boxes, various gradient options — including Sun Burst, Top to Bottom, Left to Right — become available. The Gradient Settings option displays a dialog box where you can manipulate various properties that are relevant to your gradient. Once you make a selection, you can select any filled shape tool to create a gradient-filled object.

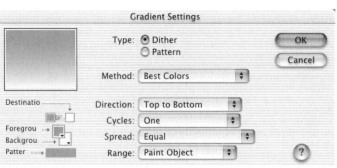

Double-clicking automatically closes any shape you are creating with the Polygon tool. It chooses the shortest distance between two points to close the polygon. Make sure the two points are close enough together so the result is not an unwanted straight edge.

Before drawing your shape, you need to change from the Normal option to the Gradient option in the Ink Effects menu located along the bottom of the Paint Editor window. As the shape is drawn, the gradient is automatically applied. Each tool can have a different Ink effect. Verify the Ink effect you want to apply before you use each tool — the effects do not carry forward from one tool to the next.

Eraser Tool

Clicking once on the Eraser tool allows you to erase any item on the canvas. To use the Eraser tool, simply drag it over the area you want to remove. If you want to start over on a completely clean canvas, double-click the Eraser tool to erase the entire paint area. This is an excellent timesaving feature.

The rectangular icon on the right is the Eraser tool.

Create a Gradient-Filled Polygon

1. Continue working in graphics.dir. Select two gradient colors in the Paint Editor. Remember, the box on the left is the starting color and the box on the right is the ending color.

2. Pick the style of gradient you prefer from the drop-down menu between the gradient starting- and ending-color boxes.

3. Select the Filled Polygon tool from the Toolbar. Make a few practice solid-color filled shapes before turning on the gradient setting.

4. When you are ready to continue, double-click the Eraser tool to erase the entire paint area.

5. Select the Filled Polygon tool. Change the Ink Effects drop-down menu on the bottom-left side of the Paint Editor to Gradient.

6. Draw a shape. The gradient colors and style you selected are automatically applied.

7. Assign a descriptive Cast name to the object. Click the plus sign (+) in the Paint Editor window to create a new canvas for the next member in your Cast.

8. Save your work and keep the file open for the next exercise.

Bitmap Text

On the Toolbar, the Text tool icon is the letter "A". The text produced with this tool is strictly bitmap text, which means it cannot be edited. If you make a mistake, you must erase the text and start again. This tool should be used only for headlines or other text that will not be updated on a regular basis. To use the tool, you can select it from the Toolbar, click on your canvas, and then start typing.

The "A" on the left is the (bitmap) Text tool.

Double-clicking the "A" displays the Font dialog box. In this box, you can choose your font and font attributes.

Using bitmap text is a simple way to create type if you don't want to worry about purchasing, licensing, and distribution issues.

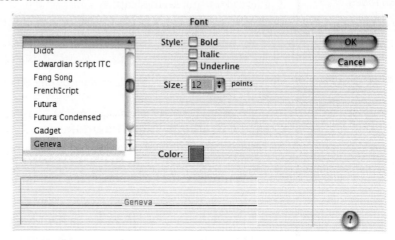

Create Bitmap Text

1. Continue working in graphics.dir. Double-click the Text tool on the Toolbar of the Paint Editor. The Font dialog box pops up.

2. Select a Font, Style, Color, and Size (a minimum of 9 pt.) and then click OK.

3. Click the white area of the Paint Editor and type your first name.

4. In the Text box at the top of the Paint window, assign a descriptive name to the object. Click the plus sign (+) to create an empty slot for the next member in your Cast.

5. Save the file and keep it open.

Magnifying Glass Tool

The Magnifying Glass tool is typically used when you need to examine or refine the details of an image. You can select the tool and then click on an object. An inset showing the object at actual size would appear in the top-right corner of the Paint Editor window. To zoom out, you can hold down the Shift key and click the object. To turn off the magnification, click the inset in the upper-right corner of your canvas.

The Magnifying Glass tool is to the right of the Hand tool.

Air Brush

Director's Air Brush tool is similar to the tool in Adobe Photoshop, with the exception of the anti-aliasing feature found in Photoshop's Air Brush tool. Its function is based on pressure. You can adjust the amount of pressure (how fast the paint comes out) by going into the Settings area. To use the tool, you would click the Paint Editor canvas and hold down the mouse button. The tool continues to spray paint until you release the mouse button.

If you were to click the Air Brush button and drag down (or click-hold), you would see six additional options: Air Brush 1 through 5, as well as a Settings option. Air Brush 1 through 5 each has preset brush sizes and pressure settings. You can either use these default settings or edit them to suit your needs. To edit an air brush, simply choose one and select the Settings option. This displays a dialog box where you can change the Flow Rate, Spray Area, Dot Size, and more.

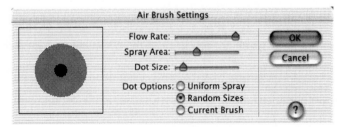

Paint Brush

The Paint Brush tool is similar to the one found in Adobe Photoshop. The Director Paint Brush tool, however, paints in strokes of 100% color, and the opacity cannot be altered (as it can in Photoshop). If you want a lighter shade of the current color, you must select a lighter color in the Foreground Color box.

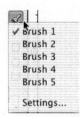

If you were to click the Paint Brush icon and drag down, you would see six additional options — Brush 1 through 5 and a Settings option. Brush 1 through 5 are preset brush sizes. You can use these presets or edit them to suit your needs.

To edit a brush, choose one and then select the Settings option. This displays the Brush Settings dialog box, where you can choose from a standard set of brushes. If you want to create a custom brush, you must change the option from Standard to Custom and then make your selection. Your selection is displayed in the large edit box to the right of the brushes. You can then click the black pixels to make them disappear (turn white), or click the white pixels to turn them black (make them visible).

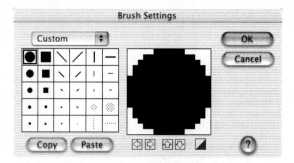

Selection Tools

The Selection tools are located at the top left of the Paint Editor window. The Lasso tool is on the top left and the Marquee tool is on the top right.

The Lasso tool is on the left and the Marquee tool is on the right.

The Lasso tool automatically shrinks to fit an object, no matter what the object's shape. To use the Lasso tool, you would drag a large circle around the object you want to select on the canvas. When you release the mouse button, the selection shrinks to fit the outline of the object you selected. If you don't want the Lasso to shrink when you use it, you can select No Shrink from the Lasso tool's drop-down menu.

The Marquee tool is a rectangular-selection tool. To use the Marquee tool, you would drag it from the top left to the bottom right of an object. When you release the mouse button, you see a selection box around the object. With the selection box in place, you can drag the object wherever you choose. You can set it to Shrink or No Shrink, as well as make it imitate the Lasso tool.

Line Tools

In the Paint Editor, there are two useful line tools called the Arc tool and the Line tool. The Arc tool creates 90-degree arcs that can be useful when drawing organic objects. The Line tool can create lines on any diagonal, as well as horizontal and vertical lines.

The Arc tool is on the left and the Line tool is on the right.

The Arc tool can make exact quarter-circles if you hold down the Shift key while you draw. The Line tool can make perfect horizontal or vertical lines if you hold down the Shift key while you draw.

The line weight, or pixel width, of both of these tools can be altered. You can choose from the different line widths listed under the color boxes in the Paint Editor. If you double-click the bottom option, it displays the Paint Window Preferences dialog box, where you can customize the width (64-pixel maximum). After you choose your line width and foreground color, you can click the canvas area of the Paint Editor and draw.

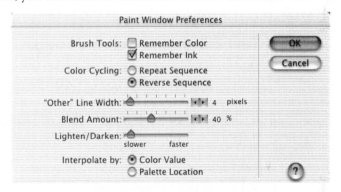

The Paint Window Preferences box.

Paint Ink Effects

Paint Ink effects can be accessed from the bottom-left corner of the Paint Editor. While creating cast members, you can apply Smudges, Smears, Gradients, and Blends.

Changing the Ink effects on the bottom of the Paint Editor window while you use the Paint Brush and Air Brush tools can create interesting effects, such as transparencies and gradations.

To apply a Paint Ink effect, select a painting tool and then select your Ink effect from the menu at the bottom of the Paint Editor window. For an effect to work, there must already be paint on your canvas. Apply a second color, and the two colors blend together to create the desired effect.

Some Ink effects work better with patterns, and some with solid colors. Some effects require you to work with a certain tool or tools; otherwise, they do not work properly. If an effect is grayed out on the drop-down menu, you probably selected an incorrect color mode or tool for that effect to work properly.

When you create sections of an object in separate areas of the canvas, you can perfect each section before you place it. You don't have to worry about making mistakes on the finished piece. You can use the shrinking Lasso tool to drag the perfected sections onto the finished piece, and place them in their exact positions.

Use Various Tools and Ink Effects

1. With graphics.dir still open, experiment with a variety of the Brush tools and Line tools in the Paint Editor until you feel comfortable using and adjusting them. Use the Magnifying Glass tool when necessary.

2. Experiment with the Ink effects. Create an object, and then choose a new tool. Set the Ink effect for that tool. Paint on top of the previous object and observe the result.

3. Use a combination of Brush tools and Line tools to create a new cast member. Make a realistic object or animal.

4. Create another design in pieces. Click the plus sign (+) to create a new cast member (which will result in a clean canvas). Create each piece in a different area of the Paint Editor window. Then, use the selection tools located at the top left of the Paint Editor to move each piece to its correct location on the final object.

5. When finished, assign a descriptive name to your object. Next, create an empty slot in your Cast by clicking the plus sign (+) in the Paint Editor.

6. You are done with this Cast and movie; however, you may want to keep the file open for further experimentation. If not, save your changes and close the file.

Text Editor and Related Tools

Director can produce vector-based text within the Text Editor. To open the Text Editor, you can select Window>Text or press Command/Control-6. This feature is very useful because it allows you to create text that can be edited at any time. Imported vector-based text files will also open in this editor, allowing for easy last-minute changes. The Tools palette and Text Inspector provide additional tools for manipulating vector-based text.

Text Editor

You'll find that Director's Text Editor is similar to most basic word-processing programs. Here, you can create editable text elements. If you create a text cast member and find a misspelled a word, it can be easily corrected in the Text Editor.

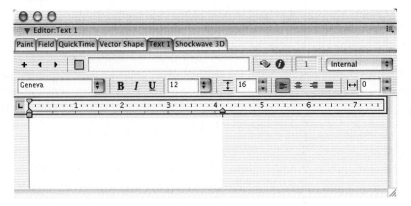

The Text Editor.

The top row of the Text Editor is similar to the top row of the Cast. It contains the Forward, Backward, and Next buttons, the text field for naming cast members, and the Cast Member Script and Cast Member Properties buttons.

The second row contains the basic specification options necessary to create text. Here, you can select a typeface, point size, alignment, style, line-spacing/leading, and kerning/tracking. It also contains rulers to help determine the correct size of your text. You can drag the arrows on the ruler to adjust the width and indents of the text.

Tools Palette

If you want your type to be a particular color, you must access the Tools palette. The Tools palette and Text Editor can both be accessed from the Window menu. Typically, the Tools palette is open by default. You can pick a foreground color (other than black) from the Foreground Color box located at the bottom of the Tools palette. When you enter text in the Text Editor, it assumes that color.

If you want to change the color of existing text, select the text in the Text Editor and choose a new color from the Foreground Color box in the Tools palette. You can also change the background color behind the text by using the Background Color box in the Tools palette.

Create and Edit a Text Cast Member

1. If it is not already open, launch Director and select File>New>Movie.

2. Access the Text Editor from the Window menu (Window>Text).

3. Select your Font, Type Size, and any other attributes you want to use from the Text Editor.

4. Type a word that describes a color, such as "Red" or "Black".

According to Macromedia, another way to include fonts without violating licensing agreements is to use the Insert>Media Elements>Font option, which permanently embeds the fonts into your Director project; they travel with your project and can be used at any time. This allows you to use the editable text you create in the Text Editor. This method increases your file size, however, so use it judiciously.

Working with white text can be difficult because you can't see it while you create it. Generally, this can be overcome by creating your type in any color other than white and placing it on the Stage. When it is exactly as you want it, change the text color to white.

5. Assign the same name to the cast member.

6. Close the Text Editor.

7. If it is not already open, access the Cast window. Double-click the text cast member you just created. This reopens the Text Editor.

8. Highlight the word. Select a new Font and Size. Then, choose a Foreground Color from the Tools palette (Window>Tools Palette) that reflects the name of the color you typed.

9. Close the Text Editor.

10. Notice that the original color of the text is replaced by the new color in your Cast.

11. Keep this movie open for the next exercise.

Text Inspector

The Text Inspector, a floating type-specification window, allows you to change all the type specifications (except color) directly on the Stage or in the Cast. It can be accessed from the Window menu (Window>Text Inspector). You cannot, however, edit the text itself from the Text Inspector. You can double-click the text sprite on the Stage to select it, and then edit the text. A blinking cursor displays in the text on the Stage, letting you know the text can be edited.

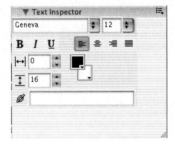

To adjust the text specifications of a cast member while in the Cast window, simply highlight the cast member and select your new specifications from the Text Inspector.

To adjust the text specifications using the Text Inspector while on the Stage, click the sprite to highlight it and then pick your new specifications from the Text Inspector. Although you are changing the sprite on the Stage, the original cast member is also changing, as well as all the other sprites you've placed in the Score from that cast member. The only way to keep this global update from happening is to create a different cast member for each set of type specifications you need.

The Text Inspector is considered one of Director's utilities. The Text Inspector palette can be grouped with other utilities or inspectors, such as the Behavior Inspector and the Object Inspector. These palettes can be stacked one above the other, or they can be torn apart and used independently of one another.

Use the Text Inspector

1. Continue working in the open file from the previous exercise. Select Window>Text Inspector to display the Text Inspector.

2. Highlight the text cast member you made in the previous exercise.

3. Make some alterations to the specifications in the Text Inspector. The Cast slot windows are very small, so changes made to cast members are often not visually obvious in the Cast. If you are not sure whether a cast member has changed, drag a copy to the Stage to view it more clearly.

4. Double-click the text on the Stage and change the text to read, "I've completed Chapter 2 today."

5. Save your changes in the **Work_In_Progress** folder as "textpractice.dir", and then close the movie and the application.

Chapter Summary

In this chapter, you learned to use some of the primary tools in the Paint Editor and Text Editor. The Paint Brush tool, Text tool, Gradient tool, and Line tool will help you create some basic graphics in the upcoming chapters. You also discovered how to correctly utilize and manipulate bitmap and vector text.

In addition, you learned how to create text and graphic cast members. Finally, you discovered how to edit your work. These new skills will help build your confidence and allow you to create more elegant and complex presentations with Director.

3 Sprites and Basic Animation

Chapter Objectives:

Director was originally designed for animation, and that continues to be one of its primary strengths. You can use Director to apply different animation methods, many of which are presented in this chapter of the book. In addition, you will learn new terms that are commonly used in the animation industry, and several tools you can use to align items on the Stage. In Chapter 3, you will:

- Explore the concept of a sprite.

- Learn how to reverse an animation.

- Discover how to create basic animations using several different techniques.

- Learn important terms used in the digital animation industry.

- Become familiar with various methods for aligning items on the Stage.

Projects to be Completed:

- Gaenzle Illustration and Design (A)

- Redi-Base (B)

- Digital Portfolio (C)

- Shaw's Portfolio (D)

- ABC's (E)

Sprites and Basic Animation

This chapter of the book explores basic keyframe animation. Several new, commonly used terms will be introduced and explained in the chapter including keyframe, sprite, and animation paths. These terms are commonly used throughout the digital animation industry – for both 2-dimensional and 3-dimensional animation.

Sprites

Sprites are cast members that have been placed in the Score or on the Stage. A sprite is a single instance of a cast member. For example, if an image is dragged to the Stage and extends from Frame 1 through Frame 10 in the Score, that particular sprite is ten frames in length. If a copy of the same image extends from Frame 11 through Frame 20, that copy might seem identical, but it is actually a separate sprite with its own set of specifications.

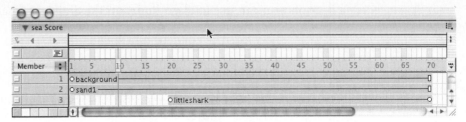

Placing Sprites on the Stage or in the Score

In Chapter 1, you placed a sprite in the Score and it automatically appeared in the center of the Stage. This technique is useful when you have backgrounds or other items that need to be centered on the Stage. This option also allows you to easily place the sprite in a specific location in the Score.

If you place a sprite directly onto the Stage, however, the sprite appears in the next available opening in the Score. Alternatively, if you highlight a particular square or cell in the Score before dragging a cast member to the Stage, the sprite starts there.

Sprite Overlays

Each sprite has its own properties, such as location on the Stage, or opacity. When you have a hundred or more sprites in the Score, it may be difficult to remember the settings for specific sprites. To help alleviate possible confusion, each sprite has its own *sprite overlay*, containing shortcut buttons used to quickly access sprite information.

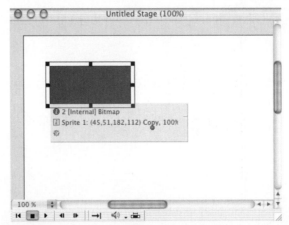

The sprite overlay is accessible from the View menu. Here, you will find three options — Show Info, Show Paths, and Settings:

- Show Info must be checked for an Overlay box to show up next to the sprite on the Stage.
- Show Paths should be checked if the sprite is animated. Checking Show Paths displays the animation path the sprite follows during its animation.
- Settings displays the Overlay Settings dialog box that contains several options. Changing the color of the type in the overlay is one of the options. If you have a black background, you don't want your text to be black because you won't be able to see it. Clicking the current color displays a Color palette.

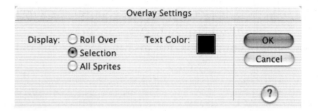

The options available in the Overlay Settings dialog box include:

- **Roll Over**. This option displays overlays and/or animation paths for sprites as you move the cursor over them. When you move away, the overlay disappears.
- **Selection**. This option displays the overlay and/or animation paths for a selected sprite.
- **All Sprites**. This option displays overlays and/or animation paths for all the sprites in the Cast. This can be confusing if you have many objects in the Cast.

Below is an example of the Overlay Info box and an animation path.

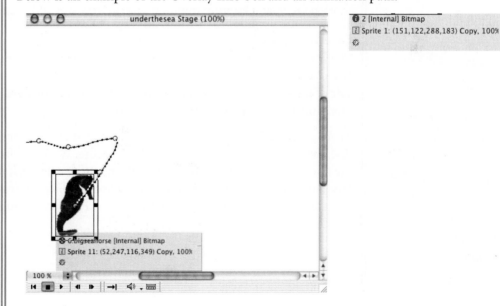

The overlay display provides important information about the sprite to which it's attached. The three icons inside the overlay are links to certain tabs in the Property Inspector. For example, if you click the top Cast Member Properties icon, it displays the sprite's basic file information in the Property Inspector. The middle icon displays the selected sprite's options and specifications in the Property Inspector. The bottom icon displays the Behavior Inspector within the Property Inspector. (We will discuss the Behavior Inspector later in this book.) The thin horizontal line on the right edge of the overlay display is a slider that changes the opacity of the display box when moved up and down.

Sprite Preferences

Macintosh users can access the Sprite Preferences dialog box from the Director menu (Director>Preferences>Sprite). Windows users can access the dialog box from the Edit menu (Edit>Preferences>Sprite). We discuss all of these options in the next few chapters of the book; but for now, we're going to focus on the Span Duration option.

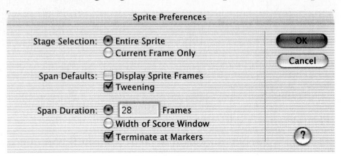

Span duration is the number of frames over which a sprite extends. The default is 28 frames, meaning that each time a sprite is placed in the Score, it extends 28 frames unless the duration is otherwise adjusted. If the majority of the work you produce is two or three frames, or if you have a monitor that is smaller than 14 in., you might want to shorten the Span Duration option to maximize space and reduce scrolling time.

Extending Sprites

There are many ways to extend a sprite. The shortcut for extending a single-frame sprite across a number of frames is to hold down the Option/Alt key while dragging the right side of the sprite. With multiple-frame sprites, there is no need to hold down the Option/Alt key while dragging.

The key command to extend a sprite is Command/Control-B. You must first Shift-click the frame where you want the sprite to end, and then press Command/Control-B.

There are two additional ways to extend a sprite after it has been placed in the Score. The first method is to highlight the sprite in the Score. While holding down the Shift key, click the frame in the Score to which you want the sprite extended; this places the Playback Head in that frame. Then select Modify>Extend Sprite, or press Command/Control-B. The sprite extends or collapses to wherever the Playback Head is currently located.

As an alternative, you can change the numbers in the two frame fields of the Sprite tab in the Property Inspector. One is for the beginning frame of a sprite (Start Frame), and one is for the ending frame (End). You can enter the frame numbers for the sprite to start and end.

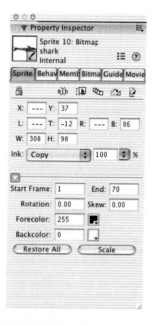

Copying and Pasting Sprites and Cast Members

Copying and pasting sprites and cast members is similar to copying and pasting objects in every other desktop application. Novice users tend to under-utilize the timesaving Copy/Paste functions. You can copy and paste whole sections of Director projects by copying and pasting whole groups of sprites.

If you want to duplicate an animation, don't redo it — copy and paste it. For example, if you want to create rain, make one drop, animate it, and then copy/paste it a few times, changing each drop's size and position. Finally, select the whole group, copy it (Command/Control-C), and then paste it (Command/Control-V) over and over again, changing the position, size, and timing of each copy.

To copy and paste a cast member while the Cast is in Thumbnail view, simply highlight the member in the Cast, copy it, highlight the empty Cast slot, and then paste it. If the Cast is in List view, copy the same as above. To paste, however, make certain nothing is selected in the list before you paste. After you paste the new item, it appears at the bottom of the list. If an existing item on the list is selected, the new item is pasted on top of the selected item, and it deletes it.

The Copy/Paste function could be used for a variety of tasks that would normally require repetitive steps. If you have one yellow flower and you also want a red and a pink flower, perform two copy/pastes of the yellow flower, access the Paint Editor window, and use the Paint Bucket tool to change the colors of the copied flowers.

Copying and pasting sprites is performed the same way. Highlight the entire sprite in the Score (by single-clicking it), copy it, select a frame to place it in (click the desired frame), and then paste it.

If the Cast is in List view, and you want to paste a new item, make certain nothing in the list is selected before you paste. If an existing item on the list is selected before the paste, the new item is pasted on top of the selected item, and it deletes it.

Use Sprite Overlays and Extend Sprites

1. If it is not already open, launch Director. If you want to view the final version of this exercise before you begin, navigate to the **RF_Director** folder and access **finsea.dir**. Otherwise, begin with Step 2.

2. Navigate to the **RF_Director** folder and open **sea.dir**.

3. Select Director>Preferences>Sprite and change your Span Duration to 2 Frames. Click OK.

4. From the Cast window, drag a copy of shark to the Score and place it in Frame 1, Channel 10. Extend the sprite to Frame 70 by dragging the right edge of the sprite (in the Score) to the right until you reach Frame 70.

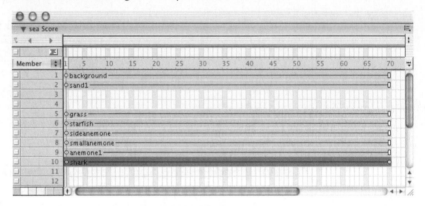

For ease of use, Director implemented a pasteboard around the Stage area so you can move sprites on and off the Stage without having to use Lingo scripts.

5. Click anywhere in the middle of the shark sprite in the Score. Go to the Stage and use the Arrow keys on your keyboard (or use your mouse, but be careful you don't click on the center dot or the outside handlebars) to drag the shark completely off the top-left edge of the Stage. His nose should barely touch the edge of the Stage. The shark will enter the Stage from this direction. To help you see where you are moving the shark, go to the bottom of the Stage and change the view percentage in the drop-down menu to 50%. Windows users can select View>Zoom>50%. This temporarily shrinks the Stage so you can see where you are placing the shark.

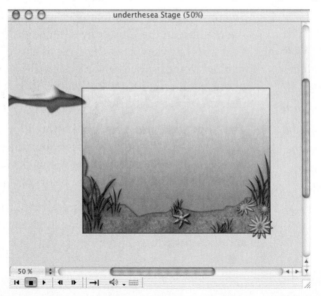

6. Click Frame 70 of the shark sprite and drag the shark off the right edge of the Stage. As you drag your sprite, you see an "elastic" line appear with dots on it. This is the animation path. Each dot represents one frame. (You will learn more about this path shortly.) If you don't see the path, select View>Sprite Overlay>Show Paths and it appears. Now the sprite is positioned off the right edge of the Stage on Frame 70 when the movie ends.

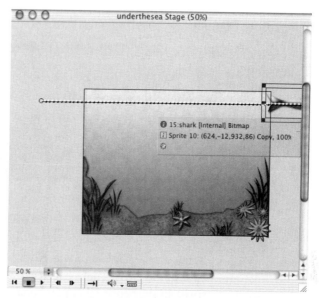

7. Return the magnification of the Stage to 100%. Rewind and play the movie using the controls in the Control bar at the bottom of the Stage. If it runs too fast, open the Control panel (Window>Control Panel), and change the Preferred Frame Rate in the Control bar at the bottom of the Stage to 7 fps (frames per second). We are using this slow frame rate because this is a beginner's exercise. Typically, you will work at 15 or 30 fps on more advanced projects.

8. From the Cast window, drag a copy of littleshark to the Score and place it in Frame 20, Channel 3. Extend the sprite to Frame 70 by dragging the right edge of the sprite (in the Score) to the right until you reach Frame 70.

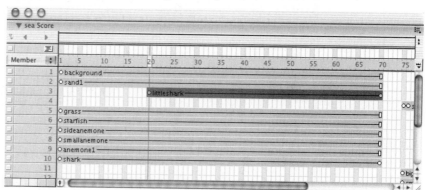

9. Click anywhere in the middle of the littleshark sprite in the Score. Go to the Stage and use the Arrow keys to drag the littleshark sprite completely off the right edge of the Stage (so his body is skimming the top of the sand and he's swimming through the grass). You can temporarily shrink the Stage if necessary.

The key command to undo a step is Command/Control-Z. Remember to use this command when necessary. Keep in mind that it only reverses the step you just completed.

There are no unlimited undos in Director. You can only undo one step.

10. Click Frame 70 of the littleshark sprite and drag your shark totally off the left edge of the Stage. Now the littleshark sprite is positioned off the left end of the Stage on Frame 70 when the movie ends.

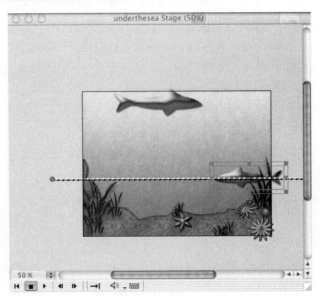

11. Rewind and play the movie. Notice how the littleshark rolled across the Stage behind the grass. That's because it was put into Channel 3, which is above the grass sprite in the Score. Channels behave very similar to layers. The items in Channel 10 (shark) are much closer to the front than the items in Channel 1 (background).

12. Save the movie as "seapractice.dir" in the **Work_In_Progress** folder. Keep the movie open for the next exercise.

Aligning Objects on the Stage

Guides, grids, and other alignment tools help produce well-balanced results for any page-layout or illustration project. A *guide* is a single horizontal or vertical line that can be used to visually align objects. A *grid* is a set of horizontal and vertical lines that create a mesh-like structure, and can be used to align text and graphics on the page.

Guides

Guides can be created in any color and are easily adjusted once placed on the Stage. Along with the grid information, guides can be found in the Property Inspector under the Guides tab.

To create a guide, drag one from the Property Inspector next to where it says "New:" and drop it on the Stage. To move the guide, select it and drag it to a new location.

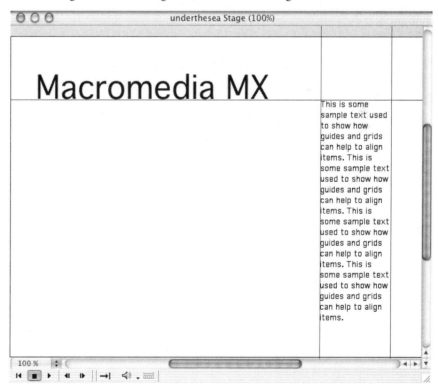

Guides and grids do not display on your projector or published file, even if you forget to turn them off or drag them off the Stage. You only see grids and guides when viewing the file on your monitor.

Grids

A grid divides the Stage into evenly spaced squares. Grids are very helpful when you must create even spaces between or precise alignment of objects on the screen. Grids can, however, also be used loosely as a guide. As an item is placed, it doesn't necessarily need to fit exactly within a specific square, unless your design warrants that type of alignment.

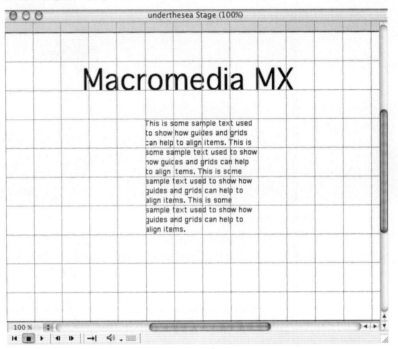

Grids offer a Snap To option. With this option turned on, if you place a cast member close to a grid line, the edge of it snaps to the edge of that line. This is useful for some projects, but not all. This feature can be turned on or off by selecting Snap To on the Guides tab in the Property Inspector.

In the Property Inspector, you can also select the color of your grid and dictate whether the lines of the grid are solid or dotted. Additionally, the width and height between the lines can be adjusted to display different square sizes. The width and height are in pixels, not inches.

Tweak

It is often necessary to move sprites on a Stage in small and precise increments. You can access the Tweak dialog box from the Modify menu (Shift-Command/Control-K). If you have various items that need to be moved and aligned, you can move the first item, and then enter the same information for the rest of the items. They will be moved the same distance, one at a time.

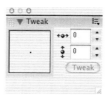

In the Tweak dialog box, you must enter a negative number to move left or up, and a positive number to move right or down.

The Tweak dialog box contains two adjustment boxes, one for vertical movements and one for horizontal. You can either enter numbers in the boxes and press the Return/Enter key, or click the directional arrows and watch until you are satisfied with its position. With the sprite selected, you can move it with the Arrow keys on your keyboard.

Align and Distribute

The Align dialog box (Window>Align) allows you to quickly align sprites. Sprites can be aligned on the vertical or horizontal axis. On each axis, they can be aligned by the their tops, bottoms, right sides, left sides, or registration points.

You can align several different sprites. You can also align a sprite to copies of itself over several frames by highlighting the sprites you want to align, and clicking the grid squares that represent the horizontal and vertical alignment.

The Align dialog box also allows you to distribute sprites across an area. You have the option of distributing them by their left sides, centers, right sides, registration points, the width of the object, or across the Stage. To do this, highlight the sprites you want to distribute and then choose the distribution method.

Animating Sprites

The background information from the beginning of this chapter prepared you for the next stage of Director development — animating sprites. Director is quite good with 2-D animation — Macromedia has been in this arena for many years. The company has worked diligently to combine elements of traditional animation with the necessary digital components, creating a blend between the two genres. This eases the transition for traditional animators who are attempting to break into digital animation.

Keyframes and Tweening

Keyframes are single frames of a sprite that can hold information. If you look at a multiple-frame sprite in the Score, you notice that the first and last frames have either a circle or a rectangle in them, whereas all the rest of the frames simply have a line that runs through them, connecting them with their first and last frames. The first and last frames are the keyframes. To select a keyframe, click the circle (or the rectangle) at the end of the sprite. To select the whole sprite, click any frame of the sprite that does not contain a keyframe.

○18 ── ▯

Keyframes store information on the size of a sprite, where it should be located, and at which angle it should be rotated when it arrives at a particular frame, among other things. You must give a sprite a defined position at a specific keyframe in order to create an animation sequence. This can be done by highlighting a keyframe in the Score and then dragging the sprite to its new location on the Stage. If you want to modify its size, highlight the keyframe and then resize the box that contains the sprite on the Stage.

By adding several keyframes and adjusting the specifications of the sprite for each one, you can create animation. All frames between two keyframes are automatically equally divided into the animated steps necessary to make the transition appear seamless. This is called "in-betweening," or "tweening" for short.

In tweening, you determine some keyframes in an animation sequence, and Director automatically completes the steps in between. When you extend a sprite, Director uses the original information to complete the tween; it simply copies and pastes the sprite into each of the frames in the extended area.

The first and last frames of every sprite are keyframes. You can add keyframes to any other frame of the sprite by selecting Insert>Keyframe; you can delete keyframes by selecting Insert>Remove Keyframe. You can add or remove keyframes from the Score wherever the Playback Head crosses the currently selected sprite.

Keyframes and Tweening

1. Continue working in seapractice.dir from the previous exercise. It is saved in your **Work_In_Progress** folder.

2. From the Cast window, drag bigseahorse to Channel 11 and extend the sprite across Frames 1 through 70.

3. Insert new keyframes into Frames 5, 15, 25, 35, and 45 of the bigseahorse sprite. Click the sprite in Frame 5 and choose Insert>Keyframe from the Main menu. Perform this action to insert each new keyframe (at Frames 15, 25, 35, 45).

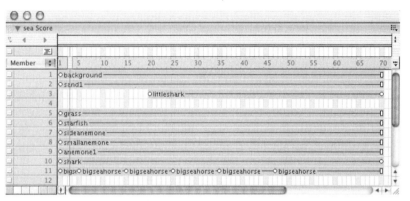

4. Next, let's position the keyframes on the Stage. First, highlight the entire sprite in the Score. Go to the Stage, and drag the sprite onto the Stage. Position it above the sand, off the left edge of the Stage (the beginning position). You might want to change the zoom percentage of the Stage to 50% to give yourself more room to work.

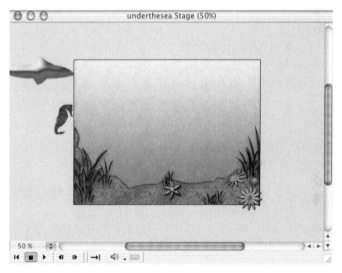

To ensure you are choosing the correct frame numbers, keep an eye on the current frame number in the Control Panel.

5. Next, highlight only Frame 5 of the sprite in the Score and go to the Stage. Move bigseahorse to where you want it to be on the Stage when the movie hits Frame 5.

6. Repeat Step 5 for Frames 15, 25, and 35. In general, you are trying to move the seahorse to the right and down toward the large grasses on the left side of the Stage. At Frame 35, you want to be approximately an inch away from one of the tall, thick blades of grass. Notice that the keyframes appear as larger colored dots along the animation path. If you don't see the animation path, select View>Sprite Overlay>Show Paths to turn it on.

7. Highlight Frame 45 of the sprite in the Score. Move the seahorse so its tail grabs onto the long stalk of grass (see image in Step 8).

8. Highlight the last keyframe of the bigseahorse sprite (Frame 70). If the last keyframe has a circle in it, press the Delete key to delete any unwanted movement. We want the seahorse to stay anchored to the grass for the rest of the movie. If the last keyframe is shaped like a rectangle, leave it alone — it is already empty of information.

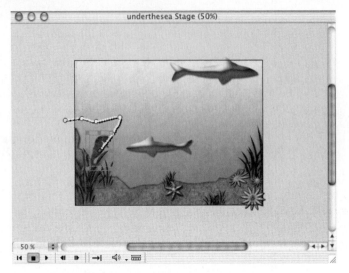

9. Rewind and play the movie. Notice that the big seahorse moves around on the Stage, then perches on the grasses and stays still until the end of the movie. If you don't like where some or all of your keyframes are located on the Stage, simply drag the colored dot representing each keyframe to a new position of your choice.

10. Next, let's work with the small seahorse. From the Cast, drag smallhorse to Channel 12 and extend the sprite across Frames 15 through 70.

11. Insert new keyframes at Frames 20, 30, 40, 50, and 60 of the smallhorse sprite.

12. To position the keyframes on the Stage, highlight the entire sprite in the Score. Go to the Stage, and drag the sprite onto the Stage. Position it above the sand, off the top-right edge of the Stage (the beginning position).

13. Next, highlight only Frame 20 of the sprite in the Score and go to the Stage. Move smallhorse to where you want it to be on the Stage when the movie reaches Frame 20.

14. Repeat Step 13 for Frames 30, 40, and 50. In general, you are trying to move the seahorse to the left and down toward the large grasses on the right side. At Frame 50, you want to be approximately an inch away from one of the tall, thick blades of grass.

15. Highlight Frame 60 of the sprite in the Score. Move the seahorse so its tail grabs onto a long stalk of grass.

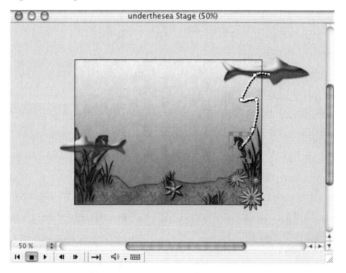

16. Highlight the last keyframe of the smallhorse sprite and press the Delete key to delete any unwanted movement (if necessary) as you did with the bigseahorse sprite.

17. Rewind and play the movie. If you don't like where some or all of your keyframes are located, reposition them as you did in Step 9.

18. Save your changes and keep the movie open for the next exercise.

Sprite Properties

The properties of each sprite can be viewed from the Property Inspector. Information such as width, height, scale, rotate, skew, Ink effects, and blend percentage is displayed. One of the most often-used tools in the sprite Properties dialog box is the Ink Effects drop-down menu. The second and third options in this menu, Matte and Background Transparent, remove the white bounding box around your graphic cast members.

The box also shows the location of the sprite on the Stage and allows you to lock a sprite so it isn't accidentally moved or edited. To access the sprite property information, select (highlight) a sprite, and then click the Sprite tab in the Property Inspector. It is not recommended for a sprite to be to scaled up or down too much, since Director requires a significant amount of RAM to size a sprite on the fly while the movie is playing. If you have many sprites, and each one is scaled up and/or down, the movie slows to a crawl. Larger sprites, such as backgrounds, affect the system the most.

Animating in Space

The Animating in Space option allows you to make identical animations look different. To do this, you can place a sprite in the Score, and then copy/paste the sprite into the same frames, but on a different channel in the Score. Then, highlight the entire newly pasted sprite and move it to a new location on the Stage. When you rewind and play the movie, you will see that two of the same animations are playing at the same time but in different locations. This produces the illusion of two different animations. The farther apart you place them, the more likely they are to appear different.

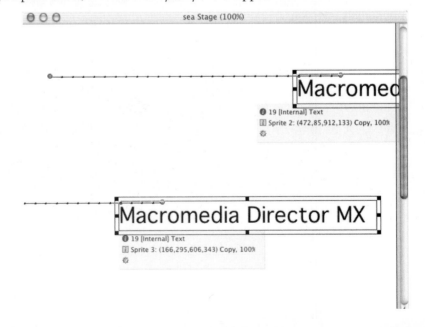

Animating in Time

The Animating in Time option involves starting duplicates of the same animation at different times. The process is similar to Animating in Space, except you paste the second sprite in the next available channel and in a different frame from the first. You can start the new sprite a few frames later than the first sprite to delay the start of the second animation.

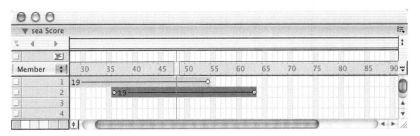

Animate in Space and Time

1. Continue working in seapractice.dir from the previous exercise. Look in the Score to find a sprite named biggerfry in Channel 13. This is the small fish that swims across the screen in the final movie.

2. Highlight the biggerfry sprite in Channel 13 and copy it. Paste a copy of biggerfry into Frame 1 of Channel 14. You don't see the second fish on the screen because it is pasted exactly on top of the first fish.

3. Drag the fish on the screen down and to the right so it looks as though it is swimming with the first fish, but trailing a little bit behind it.

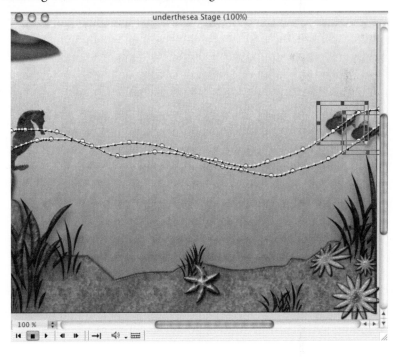

4. Now for an animator's trick: exchange the second fish for a copy of the smallfry cast member (a smaller version of the biggerfry fish). To do this, single-click the smallfry cast member to highlight it. Next, highlight the entire biggerfry sprite in Channel 14 of the Score. Finally, select Edit>Exchange Cast Members (or press Command/Control-E). Look at the Stage to verify that Director switched the fish. The small fish kept the same sprite information — Director just switched the visual picture. This method is useful if you have a lot of different cast members that need to follow the same path.

5. Rewind and play the movie. The two fish should swim together across the screen in identical fashion. By staggering their placement, you created two seemingly different animations without the effort of keyframing both fish (changing the fish image also helped). Even though it starts and ends at the same time as the first fish, you moved its animation path so it moves around in another area of the Stage. This is an example of Animating in Space.

6. Copy the sprites in Channels 13 and 14. To select both sprites, click the first sprite, then Shift-click the second sprite. Paste them into Channel 15, Frame 20, and Channel 16, Frame 20.

7. On the Stage, both fish and their animation paths should be highlighted. Drag both fish straight down so they are in front of the sand. Then drag them to the right so their animation paths are shifted to the right.

See the two pair of small fish with parallel paths.

8. Rewind and play the movie. This time, the new animation looks very different. Notice that by starting one animation later than the other, they look slightly different. This is an example of Animating in Time — staggering the starting times of identical animations.

9. Save your changes and keep this movie open for the next exercise.

Step-Recording

The Step-Recording option is the perfect way to record an unusual animation path that must be precise. When you can stop and place your objects one frame at time, you can create a very accurate animation. Director then strings together all of your object placements (using keyframes) into a smooth animation.

To create a Step-Recording animation, you would drag a cast member to the Stage and ensure the Playback Head is in the first frame of the sprite. The next step would be to turn on Step-Recording by selecting Control>Step-Recording. You know that Step-Recording is turned on when you see a red "step forward" icon next to the channel number of the channel where your sprite is located. You may also notice that the bounding box around your sprite is larger than before.

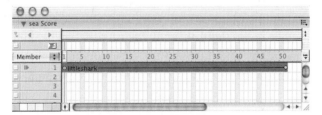

You can click the "step forward" button in the Control bar at the bottom of the Stage (or select Control>Step Forward) to advance the Playback Head to the next frame. You can now move the sprite to its next position (or leave it still if it is a slow-moving object) if you prefer. You can click the Step Forward button again to reposition your sprite. You can continue this process until you are finished with your animation. To turn off Step-Recording, you can select it again from the Control bar or Control menu.

Real-Time Recording

The Real-Time Recording option is simply recording an animation as you drag it around the Stage in real time. First, you would select a sprite in the Score that you want to animate. You must make certain it extends across at least 30 or 40 frames — you will understand why in the next exercise. Real-time recording can be turned on by selecting Control>Real-Time Recording. When you turn it on, you can see a red dot to the left of the channel where the sprite resides. You can also see that the bounding box around your sprite on the Stage now resembles a red-striped candy cane.

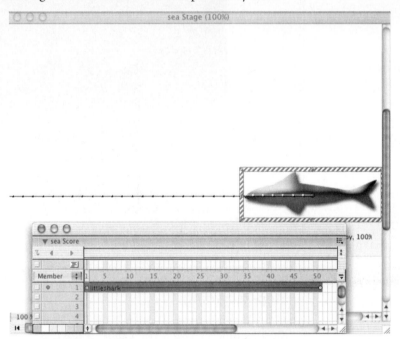

The tempo needs to be kept slow for Real-Time Recording because the Playback Head must move across the Score slowly enough to animate the object before reaching the end of the sprite. A tempo of 5 fps (set in the Control bar at the bottom of the Stage) usually works well.

You can rewind the Playback Head, go to the Stage, and then drag the sprite around the Stage in the path you want the animation to follow. As soon as the sprite on the Stage is touched, the Playback Head starts to move across the frames. When the Playback Head reaches the end of the sprite in the Score, you should stop moving your sprite.

Once this is complete, you can rewind the movie and play it to see the animation. You can also look at the animation path on the Stage and drag the Playback Head back and forth to see it frame by frame, or at whatever speed you prefer. The animation path is comprised of dozens of keyframes, all of which can be edited.

Reversing an Animation

Reversing an animation is a quick, easy way to make a copy of a single sprite animation appear different from the original. To apply this technique, you would highlight the animation and then select Modify>Reverse Sequence. The animation sequence would be reversed frame by frame, resulting in an appearance that is very different than the original.

Use Real-Time Recording and Step-Recording

1. Continue working in seapractice.dir. From the Cast, drag a copy of diver to Channel 17, Frames 1-70. Highlight the diver sprite in the Score and drag it off the bottom-left edge of the Stage (the beginning position).

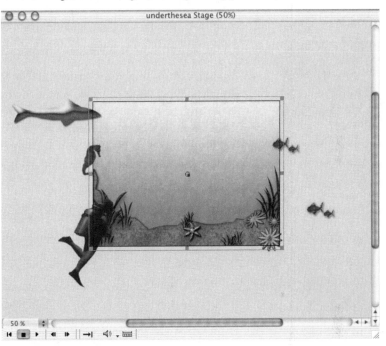

2. With the diver sprite still highlighted in the Score, drag the Playback Head to Frame 1 or click the Rewind button in the Control bar at the bottom of the Stage. Open the Control panel (Window>Control) to verify the Tempo is set to 4 or 5 fps.

3. Turn on Real-Time Recording by selecting Control>Real-Time Recording. Notice the red-and-white striped box around the sprite on the Stage, and the small red dot next to the number of the channel that contains the sprite you are about to animate. This red dot indicates you activated Real-Time Recording.

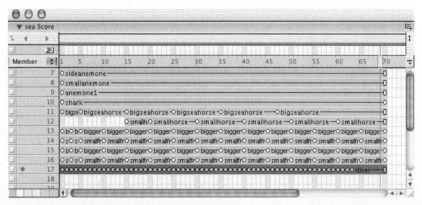

If you get into trouble, you can always close the file without saving your changes. You can then reopen the file and start over again.

4. As soon as you drag your sprite onto the Stage, the recording begins and the Playback Head starts to move across the frames in your Score. Slowly drag the sprite around the Stage and create the animation path. While you are dragging the sprite around, Director is recording the placement of the sprite as the Playback Head rolls through each frame. When the Playback Head reaches the end of the diver sprite at Frame 70 in the Score, stop dragging. Director keeps making new keyframes as long as you keep dragging the sprite.

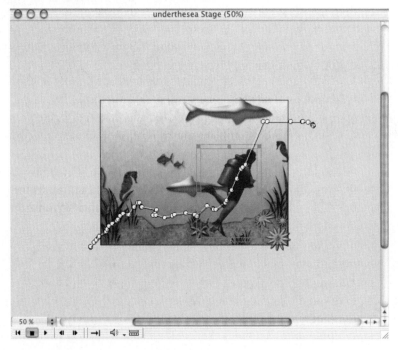

5. Rewind and play the movie. If you don't like the animation, delete the sprite in your Score and start over again, or go to the Stage and reposition the keyframes you don't like.

6. From the Cast window, drag a copy of snail to Channel 4, Frames 1-70. Highlight the snail sprite in the Score and drag it to the left side of the Stage on the sand (the beginning location where it starts to crawl onto the Stage).

7. With the snail sprite still highlighted in the Score, drag the Playback Head to Frame 1 or click the Rewind button in the Control bar at the bottom of the Stage.

8. Turn on Step-Recording by selecting Control>Step-Recording. Notice the red step-forward icon next to the number of the channel that contains the sprite you are about to animate. Also notice the bounding box around your object is larger, indicating you activated Real-Time Recording.

9. Click the Step Forward button in the Control bar at the bottom of the Stage (or select Control>Step Forward). This advances the Playback Head to the next frame. You can now move the sprite to its next position. Click the Step Forward button again and reposition the sprite. Repeat this action until you are finished with the animation. Since this is a snail, and snails move very slowly, you might want to move the snail in 1-pixel increments with the Arrow keys. To turn off Step-Recording, select it again from the Control menu or Control bar.

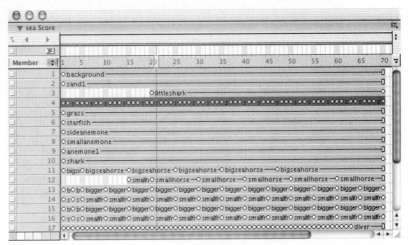

10. Rewind and play the movie. If you don't like the Step-Recording, delete the sprite in your Score and start again, or go to the Stage and reposition the keyframes you don't like.

11. Highlight the sprites in Channels 15 and 16 (biggerfry and smallfry) and select Modify>Reverse Sequence. This reverses the animation so the fish are swimming backward.

12. Highlight the sprite in Channel 15 and go to the Property Inspector. Select the Flip Horizontal icon. It is the second to last icon in the top row directly below the tabs (the first icon in the row resembles a padlock). This flips the fish so it is swimming in the correct direction. Do the same for the sprite in Channel 16.

13. Reset the Span Duration to 28 frames (Director>Preferences>Sprite for Macintosh, and Edit>Preferences>Sprite for Windows).

14. Close the movie without saving your changes, and then close the application.

Chapter Summary

In this chapter, you learned about sprites. You also discovered the use of keyframes in animation, and learned many ways to create them. As a professional, using a combination of animation techniques allows you to create a more effective result than applying each technique in isolation. Utilizing these techniques (when appropriate) also increases your animation output without spending significant amounts of additional time or effort. Finally, you discovered how to put together a basic animated Director movie.

Complete Project B: Redi-Base

4 Additional Paint Tools and Vector-Based Graphics

Chapter Objectives:

The vector format is the best choice for creating simple graphics that do not require fine detail. Vector graphics can be resized without distortion, they require less RAM and disk space than bitmaps, and they download faster from the Web than bitmaps. In situations where you could use either bitmap or vector graphics, vector is the obvious choice — if for no other reason than keeping the file size small. In Chapter 4, you will:

- Learn about additional tools in the Paint Editor.
- Discover how to manipulate bitmap graphics using these tools.
- Become familiar with the concept of onion skinning, and practice using it.
- Explore the Vector Shape Editor.

Projects to be Completed:

- Gaenzle Illustration and Design (A)
- Redi-Base (B)
- Digital Portfolio (C)
- Shaw's Portfolio (D)
- ABC's (E)

Additional Paint Tools and Vector-Based Graphics

Since Macromedia introduced the Vector Shape Editor in Director 7, two types of graphics have been available: vector and bitmap. The decision on which format to use for a particular application is simple, one that will be familiar to those who have worked with other illustration and photo-manipulation programs such as Illustrator, FreeHand, or Photoshop.

The bitmap format is ideal for working with complex images because it allows you to control the image on a pixel-by-pixel basis. Bitmaps store information about each pixel, resulting in a much larger file that occupies more RAM and disk space than a comparable vector-based graphic.

Additional Paint Editor Tools

Although Director's Paint Editor does not provide the breadth of tools that Corel Painter and Adobe Photoshop offer, it does include many powerful options. Some of its tools allow you to align and measure graphics, and others allow you to modify graphics after they have been created. We will explore some of these tools in this chapter.

Please note that the paint tools located on the bar that runs across the top of the Paint Editor can only be used in conjunction with the Marquee tool. This is because most of these tools require X,Y coordinates to calculate the types of changes these tools were designed to make. A marquee has four corner points, each of which has its own X,Y coordinates.

The Lasso tool, on the other hand, makes its selections based on the outline of the object. Most objects are not squares or rectangles — they are organic objects or complex objects with no definite corner points, so the Lasso can't be used with most of the paint tools across the top of the Paint Editor.

Rulers

Rulers are only available in the Paint Editor, and are typically used to provide information on the size of an object being created. The ruler can be set to measure in pixels, inches, or centimeters. Typically, when working in multimedia- or Web-design programs, pixels are used as the units of measurement. Director automatically defaults to pixels.

The rulers can be viewed in the Paint Editor by selecting View>Rulers. The units can be changed to pixels, inches, or centimeters by clicking the intersection point of the rulers.

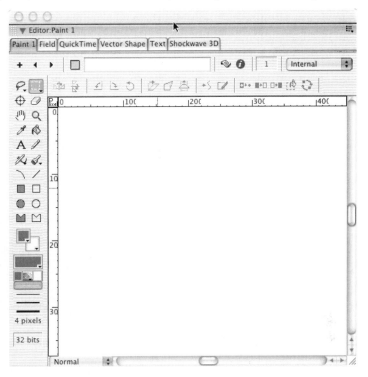

Registration Point Tool

When you place a sprite on the Stage by dragging a cast member to the Score, the sprite appears centered on the Stage; Director calculates the center of the sprite as well as the center of the Stage. The registration point is the point around which your graphic will rotate or animate. In order for Director to make this and other calculations, it utilizes each cast member's registration point. Each cast member is automatically given a registration point when it is created. In the case of animation, the registration point of your graphic is what will touch and follow all the keyframes in a sequence.

With the Registration Point tool, you can set or change the registration point of a graphic to any point within the graphic. For instance, to create a spinning ball, you should leave the registration point in the center of the ball. To make the hands of a clock rotate, however, you would move the registration point to the end of each of the hands so the hands rotate from a fixed, central point, creating correctly moving clock hands.

The Registration Point tool is located under the Lasso tool in the Paint Editor. When it is activated, it displays crosshairs that identify the position of the registration point. To change the registration point, click where the lines intersect in the Paint Editor and drag the intersection to a new point.

The Vector Shape Editor also has a Registration Point tool, and it works the same way as the Registration Point tool in the Paint Editor.

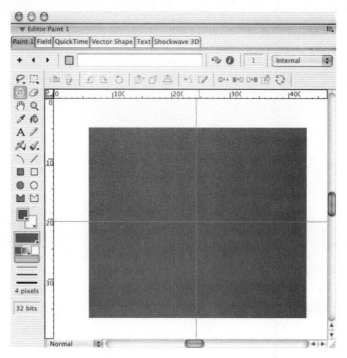

The registration point is in the exact center of this rectangle.

Flip Tools

The first group of buttons on the left edge of the bar is the flip tools group. They flip anything in the Paint Editor horizontally, vertically, or respectively. To use the flip tools, select the item to be flipped using the Marquee tool, and then click the Flip Horizontal or Flip Vertical tool.

Flip Horizontal tool on the left, Flip Vertical tool on the right.

Rotation Tools

The Paint Editor offers a set of rotation tools. To access these, or any of the tools along the top of the Paint Editor window, you must first select an entire graphic with the Marquee tool. Then you can select the rotate tool you want to use.

The Rotate Left and Rotate Right tools allow you to rotate your graphic 90 degrees at a time, clockwise or counterclockwise. The Free Rotate tool allows you to select any corner of the graphic and rotate in any amount.

From left to right: Rotate Left, Rotate Right, and Free Rotate tools.

Skew, Warp, and Perspective Tools

The next group of buttons across the top of the Paint Editor contains the Skew, Warp, and Perspective tools. These tools work the same way as the Free Rotate tool. You can click the tool you want to use, click a corner of a graphic, and then drag. Note that depending on which tool you select, the corner points of the selection box surrounding your graphic change shape.

From left to right: Skew, Warp, and Perspective tools.

Smooth and Trace Edges

The Smooth tool performs a version of *anti-aliasing* on the selected items, smoothing the transition between one color and another. The result is a blur effect. Smoothing can be increasingly applied to a graphic with each click of the Smooth tool. The Smooth effect works only on 32-bit images. To increase the bit depth of an image, you can select Modify>Transform Bitmap and change the bit depth to 32-bit.

The Smooth and Trace Edges tools.

The Trace Edges tool produces an outline of the object and deletes the original. If you repeatedly apply the effect, the result is consecutive outlines. For example, the Trace Edges effect was applied four times to create the four outlines below.

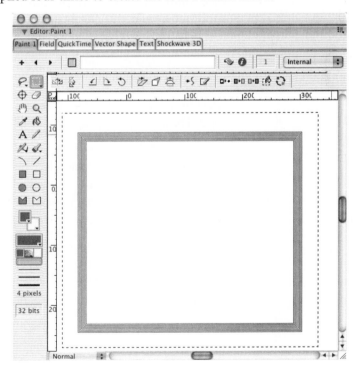

Invert, Lighten, Darken, Fill, and Switch Colors

The last group of buttons contains the Invert, Lighten, Darken, Fill, and Switch Colors effects:

- Invert reverses the colors of the selected graphic to the opposite color on the color wheel. Black becomes white, red becomes green, and so on.

- Lighten and Darken either decrease (lighten) or increase (darken) the contrast of an image, depending on which tool you choose. The behavior of these effects varies depending on the bit depth of the graphic. Both work well on 32-bit graphics, but they do not work at all on 16-bit graphics.

- The Fill option fills the selected area with the current foreground color. This effect works similar to the Paint Bucket tool.

- Switch Colors substitutes a single color in the selected area with another color. All the other colors remain unaffected. You must, however, be certain the current color of the graphic is the color located in your Beginning Gradient Color box and the new color is in the Ending Gradient Color box.

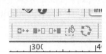

From left to right: Invert, Lighten, Darken, Fill, and Switch Colors tools.

Use Paint Tools

1. If you want to preview a completed version of this exercise file before you begin, select **finparty.dir** from the **RF_Director** folder. To start the exercise, open **party.dir** from the **RF_Director** folder. It is a partially completed project. You will complete the project in this chapter.

2. Let's start with something easy. Drag the Playback Head to Frame 81. You see an angel in the Cast. Double-click the angel to open her in the Paint Editor.

3. Select the angel with the Marquee tool. Click the Lighten tool twice to lighten the angel. The angel's details are crisper and she appears brighter.

4. Go to the middle section of the Director movie. Drag a copy of the angel cast member to the Stage and place her on the Christmas tree on the left side of the page as shown below (your Playback Head must be somewhere between Frames 81 and 144 to see the image below). Put the angel copy into Channel 15, Frames 81–144.

When working in 32-bit color, the Switch Colors tool only works on the part of the object that has been selected with the Lasso tool. Both the Lasso and Marquee tools work for other bit depths.

5. Next, let's create some special effects type. From the Paint Editor, click the plus sign (+) to create an empty cast slot.

6. Double-click the Text tool. Select a dark yellow-orange for the color of your text. Choose 48-pt. ATC Pine Heavy. Click OK to close the box.

7. Type "Christmas Party" so it is centered on two lines as shown below. Type "Christmas" on the first line, press the Return/Enter key, press the Spacebar a few times to indent the second line, and then type the word "Party". If necessary, use the Lasso tool to modify the spacing to center Party below Christmas.

8. Select the words with the Marquee tool. Before you do so, verify that the Marquee tool's drop-down menu is not set to Shrink. Leave some room around the words when you select them. Click the Trace Edges tool twice. The result should resemble the image below.

9. Click the Foreground Color box and select a dark blue color. Select the Paint Bucket tool from the Toolbar. Make sure it is set to Normal at the bottom of the Paint Editor window. You don't want any unexpected Ink effects.

10. Click the middle of each letter with the very tip of the Paint Bucket tool to fill the centers of the letters with dark blue. If necessary, use the Magnifying Glass tool to zoom in. Move slowly and carefully.

You can only undo one step in Director. If you work too fast and click in the wrong spot more than once, you won't be able to undo both errors.

11. Let's place the image. Drag a copy of the image to Channel 14, Frames 102-144. Highlight the entire sprite in the Score, then go to the Stage and drag it to the top half of the white box. It should be placed as shown below. Highlight the sprite in the Score and change it from Copy to Background Transparent in the Property Inspector.

12. Save the movie as "partypractice.dir" in your **Work_In_Progress** folder. Keep this file open for the next exercise.

Onion Skinning

Onion skinning is a term used by traditional 2-D animators. They would work with see-through paper to quickly create overlays to reference the prior position of a character or a scene while they painted the next position. This allowed them to make certain the new image was the correct size and in the correct position.

Director includes the Onion Skin palette, which can be accessed from the View menu. The Onion Skin palette is available only while you are working in the Paint Editor. You must have at least one cast member for the Onion Skin feature to work.

To use the Onion Skin feature:

- Open the Paint Editor and click the plus sign (+) in the top-left corner to go to the next empty cast slot.
- Create an object in the Paint Editor and then click the plus sign (+) to go to the next empty cast slot.
- Open the Onion Skin palette by selecting View>Onion Skin.
- Turn on onion skinning by clicking the first button on the left side of the palette.
- Set the number in the first white box in the Onion Skin palette to 1. This allows you to see one previous cast member in the Paint Editor. Even though it's grayed out and you can't access it, you can use it as a reference. You can change the number in the first white box to the number of previous cast members you want to use as references. You can change the number in the second white box to the number of following cast members you want to use as references.

The remaining three buttons on the Onion Skin palette are:

- Set Background, used to select a certain cast member for use as a background.
- Show Background, used to reference only the background you selected, no matter where it is in the Cast.
- Track Background, which basically pulls the background cast member along and always keeps it in the previous Cast window as you make each new cast member.

In the following example, we created a rectangular outline. Next, the circle was created to fit in the top half of the rectangle using the Onion Skin palette set to 1 previous cast member. This way, the rectangle was referenced for position. Finally, the triangle was created to fit into the bottom half of the rectangle. The Onion Skin palette was set to 2 previous cast members.

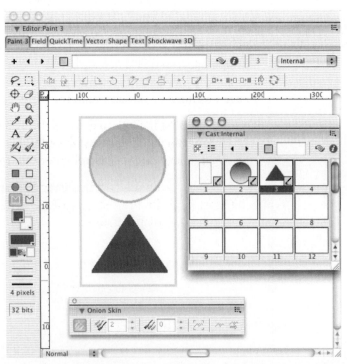

When you drag the Playback Head back and forth through the movie, it is referred to as "scrubbing" the movie.

Work with the Onion Skin Feature

1. Continue working in partypractice.dir. If you drag the Playback Head through the movie, you notice there are three main sections. We will work with the last section first, which contains the window. From the Cast, click the second empty cast slot (Slot 10). Open the Paint Editor.

2. Double-click the Text tool in the Paint Editor. In the dialog box that pops up, select 72-pt. ATC Pine Bold Italic, and a very dark red color. Click OK to close the dialog box.

3. Type "Happy Holidays!" Put Happy on the first line and Holidays! on the second line as you did with Christmas Party in Step 7 of the previous exercise. Center the words. If necessary, use the Lasso tool to select one of the words and move it to the correct location.

4. Select View>Onion Skin to open the Onion Skin palette. Click the first icon on the left of the palette to turn on Onion Skinning. Set the number in the first window to 1. You should see the window cast member.

5. Now that you can see the window, you can move the words you typed into the correct position. Select the type with the Marquee tool and move it to the upper-right pane of the window.

6. Select the Perspective tool from the row of tools along the top of the Paint Editor window. Adjust the type to make it look like it's painted on the window glass. To do this, click the bottom-right corner of the selection box and drag down until the bottom of the selection box is parallel with the wood in the windowpane. Then, click the top-right corner and drag up until the top of the box is parallel with the top of the windowpane.

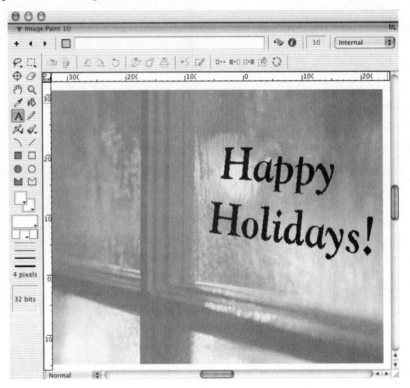

7. Drag a copy of the new Happy Holidays! cast member into Channel 5, Frames 170–190. Highlight the whole sprite and move it to the correct spot on the Stage. Scrub that section to see how it looks. Highlight the sprite in the Score and change it from Copy to Background Transparent in the Property Inspector.

8. Next, let's use the same technique to add some type to the first section (Santa Claus). Scrub the Playback Head to the first section. Click the first empty cast slot (Slot 2).

9. We need to put an introduction in the top-right corner of the image. From the Paint Editor, choose 48-pt. ATC Pine Bold Italic, and set the Color to the lightest gray.

10. The Onion Skinning should still be on and set to 1, so you should be able to see the Santa image. Enter the words, "Have you been good this year?" Stagger the words so they fit well and wrap around Santa's head.

11. Drag a copy of the text into Channel 2, Frames 2–80. Highlight the entire sprite and move it to the correct spot on the Stage. While the sprite is still highlighted, change it from Copy to Background Transparent in the Property Inspector. Scrub the Playback Head to check your movie.

12. Save your changes and keep the movie open for the next exercise.

Vector Shape Editor

As stated previously, Director includes tools that allow you to create vector shapes. Geometric in nature, vector shapes are created and displayed using mathematical formulas. These shapes consist of a series of points with connecting lines. Vectors are clean, smooth shapes that are best used for the development of simple objects. Vector images don't degrade when scaled — they can be resized without distortion or loss of quality.

The Vector Shape Editor can be accessed by selecting Window>Vector Shape.

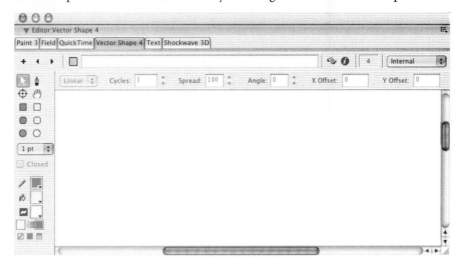

Vector Shape Tools

The Vector Shape Editor offers tools similar to those in the Paint Editor. It includes Rectangle, Ellipse, and Rounded-Edge Rectangle tools. These shapes include points and point handles that extend off the points. You can drag the different points in or out to create an infinite number of new shapes.

In the following example, the filled circle has four points. Each point has a set of handles protruding from it that determines the angle and the length of the curve. Rather than using predetermined vector shapes, these points and curves can also be created freehand with the Pen tool.

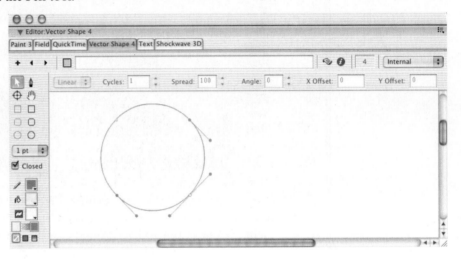

Pen Tool

Director's Pen tool is similar to the Pen tool found in Photoshop, Illustrator, PageMaker, QuarkXPress, and FreeHand. You can use the Pen tool to create lines and curves between points.

Once the Pen tool is accessed, you can click anywhere you want to place a point. For curves, click to create a point and then drag. When you drag, you create handles that determine how the line curves through the point. Extending the handles determines the length of the curve; rotating the handles determines the angle of the curve. If you plan to add color to your shape, be sure to close the shape by clicking the beginning point.

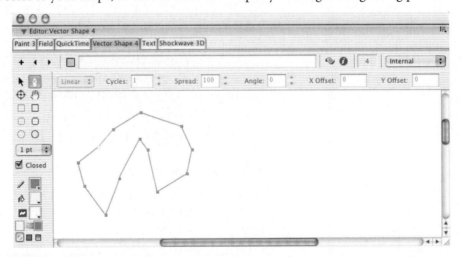

To achieve soft corners in curved shapes, drag each point to approximately 1/2 in. to display the handles. If you select the Arrow tool, you can click the ends of the handles to manipulate them.

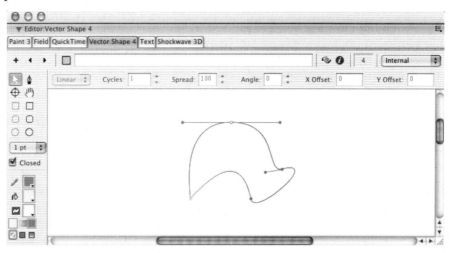

Stroke, Fill, and Background

After you have created a closed vector shape, you can fill it with solid colors or gradients. The first step in choosing a fill for a shape is to know about the three important icons located across the bottom of the left side of the Vector Shape Editor.

From left to right, the No Fill, Fill, and Gradient icons.

Before you can fill a shape, you must first choose how to fill it, and whether to fill it at all. Then you can choose the stroke, fill, and background colors. To apply stroke, fill, and background colors, you can click the button of choice, and the Color palette appears. You can then select a color, and it is applied to the stroke, fill, or background:

From top to bottom, the Stroke, Fill, and Background icons.

- Stroke changes the color of the outside line of an object. You can change the thickness of this line as well as the color. The default setting is 1 pt., but you can select an alternate line weight from the drop-down menu under the vector shapes.
- Fill applies the color you choose to the area inside the stroke of the shape.
- Background provides a background color around the shape.

Gradients

Gradients can be created within vector shapes. The bottom row of the Gradient box, from left to right, offers No Fill, Solid, or Gradient options. To create a gradient, first you must create a shape, make sure it is selected, and then click the Gradient option.

There are two available options for gradient colors. The Foreground option sets the starting color of the gradient, and the Destination option sets the ending color. You can alter the colors at any time as long as you select Gradient from the Fill options.

Across the top of the Vector Shape Editor window, there are additional options that can be assigned to a gradient. You can set the type of gradient to Linear or Radial. You can set the Cycle to determine how many times the gradient repeats inside the object (up to a maximum of seven cycles). You can set the Spread to affect the sharpness or smoothness of the transition between colors, and you can set the Angle upon which the gradient is based.

The "X" Offset (horizontal) and "Y" Offset (vertical) will offset the gradient within your shape by a specified number of pixels. It is recommended to experiment with these options; that's the best way to understand how they operate.

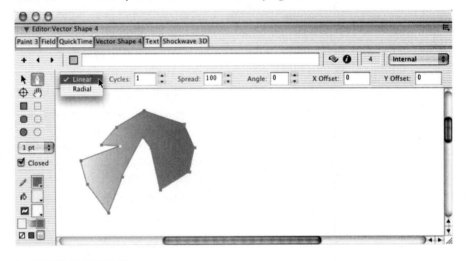

Create Vector Shapes

1. If it is not already open, open partypractice.dir from your **Work_In_Progress** folder. Open the Vector Shape Editor. Let's create a small blue Christmas ball for the tree.

2. Use the Filled Ellipse tool to create the ball. Hold down the Shift key while you draw a 1-in. circle.

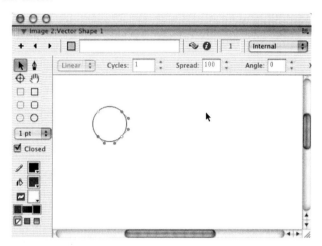

3. Set the line Width to 1/2 in.

4. Navigate to the Gradient Color boxes at the bottom of the window. Click the left box (beginning color) and choose a medium dark blue color. Click the right box (ending color) and choose a very dark blue color.

5. Click the Gradient icon — the icon in the bottom-right corner of the Toolbar. You should see the gradient on the ball. Make sure the Line tool's Color box (the top box in the vertical column of color boxes) is set to the same dark blue color used in the gradient.

6. Click the drop-down menu at the top of the window that says Linear and change it to Radial. Set the Cycles value to 2. The gradient should make the ball appear three-dimensional. If you want to change either of the gradient colors, do so now. Changing the intensity of the light or dark blue changes the appearance of the gradient.

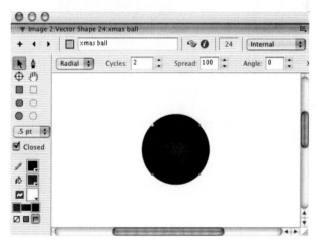

7. Drag a copy of the new blue Christmas ball to the Stage and place it on the Christmas tree. If it is too large, select a corner of the bounding box, hold down the Shift key, and drag toward the center of the Christmas ball until it is the size you prefer. It should be smaller than the other Christmas balls because you will be placing four balls on the tree.

8. After you have sized it appropriately, make sure it is placed into Channel 16, Frames 81-144.

9. Highlight the whole sprite in the Score, and then copy it. Click Channel 17, Frame 81, and then paste a duplicate of the sprite. You won't see an additional Christmas ball on the Stage because it is positioned on top of the original.

10. Make two more copies and place them into Frame 81 of Channels 18 and 19. Go to the Stage and move the balls to positions of your choice. Remember to highlight the entire sprite in the Score before you move the balls on the Stage so you don't create any unwanted animations.

11. Rewind and play the complete movie.

12. Save your movie, and then close Director.

Chapter Summary

In this chapter, you learned how to use the rest of the tools in the Paint Editor. You discovered how to modify existing graphics using these tools, and you practiced using most of the tools on a realistic presentation.

In addition, you learned about onion skinning and its importance in animation. You practiced using onion skinning to make sure cast members were the proper size and/or shape to correctly fit together when used on the Stage.

Finally, you explored the Vector Shape Editor and created a shape to use in the presentation. Whether or not you create graphics in Director, you now know how to manipulate them when they are imported to the program.

5 Manipulating Sprites and Adding Transitions

Chapter Objectives:

There are many ways to manipulate a sprite's properties to make it unique. Many of those changes can be made in the Property Inspector; others can be made from the Paint Editor. Transitioning from one frame to the next can also create the appearance of manipulating a sprite. This chapter examines the many different methods used to affect sprites and change their appearances. In Chapter 5, you will:

- Learn different ways to modify the properties of a sprite.

- Practice creating spinning objects.

- Become familiar with and create a film loop.

- Practice using the Auto Distort Xtra option in conjunction with rotation tools.

- Learn about transitions and how to apply them.

- Become comfortable manipulating individual sprites and their properties.

Projects to be Completed:

- Gaenzle Illustration and Design (A)

- Redi-Base (B)

- Digital Portfolio (C)

- Shaw's Portfolio (D)

- ABC's (E)

Manipulating Sprites and Adding Transitions

Sprites can be manipulated in many ways. Sprite properties can be found under the Sprite tab in the Property Inspector. These properties range from the length of the sprite and its placement on the Stage, to which Ink effects are attached to it, and what blend percentage the sprite has on any given frame. Each property can be modified to create interesting and unique animations.

What would you do if you needed multiple sprites to uniformly move across the Stage? For instance, let's say you animated a dog, and made his feet move, his nose sniff, and his tail wag using many different sprites; but now, you want the dog to waltz across the Stage. How would you get all of the components of the animation to accurately work together?

This can be accomplished by taking every sprite that comprise the dog and his body motions, putting them in the Score in the correct order, and then turning them all into a single cast member called a *film loop*. A film loop can be placed in the Score as a single sprite and animated across the screen using keyframes, similar to any other sprite.

In this chapter, you will also be introduced to transitions. *Transitions* are special effects that ease the change between one frame and the next. They also supply visual interest to your movie.

When used to their fullest potential, film loops and transitions can make a significant and positive impact on your movie. Knowing when and how to apply these effects is critical for every digital moviemaker.

Sprite Properties and Settings

A sprite's properties and variable settings can be found under the Sprite tab in the Property Inspector. This tab contains information about the currently selected sprite. If no sprite is currently selected, the Sprite tab is not available in the Property Inspector. The following sections explain the properties and settings that can be applied to a sprite.

Active Sprite

The icon in the top-left corner of the Sprite tab displays the sprite that is currently active. It also provides some basic information about that sprite. We know from the image below that the selected sprite is a bitmap, it is located in the first slot of the Cast, and it is part of the Internal Cast.

Start Frame, End Frame

In the lower half of the Sprite tab, you find the Start Frame and End Frame fields. The Start Frame number appears in the left field and the End Frame number is in the right field. You can enter new values in these fields to adjust the length of the sprite or move it to different frames within the Score.

Editable, Moveable, and Trails Buttons

The Editable, Movable, and Trails buttons are grouped together in the middle of the top row of the Sprite tab.

- The Editable button, found on the left of this group, is used when you want to allow a viewer to enter information in a text field, or edit text currently in a field, while a Director movie is playing. This feature might be used for an order form or a sign-in book.

- The Moveable (middle) button is used when you want a viewer to be able to drag a cast member around while a movie is playing. An example might be a digital paper doll on which a child can drop pieces of clothing to increase hand-eye coordination.

• The Trails (right) button is used when you want to make the selected sprite remain on the Stage and leave a trail of images along its path as the movie plays. If you highlight a sprite while animating, click the Trails button, and then turn on Real-Time Recording or use regular keyframes and tweening, the result is a trail of sprites behind the original.

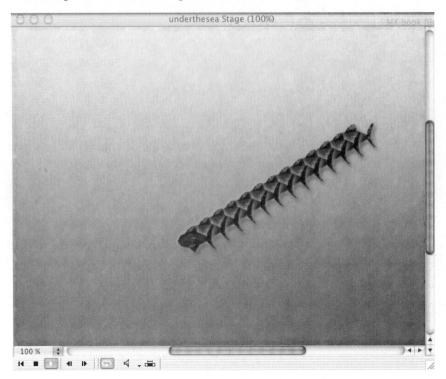

This is an example of Trails.

Ink Effects

Ink effects can be assigned to a sprite. These effects change the appearance of a sprite when it comes in contact with other sprites. Applying a particular Ink effect to the top sprite generates a new result when it comes in contact with a sprite below it.

Ink effects can be used to create special effects or to solve everyday-production problems. For instance, when used on text or a graphic, the Matte Ink effect (on the Sprite tab in the Property Inspector) removes the white box around a graphic.

If you look at the Sprite tab of the Property Inspector, you see the Ink effects value field. The effects are listed in a drop-down menu. To apply an Ink effect, you can simply highlight a sprite in the Score, and then choose the Ink effect from the menu.

Blend Percentage

The Blend Percentage setting is to the right of the Ink effects menu. Here, you can set a sprite to different blend percentages, making the sprite become more or less transparent when placed on top of another sprite. This feature is similar to the opacity slider in Photoshop.

Foreground and Background Color

Using the Foreground and Background Color swatches, you can change the colors of simple sprites and their backgrounds without accessing the Paint Editor. You can highlight a sprite in the Score and then click the color swatches to choose new foreground and background colors. You can also enter the hexadecimal values for the new colors in the Forecolor and Backcolor value fields. This method does not work with film loops (which we will discuss later), because they are made up of multiple versions of a sprite.

X,Y Coordinates

The X,Y coordinates of a sprite (in pixels) are based on the distance from its registration point to either the left side (X) or the top (Y) of the Stage. If you refer to the image below, this sprite's registration point is at 322 pixels on the X axis, and 240 pixels on the Y axis. You can move sprites around the Stage by changing these numbers and pressing the Return/Enter key to apply the changes.

Width and Height

The Width and Height boxes denote the width and height of a sprite in pixels. You can change the numbers in these fields to alter the width and height of a sprite, but your changes do not affect the original cast member.

It is not recommended that you enlarge or reduce bitmap cast members too much beyond their original size (for the entire movie) as this can dramatically slow down Director's performance, depending on the file size of the bitmap cast member. If you must apply a significant permanent change in dimension to a bitmap cast member, you can select Modify>Transform Bitmap to change the size of the original.

In general, enlarging bitmaps is not a good idea because it causes the images to become jagged and grainy. Vector cast members, on the other hand (such as those made in the Vector Shape Editor), do not display any jagged edges or graininess when resized, and result in smaller files than comparable bitmap graphics.

Flip Horizontal and Vertical

The Flip Horizontal button flips a selected sprite horizontally, and the Flip Vertical button flips a selected sprite vertically.

Flip Horizontal button on the left, and Flip Vertical button on the right.

Lock

The Lock button temporarily locks a sprite so it cannot be moved or altered during development of other pieces of the movie, or when testing your presentation. A locked sprite cannot be selected and, therefore, is nearly impossible to disrupt in any way.

To lock a sprite, you must first highlight it, and then click the Lock button. To unlock the sprite, you must highlight it in the Score, and then click the Lock button again, making it selectable and editable.

The Lock button.

Rotate and Skew

The numbers in Rotate field can be changed to rotate a sprite in either the clockwise or counterclockwise direction. You must put a minus sign in front of the number if you want your object to rotate clockwise.

The Skew field is used to set the angle of a sprite. After entering a number in either or both of these fields, you can press the Return/Enter key to apply the changes. Again, these are only sprite settings, so the original cast member is not affected.

To cause an object to rotate to the left, or counterclockwise (CCW), you must enter a minus sign before typing in the number. For example, to rotate 30 degrees CCW, you would enter -30.

Top, Bottom, Left, and Right

The numbers in the Top, Bottom, Left, and Right fields refer to the specific location of a sprite on the Stage. In the example below, the left edge (L) is at 2 pixels, the top edge (T) of the sprite is at 0 pixels, the right edge (R) is at 642 pixels, and the bottom edge (B) of the sprite is at 480 pixels. Subtract the top from the bottom and the left from the right to determine your sprite's dimensions in pixels. In this example, the dimensions are 640 pixels × 480 pixels.

Alter Sprite Properties

1. If it is not already open, launch Director. Open **undersea.dir** from the **RF_Director** folder. Save this project as "underseapractice.dir" in your **Work_In_Progress** folder. If you want to see the finished file, it is called **finundersea.dir** and can also be found in the **RF_Director** folder.

2. If you play the movie, you see that the two sharks are on a collision course. Let's fix this. Highlight the littleshark sprite in the Score. Set the Blend percentage to 50%. This makes the smaller shark appear farther away, creating perspective in the underwater scene.

3. Drag the clownfish cast member from the Cast into Channel 14, Frame 1 of the Score to create a new sprite. Make certain the entire sprite is highlighted.

4. Click the Sprite tab in the Property Inspector. Enter "50" in the End Frame field and press Return/Enter to extend the sprite to Frame 50.

5. In the Start Frame field of the Sprite tab, enter "3" and then press Return/Enter. Your sprite now begins at Frame 3 and extends to Frame 50.

6. Highlight the entire sprite in the Score and place the clownfish on the left edge of the scene above the sand (refer to the image in Step 7).

7. Highlight the first keyframe of the sprite (Frame 3). Then, hold down the Shift key and select the corner of the bounding box. Drag it toward the center of the fish. This makes the fish proportionally smaller.

The clownfish is the small fish on the upper-left side of the Stage.

8. Highlight the last keyframe of the sprite (Frame 50). Drag the small clownfish toward the center of the screen (drag the fish itself — don't drag any of the corners). Once the fish is in the center of the screen, hold down the Shift key while you select a corner of the bounding box and enlarge the fish again. The fish should now swim in from the left toward the center of the screen, getting larger as it swims, as if it were swimming toward you. This is another useful way to create perspective in a scene.

9. To make the fish appear a little more realistic while it swims, insert a keyframe into Frame 22. With Frame 22 highlighted, select the fish and drag it up so the animation path becomes an arc instead of a straight line.

10. Look at the snail in the Score. The snail already has an animation path and many keyframes, but it is moving in a perfectly horizontal line. It appears to be running into the slopes of the sandy floor instead of gliding over them. To fix this, let's add various amounts of rotation to some of the keyframes. (All keyframes are currently set to 0 degrees of rotation.) Highlight the first keyframe in Frame 1. Click the Sprite tab in the Property Inspector and enter "5" in the Rotation field. Press Enter/Return to apply this change. You see the snail tilt slightly to the right. In the second keyframe (Frame 3), enter "30" in the Rotation field. The snail should tilt more and appear to crawl downhill.

11. In the fifth keyframe (Frame 23) enter "–20" in the Rotation field. Remember that you must enter a minus sign (–) to rotate to the left or counterclockwise. Now the snail is crawling uphill.

12. To finish the snail's path, select Frame 29, and enter "10" degrees for the Rotation of the snail sprite. Frames 11, 18, 40, and 50 should remain at 0 degrees rotation.

13. Use the shark sprite to experiment with the Flip Horizontal and Flip Vertical options. Unfortunately for the shark, this makes him swim backward unless you combine this change with Modify>Reverse Sequence. Explore these options now if you prefer.

14. Open the shark sprite in the Paint Editor. Select the Registration Point tool and move the registration point to a different location. Note the result. To reset the registration point, simply double-click the Registration Point tool in the Paint Editor window.

15. Continue using the shark sprite. In the Skew field in the Property Inspector, enter "20" and then press the Return/Enter key. This skews the shark in an unnatural manner. Select Edit>Undo to undo the skew on the shark.

16. Highlight the bigseahorse sprite in Channel 6 and click the Moveable button. Now click the Loop option in the Control panel or at the bottom of the Stage to turn on looping.

17. Rewind and play the movie. As it plays, drag the bigseahorse around the Stage. You won't be able to move any of the other sprites.

18. Save your movie and keep it open for the next exercise.

Film Loops

Film loops are useful for animating repetitive motions. You can use film loops to take a repetitive sequence that covers several frames and turn it into a sprite that can be as small as one frame. A film loop would be useful to make a dog's tail wag or a ball roll along the floor.

After you have created a film loop, you cannot move or rename any of the original cast members in the loop. It is also impossible to apply Ink effects to a film loop. If you want to apply an Ink effect, such as Matte or Background Transparent, you must apply the effect to the individual sprites before you convert them into a film loop.

There are four basic steps to creating a film loop:

- In the Score, highlight the sprites you want to include in your film loop.
- Select Insert>Film Loop.
- Name the film loop in the dialog box that appears and then click OK. The film loop appears in your Cast as a separate cast member.
- Return to the Score and erase the sprites you highlighted to make your loop; you no longer need them. Do not delete your original cast members by accident.

Create a Film Loop

1. Continue working in underseapractice.dir from the previous exercise. Click on the next open slot in the Cast, then open the Paint Editor and create a small ball using the Filled Ellipse tool set to No Line. Use a brown-and-white gradient as the fill. Use the Line tool to add brown spikes to the ellipse so it resembles a sea urchin. In the Name field of the Paint Editor, enter "Sea Urchin".

2. Select the Marquee tool from the Toolbar. Ensure the tool is set to Shrink by click-holding on the tool to access the pop-up menu. Select the sea urchin with the Marquee tool.

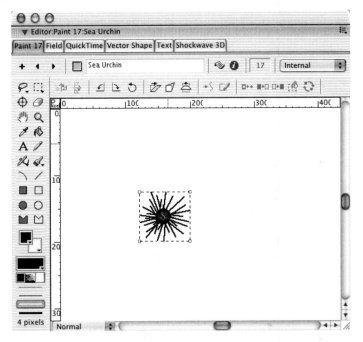

3. Click the Rotate Left button four times (each click results in a 1/4 turn). After the fourth click, the urchin is upright again. You created a full revolution of the urchin, which Director has temporarily placed into memory.

4. From the Menu bar at the top of the screen, select Xtras>Auto Distort. Enter "7" in the Generate New Cast Members field and click Begin. Director takes the full revolution (rotation) from its memory and generates 7 new cast members. Each new cast member is in the Cast. Notice that one full revolution of the ball is now divided into 8 steps.

5. The last cast member (8) is identical to the first. Since it is identical, it is not needed. Select it and press the Delete key to remove it.

6. Now highlight the first cast member, hold down the Shift key, and highlight the seventh (urchin) cast member. This should select all seven urchin cast members. Next, select Modify>Cast to Time, and notice the new sprite in your Score. The sprite contains the seven cast members in a row. It doesn't matter where the new sprite is located in your Score because it is only temporary.

7. With the sprite still selected, choose Matte or Background Transparent. Remember, you must add any Ink effects to the sprite before it becomes a film loop — Ink effects cannot be added afterward. If you forget to add Ink effects, you must delete the film loop and then re-create it. If you played the movie right now, you would see the urchin spin, but it is not yet a film loop; it is still a simple sprite.

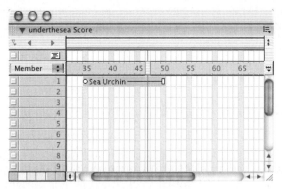

8. Let's turn the sprite into a single cast member. With the spite still highlighted, select Insert>Film Loop.

9. Name the film loop "Urchin" and click OK.

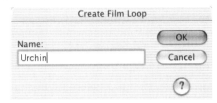

10. Notice that the film loop is placed into the first empty cast slot. Return to the Score and delete the sprite you used to make the film loop.

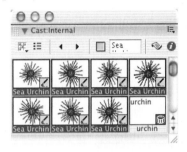

11. Drag a copy of the film loop into Channel 15, Frame 1 of the Score, and make it 50 frames long. Rewind and play the movie. Your sea urchin should spin in the center of the Stage. Highlight the whole sprite in the Score and drag the urchin off the left edge of the Stage about halfway up the sand.

12. Highlight the last keyframe (Frame 50) and drag the urchin to right side of the Stage (refer to the image in Step 13).

13. Insert two keyframes into Frames 15 and 31. Drag the two keyframes on the stage into the path you want the sea urchin to take as it rolls across the screen.

14. To help achieve a soft or hard edge on your keyframes, select Modify>Sprite>Tweening to display the Sprite Tweening dialog box. Adjust the Curvature slider to sharpen or soften the edges or arcs your keyframes form.

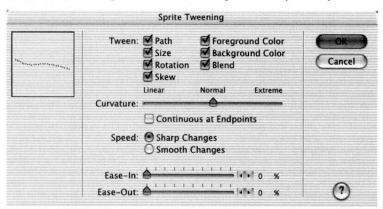

15. Play your movie to view the result. Save your changes, and then close the file.

Transitions

Most people have seen a television show where the camera switched from one scene to another using an interesting effect for the transition. Dissolves, wipes, and fades are three of the most commonly used transitions in traditional filmmaking. Transitions are used to reveal new objects or to make objects disappear from the Stage. A dissolve gradually deletes the pixels of objects on the Stage to allow new objects to show through, providing smooth transitions from one frame to the next.

There are aesthetic issues to consider when choosing a transition. Just as *Charlie's Angels* reruns appear dated, so, too, will your production if you make poor choices for transitions.

Keep your subject matter in mind when selecting transitions. A checkerboard transition is inappropriate for a professional business meeting, but may be perfect for a children's interactive CD.

Transition Channel

In the Special Channels section of the Score, there is a channel with an icon that resembles a black bow tie. This is the Transition channel. If the Special Channels section is not visible, click the Hide/Show button, shown below.

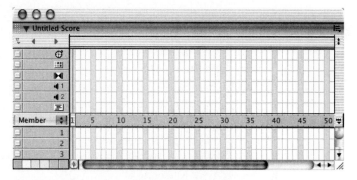

The Hide/Show button is the double arrow (Macintosh) or double "+" (Windows) in the upper-right corner of the window.

Transitions should always be placed in the Transition channel of the frame to which you are transitioning. For example, if you want a red box in Frame 1 to dissolve into a purple diamond in Frame 2, you would put the transition in the Transition channel of Frame 2.

Transition Dialog Box

The Transition dialog box provides a variety of categories and transition selections. Double-clicking in the Transition channel of the frame where you want the transition to be placed causes the Frame Properties Transition dialog box to appear.

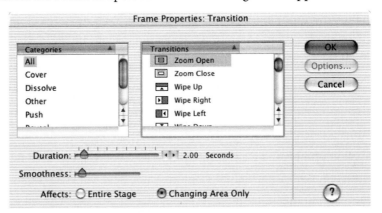

You can select the transition and adjust its duration and smoothness from this dialog box. The Duration slider indicates the length of the transition. The Smoothness slider allows you to set the transition anywhere from very choppy to so smooth that you barely realize it's happening. The Affects option allows you to select whether you want the entire Stage, or only the objects on the Stage, to transition to the next frame.

After you have chosen a transition, you should notice that Director created a cast member from your transition, and placed it in the Cast. If you need this transition again, you can simply pull it out of the Cast and place it in the Transition channel, rather than recreating the transition from scratch.

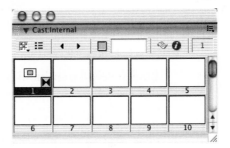

Types of Transitions

The transitions appear on the right side of the Transition dialog box. You can choose from many types, which are divided into categories and listed on the left side of the dialog box. If a category is not selected, it is automatically set to the default of All, which provides a complete list of categories from which to choose. This list appears on the right side of the palette. If you know which category you're looking for, make your selection in advance to display a shorter list of available transitions. This makes the category selection process more efficient.

Listed below are the various transition categories with brief descriptions:

- **Cover**. A Cover transition acts like a blanket to cover old objects with new ones. Covers can enter from the top, bottom, right, or left.

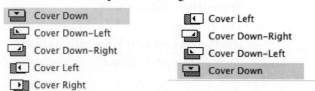

- **Dissolve**. Dissolve transitions dissolve the current objects while allowing the new objects to show through from below. You can dissolve at various speeds and with different shapes, such as pixels, bits, squares, or rectangles.

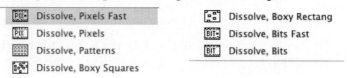

- **Other**. The Other category contains a group of specialty transitions that don't fit into any other category. These include the Checkerboard, Vertical Blinds, and Venetian Blinds transitions.

- **Push**. Push transitions make the new frame of objects push the old frame off the Stage. These can come across the Stage from the top, bottom, left, or right.

- **Reveal**. Reveal transitions are the opposite of Cover transitions — the blanket that is over the old objects is removed to reveal the new objects.

- **Strips**. Strips transitions slide across the Stage and build on top of one another to cover it. They can start and build from any side of the Stage.

- **Wipe**. Wipe transitions remove the old objects and leave behind the new. They can wipe from the center out and from the edges in, as well as from the right, left, top, and bottom.

Wipe Up		Edges In, Vertical	
Wipe Right		Edges In, Square	
Wipe Left		Edges In, Horizontal	
Wipe Down		Center Out, Vertical	
		Center Out, Square	
		Center Out, Horizontal	

Use Transitions

1. To preview the finished file before you begin this exercise, select **RF_Director>fincedarmtn.dir**.

2. From the **RF_Director** folder, select **cedarmtn.dir**.

3. Save this movie as "transition.dir" in your **Work_In_Progress** folder.

4. Click the Movie tab in the Property Inspector. Click the color swatch to the right of the Paint Bucket icon and change the Stage Color to Black. While you are in the Movie tab, ensure the Stage Size is set to 640 × 480 pixels.

5. Select Window>Control Panel and verify that the Loop option is turned off. Set the Frames Per Second to 5.

6. Place the following cast members in Channel 1:

cedarmtn	Frames 1-15
hiking	Frames 16-30
camping	Frames 31-45
canoe	Frames 46-60
snowboard	Frames 61-75
picnic	Frames 76-90
biking	Frames 91-105
resting	Frames 106-120
backpack	Frames 121-135
end	Frames 136-150

7. In Frame 16, double-click in the Transition channel to bring up the Transition dialog box. Highlight Cover in the list on the left, and select Cover Down-Right from the Transitions list. Ensure the Duration is set to 2 seconds. Set the Affects option to Changing Area Only, and then click OK.

8. In the Transition channel of Frame 31, set the Category to Dissolve and then select Dissolve Bits with the same settings from Step 7. Place the following transitions in the frames identified:

Frame: 46	Category: Wipe	Type: Center-Out Horizontal
Frame: 61	Category: Push	Type: Push-Left
Frame: 76	Category: Reveal	Type: Reveal-Down
Frame: 91	Category: Strips	Type: Strips on Top, Build Left
Frame: 106	Category: Wipe	Type: Edges in, Vertical
Frame: 121	Category: Other	Type: Vertical Blinds
Frame: 136	Category: Other	Type: Random-Rows

9. From the Control panel, rewind and play the movie to view a sampling of the transitions Director has to offer. Some of these transitions are fun to work with, but are rarely used in actual production.

10. Save your file and close Director.

Chapter Summary

In this chapter, you learned a variety of ways to manipulate sprites. You discovered how to modify a sprite's animation using various items in the Property Inspector, making it unique.

You also learned about film loops and the correct way to make them using the Cast to Time option. You practiced making a sprite spin using the Rotate features of the Paint Editor and the Auto Distort Xtra option.

Finally, you learned about transitions and how to apply them to frames of a movie. Now that you have learned many of the basics, it's time to explore a more advanced technique — interactivity.

Interactivity, Navigation, and Buttons

Chapter Objectives:

Navigation buttons and interactive elements are found in virtually every multimedia production. It is possible to create buttons in Director, but many users develop buttons in some other application — Photoshop, Illustrator, or FreeHand — and then import them into Director as cast members. Whether you create buttons in Director or another graphics program, you must use the Lingo scripting language to make the buttons work in a Director movie. In Chapter 6, you will:

- Become familiar with the concept of a Main menu.

- Discover how to turn cast members into interactive buttons.

- Learn about and use markers.

- Explore some of the various ways to navigate through a project.

- Examine and use some basic Lingo scripts.

Projects to be Completed:

- Gaenzle Illustration and Design (A)

- Redi-Base (B)

- Digital Portfolio (C)

- Shaw's Portfolio (D)

- ABC's (E)

Interactivity, Navigation, and Buttons

Before beginning any multimedia project, it is recommended you create a flow chart and plenty of hand-drawn sketches. These items allow you to sort through your ideas, and ensure your design is logical and complete. There comes a point, however, when you must put aside those visual aids and begin development.

This chapter explores some of the steps you must follow to turn Director movies into interactive experiences.

Basic Interactivity

Have you ever seen a computer in a music store that lists various musical selections you can sample? You can interact with the computer's software, clicking here and there, and choose what you want to hear.

The screen that lists all of the options is called the *Main menu*. It's typically the first list of options you see if you're using a piece of interactive multimedia.

If the only purpose of your movie is to be viewed, with no interaction, there may be no need for a Main menu.

Exercise Setup

Since the Main menu is typically the first screen you can access in an interactive piece, we will use it to begin our exploration of interactivity. To become familiar with how a Main menu works, you will view a partially completed example in this exercise. Later in the chapter, you will learn how to complete the Main menu and make it functional.

Note: Make sure to load your ATC fonts before beginning this exercise.

Look at a Main Menu

1. If you want to view the finished version of this exercise before you begin, open **findeco.dir** from the **RF_Director** folder. To begin this exercise, open **deco.dir** from the **RF_Director** folder.

2. Choose File>Save As, and save this file as "decopractice.dir" in your **Work_In_Progress** folder.

3. Play the decopractice movie. Watch as it moves through a series of screens and transitions (dissolves) and ends with a map of the New York City streets. The map resembles a grid with some colored squares on it. This is the Main menu for this movie. Notice that some of the buttons are missing. Gray boxes mark the spots where the buttons should be.

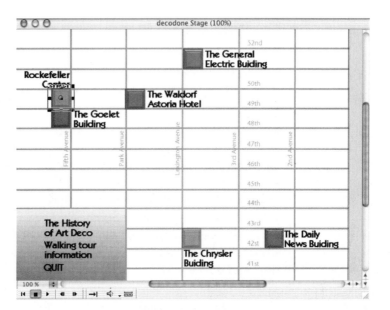

4. Keep this file open for the next exercise.

Using a Frame Script to Pause a Movie

When you first create a Main menu page, you notice that after clicking Play to start the movie, the Playback Head starts on the sprite containing the Main menu and keeps rolling right over your sprites. It is impossible to select anything.

This problem can be resolved in a few different ways. For now, we will discuss two solutions, both of which require the use of the Script channel, located in the Score directly above the frame numbers in the Special Channels section.

To access a script, you can double-click the Script channel in the frame where you want your script to be placed. Double-clicking the Script channel opens the Behavior Script window. The cursor should already be in the correct position. In the example below, we entered "go to the frame" and then closed the window.

Notice in the image above that there is some text in the dialog box that reads *on exitFrame* and *end*. These are known as *handlers*. They notify Director to pay attention to the instruction that was entered. We simply instructed Director that when it is ready to leave this particular frame, it should go back around and enter the same frame again. We are effectively looping the Playback Head on this single frame.

*If **on exitFrame** is not showing in the Behavior Script window, click the "L" button (Lingo) and look under "E" for exitFrame. When you choose the command, it is automatically inserted into the window.*

*A **go to the frame** command stops a movie until another script tells it to continue. Using a Pause command can cause a problem: if music is playing and an animated loop is running on the frame, it will stop both, whether that is your intention or not. To work around this problem, you can use the second option, a go to the frame script, to make the Playback Head repeat only the current frame.*

Creating a Main Menu

Be aware of how many and what kind of options your users can access on the Main menu. For instance, rather than displaying all 52 states on a menu at once, you can provide regional options such as Northeast, Mid-Atlantic, and Pacific Northwest to narrow down the viewers' choices.

As a general rule, it is a good idea to keep your Main menu options to six or fewer for ease of use and navigation. Use general categories for the six options on a Main menu, and offer more specific choices within those categories as you travel down the navigational structure. As stated above, one might start by dividing the United States into quadrants: Northeast, Southeast, Northwest, and Southwest. If a user were looking for Florida, the choice would be Southeast. Then, on the next screen, the Southeast category would be further subdivided: states that start with A-F, G-M, N-R, and S-Z. The user would click on the first option because Florida starts with an "F." From the list of states displayed on the next screen, Florida would be selected.

Complete a Main Menu

1. If it is not already active, open decopractice.dir from your **Work_In_Progress** folder.

2. Double-click the Script channel of Frame 200 in the Score and type *go to the frame* in the script, inserting the instructions between the *on mouseUp* and *end mouseUp* handlers. Close the window. This places the command in the Script channel so the channel stays still long enough for you to work on it and for end users to click it.

3. Rewind and play the movie and you see that it stops on Frame 200. If you click any of the buttons on the menu, the movie continues to play.

4. Find the missing buttons in the Cast and place them where they belong on the Stage. The Wald button (86) belongs on top of the gray square next to The Waldorf Astoria Hotel. The Rock button (84) belongs on top of the gray square under Rockefeller Center, and the Daily button (88) belongs on top of the gray square under The Daily News Building. There is room for each button in the Score above each corresponding building's text sprite.

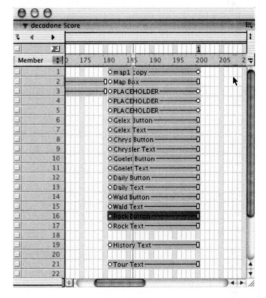

5. Extend all of these sprites to the same length as the rest of the sprites in the Main menu, from Frames 181-200.

Graphics will not react with the Highlight action until they contain a script that turns them into buttons. Do not be alarmed if you try this and the buttons don't initially work.

6. All the other finished buttons on the map become highlighted when they are clicked. To make our new buttons react in the same manner, select them one at a time in the Cast, and click the Bitmap tab in the Property Inspector. Next, check the Highlight option.

7. Save your movie and keep it open for the next exercise.

Interactive Buttons

Director provides a few button shapes, which can be found in the Tools palette. Additionally, any graphic cast member can be assigned a script to make it behave like a button.

Creating Buttons with the Tools Palette

Buttons can be created from the Tools palette using any of the Button options. Selecting the Push Button tool and dragging it onto the Stage allows you to create a smooth-cornered rectangular button. You can name the button and specify its width. The button's height, however, is determined by the point size of the text within the button.

To change the background color of the rectangular button, you can double-click the button on the Stage and choose a background color from the Tools palette.

The Push Button tool is located above and to the right of the Color boxes.

For use in online forms and charts, Director also provides ready-made check boxes and radio buttons. For radio buttons, there is even a pre-scripted behavior listed in the Control section of the Library palette (which you will learn about in a later chapter) that allows you to select only one radio button from a group at any given time. For instance, if you provide an online payment form, and you want a user to check whether he is paying by Visa, MasterCard, Discover Card, or check, this script allows the user to choose only one method. This can control a user's reaction to your online question. You will learn more about how to apply and work with behaviors in a later chapter of this book.

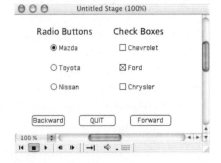

Scripts can be added to buttons by clicking the cast member Script button in the Cast and inserting the instructions between the *on mouseUp* and *end mouseUp* handlers.

Turning Cast Members into Buttons

Almost any type of cast member can be assigned a script to make it behave like a button. To do this, you can highlight the appropriate cast member and click the Script button in the upper-right corner of the Cast. After the Lingo script to direct the button has been entered, the cast member displays a miniature icon of the Lingo script on the left side of the Cast slot.

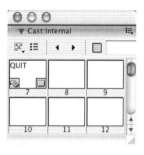

Make the Menu Buttons Work

1. Continue working in decopractice.dir. Scrub along the Score to Frame 500 where the Waldorf Astoria sprites begin. In the Cast, highlight the Wald button, and then click the Script button in the upper-right corner of the Cast to open its Lingo Script window. Type *go to frame 500*. Don't move the cursor. When you are done, close the Script window. Now click Play on the Control panel to play the movie and try the button. If it works (it should jump to Frame 500 when clicked) move on to Step 2; if it doesn't work, retrace your steps and try again.

2. Locate the Rockefeller Center sprites in your Score. These begin at Frame 220. Go to the Cast and highlight the Rock button. Open the Script window and type *go to frame 220*. Close the Script window.

3. The last button is for the Daily News Building sprites, which begin on Frame 752. Use the same procedure to open the Script window, type *go to frame 752*, and then close the Script window.

4. Save your changes. Play the movie and click the new buttons. Keep this movie open for the next exercise.

Markers

Markers provide another way to travel through a Score — particularly useful when your Score is very long. When a movie is short, it is easy to locate a specific frame; but as movies become more complex, it becomes difficult to keep track of exactly what is happening, and where. For this reason, Director offers an unlimited supply of markers, which provide an excellent way to label points of interest and navigate within your Score. Markers work similar to tabs in a word-processing or page-layout program. There's an area across the top of the Score where you can create as many markers as necessary.

Marker names must be placed within quotes in a script because Lingo recognizes them as proper names.

Lingo and Markers

You can edit, relocate, and delete markers at any time. You can also add or delete frames before or after a marker, and the marker moves along with the frame to which it is attached.

This feature can be extremely useful. In the previous exercise, you learned how to use a script to go to a particular frame. If you then add or delete a frame, there might be some confusion about the correct frame number — the sprites that were once in Frame 135 might now be in Frame 134, leading to possible scripting errors. To avoid all confusion, you can place a marker at Frame 135 and assign a specific name to it. This way, even if you add or delete a frame, your script still works because the marker moves along with the frame.

Marker names must be placed within quotes in a script because Lingo recognizes them as proper names.

Creating Markers

There is a white strip above the Special Channels section of the Score. To create a marker, you can click in this strip directly above the frame you want to mark. A triangle and a cursor appear, allowing you to name the marker. You can then slide the triangle to the left or right to move the marker. You can drag the triangle straight down toward the Visual channels to delete the marker.

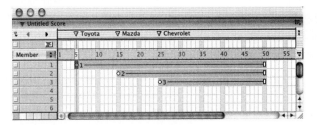

Navigating to Markers

Customized markers are good for clarity and Lingo scripting, but they also serve another purpose — for navigation. Creating markers while you work is similar to creating a road-map for your project. In the Markers palette, which is accessed from the Window menu, you can highlight the marker you want to jump to, and that frame displays on the Stage.

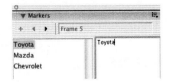

Another way to use markers for navigation is to use the Marker Menu button. This is the button located farthest to the left on the Marker bar in the Score. Highlight the marker you want to go to, and it automatically advances the Playback Head to that point in the Score.

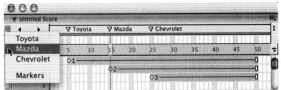

Add Markers

1. With decopractice.dir still open, let's add a couple of markers to the Score.

2. Locate Frame 808 on the Score and click the Marker bar. Name this new marker "History".

3. Move to Frame 836 and create a new marker named "Tour Info". These two markers identify where the information begins.

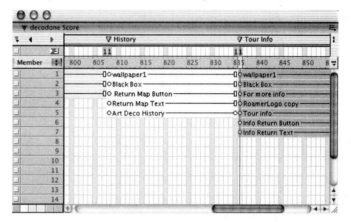

Let's go back to the Main menu and add buttons with scripts to automatically take you to these markers so you won't have to navigate through the frames.

4. Move the Playback Head to the Main menu (Frame 181). Go to your Cast and locate the History button. Place the button on the Stage to the left of The History of Art Deco. Locate the Tour button and place it on the Stage next to Walking tour Information. Locate the Quit button and place it on the Stage to the left of QUIT.

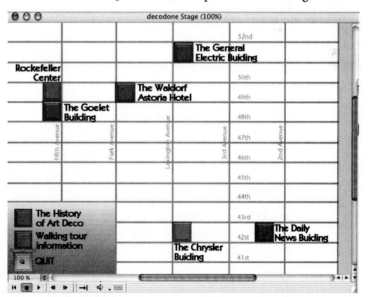

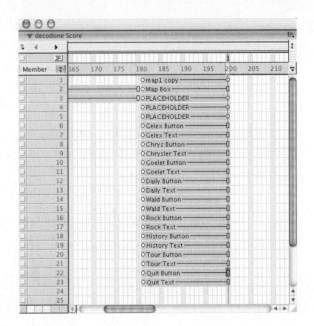

*If **on mouseUp** is not showing in the Script window for Step 5, click the "L" button and look under Mo to Move for **mouseUp**. The command is automatically inserted into the window when you choose it.*

5. Save your changes and leave the file open for the next exercise.

Navigate with Markers

1. Continue working in the open file. Highlight the History button in the Cast and click the Script button. Type *go to "History"* in the Script window. (Remember that Lingo requires the names of buttons to be placed in quotes.) The Tour button needs a script that says *go to "Tour Info"*. (If you don't see the *on mouseUp* handler in the Script window, refer to the hint in the sidebar.) Don't forget that spelling, spaces, quotes, and case all must be accurate in a Lingo script for it to work properly. Work carefully to ensure accuracy.

2. The Quit button needs a script that says *quit.*

3. Select Window>Markers to display the Markers palette. Click the different markers you created and watch your Score and Stage. The Playback Head automatically jumps to each position. As you can see, markers are similar to customized shortcuts.

4. Rewind and play your movie. It should look and act like the final version, **findeco.dir**, provided in the **RF_Director** folder.

Chapter Summary

In this chapter, you gained an understanding of the Main menu and know when it is necessary (or preferable) to include one in a movie. You learned about basic interactivity and discovered how to include interactivity with Lingo scripts.

You learned about markers and how to use them to navigate through your work. You also learned how to turn a normal cast member into an interactive button. These are the basics that prepare you to create full-sized, animated, interactive projects.

Complete Project C: Digital Portfolio

7 Adding Sound and Video

Chapter Objectives:

The addition of sound and/or video to a Director presentation can greatly enhance its effectiveness. Director can import virtually every type of sound and video file commonly used today. To successfully add audio and video components, you must know which file types are acceptable, how to import them into Director, and how to manipulate these elements to suit your particular needs. In Chapter 7, you will:

- Become familiar with audio and video files.

- Learn different ways to play the various types of media files.

- Discover how to utilize the QuickTime window.

- Explore the many preferences available for audio and video files.

- Practice importing and playing these media files.

Projects to be Completed:

- Gaenzle Illustration and Design (A)

- Redi-Base (B)

- Digital Portfolio(C)

- Shaw's Portfolio (D)

- ABC's (E)

For Macintosh only: If you want to use Director to capture sounds from an outside source — such as CD, DVD, or microphone — follow these steps. First, start playing the music well before the section of music you want to record. About 20 seconds before you want to start recording, select Insert>Media Elements>Sound. When the music reaches the correct location, click Record. When you are finished recording, click Stop. Director automatically places your sound clip in the Cast. Catching the precise spot in the music may take a few tries. To play the sound clip in the Director movie, drag a copy of it from the Cast to one of the Sound channels in the Special Channel section of the Score. This is discussed in more detail in the Sound Channels section of this chapter.

Adding Sound and Video

Until now, we have focused on working with graphics; but to make Director movies appear more professional, sound and video components can be added. These elements add depth and complexity to your work, as well as create moods for your viewers.

Designers must be careful when matching sounds to animations, graphics, and videos. When the match is appropriate, the result is greater than the sum of its parts; the viewer is drawn into the movie, compelled to watch the action. When there is a mismatch, the result can distract and confuse the viewer.

Sound

CD-quality sounds can be imported into Director from a variety of external software applications, some of which are mentioned below. Director can capture sounds internally only on the Macintosh platform; the sounds won't be digital quality, but they are usually acceptable for the average user.

When capturing audio in general, it is best to keep sound clips short. Short clips use a small amount of memory, which provides quick playback; long clips slow your movie to a crawl. A variety of compression methods can be used; similar to graphic-compression methods, there's always a trade-off when you apply them. Even though a compressed file is smaller, the reduction is achieved at the expense of either sound quality or access speed.

Macromedia Shockwave Audio is proven technology that maintains quality when used to compress sounds. This technology supports *streaming audio* — a sound starts to play as soon as the first part has been loaded. The rest of the sound continues to load as the sound plays. The sound plays smoothly but doesn't clog your computer's memory. You can create Shockwave files in most sound applications, including Sound Forge XP (Windows), Peak LE (Macintosh) and Sound Edit (Macintosh).

Recording Sound

Director can record sounds from any medium a Macintosh computer can play, such as CDs and DVDs. Simply cue your CD or DVD using whatever program you would normally use on your machine to play it.

If you are running Windows 98 or NT, you must use an external software application to capture sound, as Director doesn't support audio on the Windows platform.

Director's Multimedia Studio comes with fairly capable audio programs, including Peak LE (light edition) and SoundEdit for Macintosh, and Sound Forge XP (streamlined version) for Windows. Another popular sound-capture application is Adobe Premiere, which can capture audio or video and edit the files.

Importing Sounds

Sounds can be linked or embedded. When sounds are linked, whether by default or design, you must keep a copy of the sound file in the same folder as your project. If you don't, Director won't be able to locate the file. It is best to embed only small sound files, such as beeps or chirps, to keep your movie file size small. Director automatically links large files, but in case the program embeds a file you believe should be linked, you can delete it from your Cast and import it again. Upon import, you can choose the Link to External File option from the Media drop-down menu.

The exercises in this book start from the point of importing sounds, not capturing them, since the procedure for capturing differs depending on the software and platform you use.

Director can import various types of sound files:

- AIFF files
- WAV files
- Sun AU files
- Shockwave Audio files
- MP3 files
- IMA files, compressed
- System 7 sounds (Macintosh only)
- RealAudio files

Multimedia sound commonly offers two bit-depth modes: 8-bit or 16-bit. At 8-bit depth, a sound sample has 256 possible values; at 16-bit depth, the sample has 65,536 possible values. Although the 16-bit option is twice the size, it is well worth the space. Using 16-bit depth provides the best result for the least amount of trouble — especially over the Internet. Be certain to set the sampling rate between 44.1KHz and 11.025KHz for adequate playback quality. CD-quality sound is 44.1KHz.

Sound Channels

Director has two Sound channels. You can play any two sounds at the same time — you might play mellow background music while birds chirp.

These Sound channels are special channels located above the numbered frames in the Special Channels section of the Score. Icons that resemble loudspeakers identify these channels.

The numbered channels above are the Sound channels, identified by the loudspeaker icons.

Placing sounds in the Sound channels is no different than creating any other sprite. The sound is dragged from the Cast to one of the channels. The sprite can be extended across as many frames as necessary to play the entire sound.

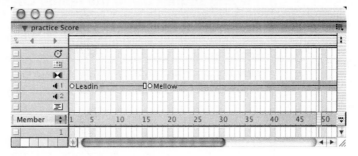

Sound Properties

To preview sounds before placing them in a Score, access their sound properties from the Property Inspector. The Sound tab contains a Play button and a Loop check box. If this box is checked, the sound continues to play as long as the Playback Head remains on the sprite in the Score.

Playing Sounds

There are many ways to play sounds in Director. There is no right or wrong method; the decision on which method to use is simply a matter of which one best fits your project or personal style.

Extending Sound Across Many Frames

One way to play a sound is to place the audio in the Score and extend it across as many frames as necessary to play the clip in its entirety. This method is *not* recommended for a clip that is very long, as it needlessly utilizes a very large number of frames.

Playing Sounds Using the Tempo Channel

A sound can take up only one frame and still play well. There are two ways to do this. The first involves using the Tempo channel. When using this method, you would place a sound in the Score so it covers only one frame. You would then double-click the Tempo channel, and then click the Wait for Cue Point radio button. From the Channel drop-down menu, you would choose the name of your sound, and select End from the Cue Point drop-down menu.

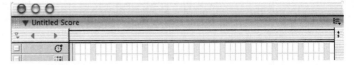

The Tempo channel is the one with the stopwatch icon

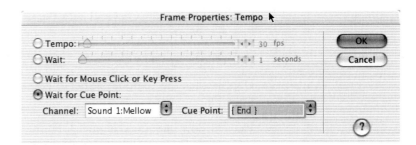

Playing Sound Using Lingo

The second way to play audio across one frame requires a *go to the frame* Frame script. To use this method, you would drag a copy of the sound into a single frame of one of the Sound channels in the Score, and place the Frame script in the Script channel of the same frame. This tells Director to repeatedly play the frame.

You would need to add buttons to this frame so viewers could move on to the next part of your presentation after the sound clip finished playing; otherwise, Director would indefinitely play this frame. Unless you choose Loop from the Sound tab of the Property Inspector, the sound would stop after it plays through once, leaving a lot of quiet time.

Playing Sound Using Buttons

There are times when it is necessary to create buttons to start and stop a sound rather than allow the Playback Head to take control.

You might need buttons on a menu that contain *go to frame* scripts to take you to the exact frame that starts the sound.

You may also want to include Play and Stop buttons on the frames that contain the audio clip. These buttons allow the viewer to stop the audio during playback. The script for a Play button is *continue*; the script for a Stop button is *pause*.

Import and Play Sounds

1. Launch Director if it is not already running. Turn on your computer speakers before you begin.

2. If you want to view the finished version of this movie, select **finsounds.dir** from the **RF_Director** folder. To begin the exercise, open **sounds.dir** from your **RF_Director** folder.

3. Select File>Save As and save the movie as "soundpractice.dir" in your **Work_In_Progress** Folder.

4. Select File>Import, or press Command/Control-R, to import the **mellow.aiff** and **leadin.aiff** sounds from the **RF_Director** folder.

5. Select mellow in the Cast and click the Loop check box on the Sound tab of the Property Inspector.

6. Open the Score and place leadin in Sound channel 1, Frames 1-15.

7. Double-click the Tempo channel in Frame 15 and set the Wait option to 4 seconds. Click OK.

8. Place mellow in Sound channel 1, Frame 16. To extend the sprite to Frame 150, enter "150" in the End box in the Sprite tab in the Property Inspector, and then press Return/Enter.

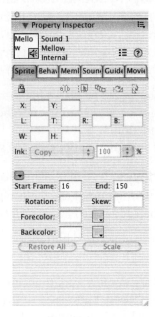

9. Open the Control panel and set the Frame Rate to 5 fps if it isn't already set at that rate. The Loop option should be turned off.

10. Use the Control panel to rewind and play the movie. Keep Director open for the next exercise.

Your music may sound a bit choppy the first time you play it; this is because it isn't streaming. Director is trying to quickly put the whole sound file in RAM, but it sometimes can't keep up. This causes the music to skip. Playing the music a second time should resolve this problem because the sound file will be loaded into RAM. Run the movie from your hard drive, not a removable disk. The transfer rate on most removable media slows down the playback.

Video

There are several programs that allow you to capture and edit video. As of this book's publishing, the most popular cross-platform program is Adobe Premiere.

For the Macintosh platform, there is a low-cost solution available in iMovie, which comes free of charge with the Mac OS X operating system. FinalCut Pro is available for movie-editing professionals, but it is not free.

Importing Video

Video is imported the same way as sound. Digital video files are usually large, so they are automatically imported as linked cast members (rather than embedded). As such, you should always place the linked file in the same folder as your Director movie before importing to save the time and trouble of having to update links later.

Director supports QuickTime, RealVideo, and AVI digital video formats. QuickTime must be installed on any computer playing or creating a movie containing QuickTime video. On the Macintosh platform, Director automatically converts any AVI or RealVideo to QuickTime as it plays.

Exchanging Linked Video Files

If you import a video file and then discover it's not the one you want, Director provides a useful button in the Property Inspector for replacing an incorrect file with the correct one. You can find this button on the Members tab. It is oval with three dots on it, directly below the Filename field, as shown in the following image.

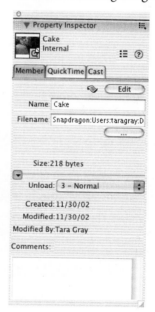

The button used to exchange linked video files is the small oval button with three dots on it.

When clicked, the button displays a dialog box that allows you to browse for and select the correct video.

QuickTime Window

When a video cast member is double-clicked, the QuickTime window is displayed. You can click the Play button in the bottom-left corner to preview the movie.

Video Properties

Video properties can be found in the Property Inspector under the QuickTime tab. In this area, you can choose to allow scaling or cropping of the video, as well as to show the video, play its sound, stream it, loop it, or show the Controller. The Controller features Play and Rewind buttons.

Placing Video in the Score

Unlike sound, video does not have its own special channel. Video is considered a visual item and, therefore, is placed in a Visual channel, the same as any other graphic.

There is one important fact about video you must understand before you design a movie: Unless you turn off the Direct To Stage (DTS) option on the QuickTime tab of the Property Inspector for each video, the videos will act similar to separate layers that float above everything else on the Stage, and you will not be able to place graphics on top of them and, therefore, make it appear as though you have altered their shape.

Unless you turn off the Direct To Stage option on the QuickTime tab of the Property Inspector for each video, the videos will act similar to separate layers that float above everything else on the Stage, and you will not be able to place graphics on top of them.

After you've turned off the Direct To Stage option, a video behaves similar to any other graphic. It can be moved back or brought forward by changing its location in the channels. The only drawback to turning off Direct To Stage is that it can slow down your video playback if there are graphics layered over it. It requires more RAM to process each frame of a video with layered graphics.

Playing Video

When it comes to playing video, there are several issues to consider. The size of the video clip (in dimension), the size of the file, and the speed of the viewer's machine are just a few of these considerations.

As a rule, smaller, shorter video clips are better. Be selective and tell your story with the fewest frames. If you have several small clips you want to use, combine them with a video-editing program, or place them one after the other to play in sequence.

Next, let's take a look at a few different methods to play and control a video clip in Director. They are essentially the same methods that were introduced in the Playing Sound section of this chapter.

Extending Video Across Many Frames

One way to play a video is to place the video in the Score and extend it across as many frames as necessary to play the entire clip. This method is *not* recommended for a clip that is more than two or three seconds long. A two- or three-second clip at 30 fps (frames per second) occupies 60 to 90 frames. A one-minute clip occupies 1,800 frames — far too many to work with.

Playing Video Using Tempo

A video can take up only one frame and still play well. There are two ways to accomplish this. The first involves using a Tempo channel (the one with the stopwatch icon). First, you would place a video in the Score so it covers only one frame. Then you would double-click the Tempo channel and click the Wait for Cue Point radio button. From the Channel drop-down menu, you would choose the name of your movie, and choose End from the Cue Point drop-down menu.

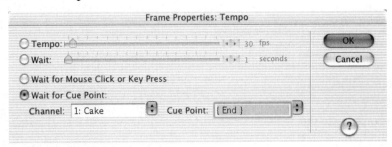

Director plays the video clip until it ends, and then continues to move through the rest of the frames in the movie.

Playing Video Using Lingo

The second way to play video across one frame requires a *go to the frame* Frame script. You would drag a copy of the video into a single frame of the Score and place the Frame script in the Script channel of the same frame. This tells Director to repeatedly play the frame.

You must add buttons to this frame so your viewers can move to the next part of your presentation after the video clip has finished playing; otherwise, Director would indefinitely play this frame.

Playing Video Using Buttons

There are times when it is necessary to create buttons to start and stop a video rather than allow the Playback Head to take control. You might need buttons on a menu that contain a *go to frame* script to take you to the exact frame that starts the video.

You may also want to include Play and Stop buttons on the frames that contain the video clip. This allows the viewer to stop the clip during playback. The script for a Play button is *continue*. The script for a Stop button is *halt*.

Exercise Setup

QuickTime must be installed before attempting to complete the next exercise. QuickTime comes pre-installed on most Macintosh systems. If you have a Windows-based system, you can download a free version of QuickTime from www.cnet.com for Windows 98 and above.

Import and Play Video

1. To preview a finished version of the movie developed in this exercise, open **fintheatre.dir** from the **RF_Director** folder. To begin this exercise, open **theatre.dir** from the **RF_Director** folder.

2. Select File>Save As and save the movie as "theatre.dir" in your **Work_In_Progress** folder.

3. If they are not already in the Cast, import the QuickTime **sol.mov** and **emily.mov** video clips from the **RF_Director** folder.

4. This amateur film project is partially complete. All the pieces are included, but the video clips must be placed, and all the buttons must have scripts attached in order to work. The film includes a menu called Coming Attractions, located in Channel 6, Frames 57-82. The goal is to allow your viewers to choose a film. Double-click the Script channel of Frame 82 and type *go to the frame*. Then close the Script window.

5. Place the sol.mov QuickTime video clip (Cast Member 15) in Channel 9, Frame 85. In this movie, you play the video in one frame using the *go to the frame* Frame script. In the Script channel of Frame 85, type *go to the frame*. Move the Playback Head to Frame 85 and play the movie to make sure it works.

6. Place the emily.mov QuickTime video clip in Channel 9, Frames 83-84. To allow this clip to play in its entirety, use the Tempo channel. In the Tempo channel of Frame 84, choose the Wait for Mouse Click or Key Press option, and then close the window. These commands hold the movie on the current frame (allowing emily.mov to continue to play) until the Stage is clicked.

7. Now let's add some functionality to the buttons. Drag the Playback Head to the Coming Attractions screen. You see two buttons — one for the Little Girl Easter (emily.mov) and one for the Sol's Life (sol.mov) video clips. We want the Playback Head to go to the frame where the emily.mov video starts (Frame 83) when we click the Little Girl Easter button (Emily button). Go to the Cast and highlight the Emily button. Click the Script button in the upper-right corner of the Cast. Type *go to frame 83* and then close the window.

8. Next, let's add a *go to frame* script to the Sol's Life button. The sol.mov video clip starts in Frame 85.

9. Drag the Playback Head to Frame 83. You see two buttons at the bottom of the screen, Attractions and The End. These two buttons need scripts to make them work. The Attractions button should take you back to Frame 82, where the Coming Attractions screen pauses. Enter *go to frame 82* as the script for the Attractions button.

10. The last button is the End button. Drag the Playback Head past the videos and you see that the rest of the sprites in the Score show the screen pulling up and the curtains closing. The button should go to the beginning of this section, Frame 87. Enter *go to frame 87* as the script for the End button.

11. Set the Tempo in the Control panel to 15 fps.

12. Rewind and play your movie. Save the movie and close Director when you're finished.

RealMedia

Director allows you to integrate RealMedia within a Director project. RealAudio and RealVideo have become standards in streaming media on the Web. RealAudio, for the most part, is played through the ever-present RealNetworks' RealPlayer Basic (the free version), which can be found at www.real.com. Additional information is available at www.realnetworks.com.

RealNetworks offers its own quality application, RealSystem Producer Plus, for adapting any form of audio or video to the RealMedia format. The new RealMedia files can then run on RealPlayer, or they can be imported into Director. RealPlayer is quite simple to use, very reliable, effective on almost any audio or video file type, and attractively priced.

Located in Director's Property Inspector, the new RealMedia tab includes some general options you can select, including the Sound channel where RealAudio will be placed, and whether or not to display the "Real" logo.

Be aware that streaming audio works best over a T1 line, and streaming video runs at its optimum level on a T3 line. Try to keep your consumers in mind, and be aware of the bandwidth they will have when they access your site.

Movie in a Window (MIAW)

If you want more than one video clip playing at the same time, some Lingo scripting is required. In Director, you have the option of using a Movie in a Window (MIAW). With a MIAW, one video clip remains open at all times while others are opened and closed. MIAWs are typically used as floating tools palettes or custom dialog boxes that can be used for almost anything. Each window can be completely interactive, which means you can click buttons in the window and the movie responds.

Using MIAWs can be challenging because their scripting sometimes interferes with the movie scripting. Some scripts will work only for the movie that contains the Lingo script, but others will command any movie that is currently open. When creating MIAWs, it is important to recognize which script elements are shared between movies and which are not. This is accomplished through the use of advanced Lingo commands.

MIAWs can be very temperamental, and they are not widely used in everyday productions. Due to these facts and the complexities of Lingo script commands, we do not address the creation and use of MIAWs in this book. If you want to learn more about MIAWs, please refer to the Macromedia Director MX users manual that came with your software.

Copyright Laws

Copyright laws concerning digital files are very complex. With the advent of the Internet and the ability to access images and copy them with a click of the mouse, there are clearly a lot of gray areas that are still being defined.

The only way to be completely safe from any possible copyright repercussions is to create original sound, video, and graphics for your movies. If that is not possible because of lack of expertise, materials, or equipment, there are other available options.

There are many companies that sell low- and high-resolution stock images. These images can be purchased in bulk on CD-ROM or one at a time over the Internet. Many of the images used in this book were purchased from PhotoDisc, a stock-photography company in Seattle, WA, and from Photospin.com.

Stock music is also available. The music used in many of the exercises in this book was purchased from The Music Bakery, a provider of royalty-free music and sounds located in Dallas, TX.

Chapter Summary

In this chapter, you learned about the different types of audio and video files that Director can import. You practiced importing and playing audio and video files. The various audio and video preferences were also discussed.

In addition, you learned about the potential benefits you can gain from using audio and video in your presentations. With a little trial and error, you are now able to add depth and complexity to your presentations. Use restraint when you add special elements to your movies, however, and remember that oftentimes, less is more.

8 Masks and Alpha Channels

Chapter Objectives:

Alpha channels store additional information for each pixel of an image. Alpha channels can be made up of any pattern of grayscale pixels that you want to interact with a graphic. The pattern of pixels is called the mask. This new Director feature allows you to improve graphics and create spectacular effects. In Chapter 8, you will:

* Learn different ways to create masks.

* Discover how different types of masks can enhance a project.

* Become familiar with and use different types of masks.

* Explore the Mask Ink effect and use gradients to create masks.

* Learn to utilize masks to create realistic effects.

Projects to be Completed:

* Gaenzle Illustration and Design (A)

* Redi-Base (B)

* Digital Portfolio (C)

* Shaw's Portfolio (D)

* ABC's (E)

Masks and Alpha Channels

Director offers a special sprite Ink effect called Mask. Mask allows you to simulate alpha channels. If you are familiar with Photoshop or FreeHand, you have probably worked with channels and may have created an alpha channel in one of those programs.

You can work with alpha channels to fade out images, make objects appear out of a haze, merge images (similar to morphing), vignette images, make images appear within type, and even create glassy or watery effects.

To do this, a black-and-white or grayscale gradient image — the mask — is created in the Paint window in the shape of the object you want to show or to hide. The image to be affected by the mask is placed in the Cast slot directly preceding the mask. After you drag the image to the Stage or Score, you can turn on the Mask feature by choosing Mask from the Ink effects menu in the Property Inspector. The image should interact with the mask you made, creating an all-new appearance.

Masks only work when you use 32-bit graphics.

Using Type to Create Masks

You can effectively place images into type by creating a type mask. This technique works best if the type is large enough to contain a sufficient amount of an image so viewers can recognize it. Running video or images inside 9-pt. type would not be useful. On the other hand, a 200-pt. bold or ultra typeface could potentially display a considerable amount of an image, and create an interesting effect.

Exercise Setup
The exercises in this chapter are all related to the same finished product. You continue to use one file throughout the chapter. In the following exercise, you explore the use of type masks. You will probably find it easier to work with your Cast in Thumbnail view.

Mask Images into Type

1. Launch Director if it is not already running. If you want to view the final piece before starting the exercise, open **finmask.dir** from the **RF_Director** folder and play it. When you are ready, open **mask.dir** from the **RF_Director** folder.

If you don't like the placement of the image within the type outline, click the Out mask cast member to bring up the mask in the Paint Editor, and select the Registration Point tool. This displays the registration point (intersection) in the window. Drag the registration point in the direction you prefer, and then go back to the Stage to view the change. Keep tweaking until you are satisfied with the result.

2. Drag a copy of the canoe cast member to the Score and place it in Channel 2, Frames 1-87. Center it on the upper third of the Stage. While the sprite is still highlighted, navigate to the Property Inspector and choose Mask from the Ink Effects drop-down menu.

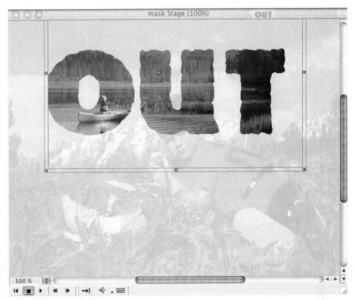

3. Insert a keyframe in Frame 34 of the canoe sprite. Highlight the first keyframe of the sprite and set the Blend percentage (next to the Ink Effects menu) in the Property Inspector to 0%. Highlight the second keyframe (Frame 34) and set the Blend percentage to 100%. Now the child fades into the background as the word OUT fades into full color.

4. Drag a copy of the camping cast member to the Score and place it in Channel 3, Frames 35-87. Center it on the middle third of the Stage and slightly overlapping the bottom of the word OUT. While the sprite is still highlighted, navigate to the Property Inspector and choose Mask from the Ink Effects drop-down menu.

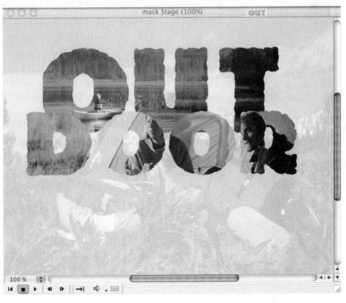

5. Insert a keyframe in Frame 60 of the camping sprite. Highlight the first keyframe of the sprite and set the Blend percentage in the Property Inspector to 0%. Highlight the second keyframe in Frame 60 (the new one you just made) and set the Blend percentage to 100%. Now the word DOOR slowly fades into full color to join the word OUT.

6. Next, let's add the word LIFE to the Stage and Score. The Life text cast member was created for this purpose. Place the Life text cast member in Channel 4, Frames 61-87. Add keyframes to Frames 70 and 73. In the Property Inspector, set the Life text sprite to Background Transparent in the Ink Effects drop-down menu.

7. The goal is to make the word LIFE start as the size of a pinhead, grow to a very large size, and then shrink to an acceptable size. To do this, highlight the first keyframe and shrink the word LIFE to a small dot. Use your Arrow keys to center the word on top of the other keyframe dots on the Stage. This ensures you don't get any vertical or horizontal movement.

8. At the first new keyframe (Frame 70), make the word LIFE very large, and center it on the keyframe dots on the Stage.

9. At the next keyframe (Frame 73), make it shrink to approximately the same size as OUT and DOOR and center it. It will stay centered until the Playback Head reaches the end of the sprite. So far, the top row of your Cast should resemble the following image:

10. Next, add the Magazine text cast member to the Stage as shown in the following image. It should be placed in Channel 5, Frames 83-87. In the Property Inspector, set the Magazine text sprite to Background Transparent in the Ink Effects drop-down menu.

11. Save your changes and keep the file open for the next exercise.

Add Scrolling Text

1. Continue working in the open file. Drag a copy of the Website text cast member into Channel 5, Frames 1-82. Add a keyframe to Frame 9. Move the text to the bottom of the screen as shown in the following image.

2. At the first keyframe, set the Blend percentage to 10%. At the second keyframe (Frame 9) set the Blend percentage to 70%. Now the Web site information slowly appears and gets darker until it reaches 70%.

3. To make it scroll, let's apply a behavior from the Library palette (we discuss behaviors in more detail in the next chapter of the book). Open the Library palette from the Window menu. The Windows version of the Library palette may look slightly different than the image shown below. Click the box to the left of the word Accessibility, and select Text from the pop-up menu. Then select the Tickertape Text option.

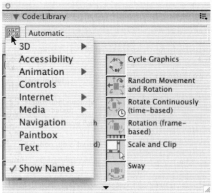

If you can't see it in your window, click the down arrow at the bottom of the window or drag the bottom-right corner of the window to enlarge it.

4. Drag a copy of the Tickertape Text behavior to the Score and drop it on top of the Website text sprite. The Parameters dialog box pops up. Set the slider to 5 and click OK. Now your text scrolls from right to left until the Playback Head reaches the end of the sprite.

5. Double-click the Tempo channel in Frame 87 and choose the Wait option. Move the slider to 3 seconds. This tells Director to wait an additional 3 seconds after everything has moved into place before advancing to the next section. This pause provides enough time to read the screen.

6. Save your changes and keep the file open for next exercise.

Gradient Vignette Masks

You can use a black-to-white gradient as a mask. The resultant effect — a solid image that fades in one or more directions — is called a *vignette*. It's similar to putting a square picture into an oval frame. The darker areas of the gradient allow the image to show through, and the lighter areas are where the image fades away.

In the next series of exercises, you'll apply a combination of gradient masks and images to gain experience working with this popular technique.

Exercise Setup
The first mask you will use was created for you. You can use this mask as a reference for other masks you create. The sample mask is for the backpack image, named Mask-Backpack. It is a gradient circle (black in the center, white at the edges).

Use Masks to Create Vignettes

1. Continue working in the open file. Drag a copy of the backpack cast member into Channel 2, Frames 88-107 of the Score. Center it on the Stage. Set the Ink effect for the sprite to Mask, and watch what happens on the Stage. If you are not satisfied with how the image is centered in the circle, adjust the registration point of the circle.

Create Gradient Masks

The Mask Ink effect only works when the mask is immediately to the right (in the Cast) of the image to which it is applied.

1. Let's create the rest of the gradient masks for the hiking, biking, and snowboard images in the Cast. First, highlight the empty cast slot to the right of hiking. If it is not empty, rearrange your cast members so it is. From the Paint window, access the Gradient Settings dialog box. Choose the settings shown below.

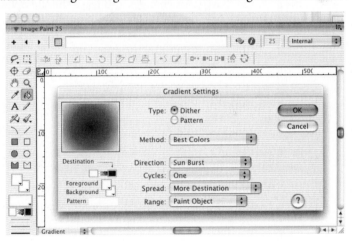

To ensure success, make certain your gradient colors are set to white and black.

2. Select the Filled Ellipse tool and choose Gradient from the Paint Ink Effects drop-down menu at the bottom of the Paint window.

3. Select View>Onion Skin and turn on onion skinning. Set it to 1 Preceding Cast member. Use this cast member as a reference to create a tall ellipse over the hikers. If you are not satisfied with your first attempt, double-click the Eraser tool to delete the ellipse, and then start again. The finished ellipse should resemble the following image. (Remember, onion skinning is turned on).

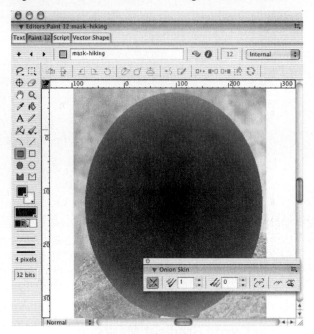

4. Next, let's create the same type of gradient masks for the biking and snowboard images. One at a time, select the cast slot to the right of each image and create an appropriate gradient shape for each one (long, horizontal ellipses are suitable for both the biking and snowboard images).

5. Save your changes and leave the file open for the next exercise.

Create Vignettes

Before you put the next vignette in the Score, you need to add some type to the backpack vignette you already placed in the Score/Stage.

1. First, click the Guides tab in the Property Inspector and drag a horizontal guide to the bottom of the page. Next, drag a copy of the Your text cast member to the Score and place it in Channel 3, Frames 88-155. On the Stage, align the baseline of the type with the guide. Set the Ink effect for this sprite to Background Transparent.

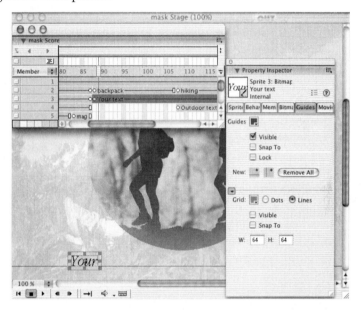

2. To create the next vignette, drag a copy of the hiking cast member into Channel 2, Frames 108-123. By doing so, it should be automatically centered on the Stage. With the hiking sprite selected, change the Ink effect to Mask.

3. Add the Outdoor text sprite to the Score in Channel 4, Frames 108-155. Place it as shown in the image above. With the Outdoor text sprite selected, set the Ink effect for this sprite to Background Transparent.

4. To create the next vignette, drag a copy of the biking cast member to Channel 2, Frames 124-138. It is automatically centered on the Stage. With the biking sprite selected, change the Ink effect to Mask.

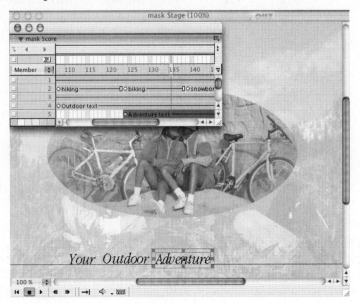

5. Add the Adventure text sprite to the Score in Channel 5, Frames 124-155. Place it as shown in the previous image. Set the Ink effect for this sprite to Backgro und Transparent.

6. To create the last vignette, drag a copy of the snowboard cast member into Channel 2, Frames 139-155. With the snowboard sprite selected, change the Ink effect to Mask.

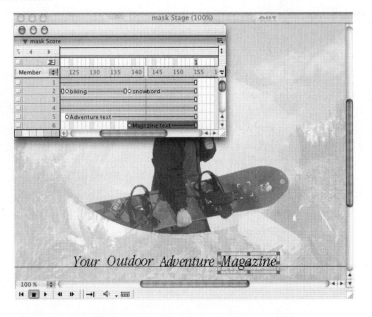

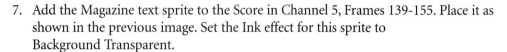

7. Add the Magazine text sprite to the Score in Channel 5, Frames 139-155. Place it as shown in the previous image. Set the Ink effect for this sprite to Background Transparent.

8. Save your changes and leave the file open for the next exercise.

Adjust the Tempo and Add Transitions

1. Double-click the Tempo channel in Frame 107. Choose the Wait for Seconds option and set it to 1 second. Do the same for Frames 123 and 138.

2. Double-click the Transition channel in Frame 88 and choose Dissolve, Pixels from the list of available transitions. Leave the other settings at their defaults and then click OK. Do the same for Frames 108, 124, and 139. This allows for smooth transitions between sections. Your Score with the Tempo channel adjustments and the transitions in the Transition channel should resemble the following:

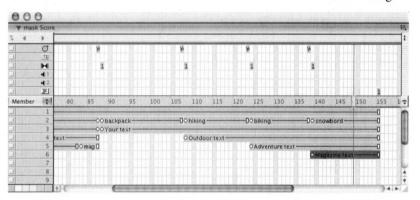

3. Rewind and play the advertisement. When it reaches the end, it should automatically return to Frame 1 and start again because of the Frame script inserted in Frame 155. If you have any questions, refer to the finished version at **RF_Director>finmask.dir**.

4. Save your changes and close the file.

Chapter Summary

In this chapter, you learned the basics of using alpha channels to create masks and masked images. You learned how to create two different kinds of masks. You discovered how to use masks to create vignettes for images. You also learned how to use a mask to create type from images and how to create tickertape text.

Free-Form Project #1

Assignment

The Copper Creek Mall is a new shopping mall that is scheduled to open in your area in two months. Your design firm was selected to produce a multimedia presentation that will be displayed on large screens located at the mall's main entrances. If the client likes the work, you will also have the opportunity to produce an interactive map of the various floors to showcase individual stores.

You were asked to create a self-playing loop. The movie must be very eye-catching and have a clear beginning and end. Passers-by who see the movie should gain an understanding of the mall, and have a good idea of what sorts of shops they will find when they enter.

Applying Your Skills

To develop the presentation, use the following features, methods, and functions:

- Use all the images currently located in the Cast in **coppercreek.dir**, located in your **RF_freeForm_DirectorMX** folder.

- Use tasteful transitions to move from one section of the movie to the next.

- Use the sounds provided in the Cast.

- Create at least six animations — the more the better.

- Come up with an idea for a mall mascot; create it and then use it in the animations.

- Use the name Copper Creek Mall and create a vector graphic that contains those words that can be used throughout the project.

- Create several bitmap images, either as backgrounds or cast members. Apply several different Ink effects to the graphics you create.

- Use a tempo command from the Tempo channel to separate the end of the loop from the starting frame.

- Use the Text window to create the copy for the project.

- Use the Paint window to create headlines.

Specifications

The total play time of the piece should be more than 30 seconds, but less than 60 seconds.

Add a *Wait for 10 Seconds* command in the Tempo channel of the last frame so the movie doesn't replay without a break between loops. In the Script channel of the last frame, add a *go to frame 1* script so the movie will return to the first frame and begin again after the 10 second pause.

Included Files

We supplied a Cast in **coppercreek.dir**. If you want, you can use the sounds and cast members from this file as the basis for your project. As an alternative, you can collect your own images and/or create your own sounds. If you choose to use the materials we provided, they can be found in the **RF_FreeForm_DirectorMX** folder on your Resource CD-ROM.

Publisher's Comments

The difficult part of creating this sort of project is finding a way to grab people's attention so they will take the time to watch it. Consider making your text grow out of, or dissolve into, a solid background. Make certain you time the sounds properly to create the correct feel and tempo for the loop.

Remember that malls are places where parents take their children, and children can be very demanding when they want to see something. Consider playing to the children to capture their attention. Adults, on the other hand, need something that will catch their interest and hold it for the entire length of the presentation.

Review #1

Chapters 1 through 8

In the first eight chapters of the book, you explored the Director interface and became comfortable with its windows and palettes. Next, you explored the Paint and Text Editors and learned how to use them to create cast members. You then found out how to use Director to develop basic animations using sprites. You discovered the benefits of using vector-based graphics in your movies, and created some vector graphics using the Vector Shapes editor. The Property Inspector was introduced, and you learned how to apply effects and modify the characteristics of sprites. The topic of interactivity was discussed, and you learned how to create navigation bars and buttons for Web-based presentations. You found how the addition of audio and video clips can add dimension and overall depth to your work. And finally, you were introduced to the concept of alpha channels and how they can be used to create extraordinary special effects. Through this series of discussions, exercises, and projects you should:

- Be familiar with the Director interface, including all the palettes, windows, and icons.

- Be able to apply text and graphical elements to your movies.

- Know how to use sprites and apply basic animation techniques to them.

- Understand how to use the paint tools and be able to create graphics with them.

- Be able to change the characteristics of sprites using the Property Inspector.

- Be comfortable adding interactivity to your presentations, including navigation bars and buttons.

- Know how to add sound and video clips to your work, adding complexity, depth, and interest.

- Understand how to apply masks and use alpha channels to create special effects.

9 Applying Behaviors

Chapter Objectives:

In the earlier chapters of this book, you used fairly simple Lingo commands to add interactivity to your Director presentations. The Library palette, which contains an abundance of pre-scripted Lingo behaviors, allows you to apply commands that would prove very difficult to script by yourself. The Library palette offers many categories of Lingo scripts that are arranged in a logical manner. Most of the behaviors are fairly easy to use, and when applied appropriately, can greatly enhance your presentations. In Chapter 9, you will:

- Learn about the Library palette and it's contents.

- Become familiar with the different categories contained in the Library palette and their general uses.

- Discover how to apply some of these behaviors to sprites or Frame scripts.

- Learn how to change the order of behaviors when more than one is applied to a sprite.

- Become familiar with the Behavior Inspector.

Projects to be Completed:

- Gaenzle Illustration and Design (A)

- Redi-Base (B)

- Digital Portfolio (C)

- Shaw's Portfolio (D)

- ABC's (E)

Applying Behaviors

Behaviors offer a quick and efficient method to add interactivity to sprites and frames without having to venture into the complex world of Lingo scripting.

A *behavior* is a script that is attached to a sprite or frame. When you drag a behavior on top of a sprite or to a Frame script channel, you can quickly apply special effects and actions that would otherwise require a sequence of complicated Lingo codes. Multiple behaviors may be attached to a sprite at one time.

Library Palette

The Library palette contains pre-scripted Lingo behaviors. To attach a behavior, you can drag it from the Library palette and drop it onto a sprite or frame. You can access the Library palette from the Window menu.

The image below shows how the Library palette looks when you first access it. Each behavior is identified and defined. If you place your cursor over any of the behavior buttons, a tool tip containing a detailed explanation of the behavior's function appears, and some general tips about how to apply it.

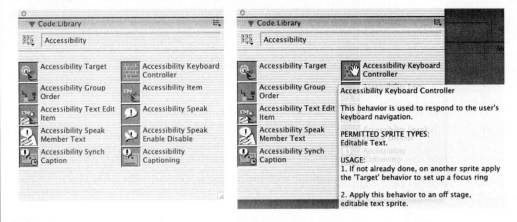

The button in the top-left corner of the Library palette displays a list of libraries you can choose from, including various Internet forms and Animation behaviors.

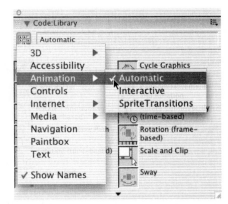

3-D Behaviors

There is a group of 3-D behaviors in the library that is split into two categories: Actions and Triggers. 3-D behaviors are typically used in pairs — one action and one trigger must be used in each instance. You will learn much more about 3-D behaviors and practice using them in the "3-D and Director" chapter of this book.

Actions

Actions are behaviors that 3-D animations can make, or they can be events that happen to the animations. Triggers are attached to the sprite to make the actions work. Actions are broken into three categories: Local, Public, and Independent. Local and Public actions require triggers, while Independent actions do not. We discuss actions in more depth in the "3-D and Director" chapter of this book.

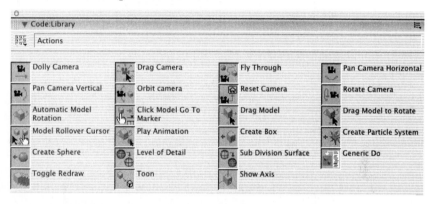

Triggers

Triggers are attached to sprites that have actions; they allow the actions to be initiated. Local and Public actions require triggers to work. Clicking the mouse and pressing a certain key on the keyboard are examples of triggers.

Accessibility Behaviors

The Accessibility category, first on the behaviors list, is new to Director MX. The addition of this category is considered a major upgrade to Director because it allows you to create presentations that meet the needs of hearing- and sight-impaired users.

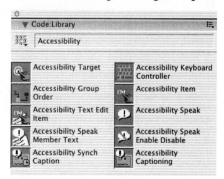

Animation Behaviors

The Animation category consists of Automatic behaviors, Interactive behaviors, and Sprite transitions. These are all behaviors that relate to animating sprites or animation in general:

- **Automatic Animation Behaviors**. The Automatic Animation behaviors include Rotate Continuously, Random Movement and Rotation, Color Cycling, and Waft. These behaviors happen automatically and require no user input.

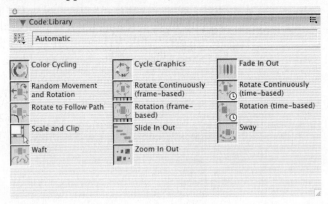

- **Interactive Animation Behaviors**. With these options, you can create interactive graphics. For example, you can set up a graphic to avoid the mouse — the graphic stays one step ahead of the pointer, no matter how fast it is chased. If you set a graphic's behavior to Sprite Track Mouse, the graphic chases the mouse pointer.

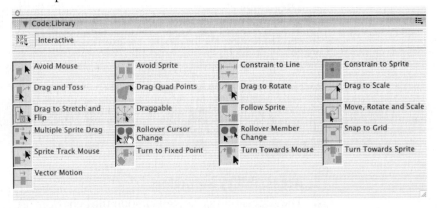

- **Sprite Transition Behaviors**. The Sprite Transition behaviors are very similar to the transitions you learned earlier in this book, except these affect an individual sprite, not the whole frame.

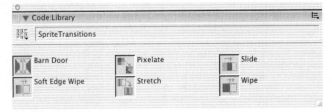

Controls Behaviors

The Controls section of the Library palette provides behaviors that control a movie and allow you to set buttons to Jump Forward, Jump Back, Jump to Marker, and more.

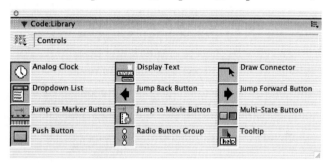

Internet Behaviors

The Internet behaviors category consists of Forms behaviors and Streaming behaviors. These are all behaviors related to publishing your Director piece on the Web:

- **Internet Forms Behaviors**. Internet Forms behaviors deal specifically with forms that can be created on the Internet and posted on a Web server.

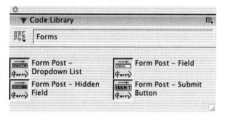

- **Internet Streaming Behaviors**. Internet Streaming behaviors allow you to stream media over the Internet, continually feeding small, consecutive amounts of information to a viewer. This category enables you to place progress bars, jump to other frames, and loop until your media is done playing, to name a few of the options.

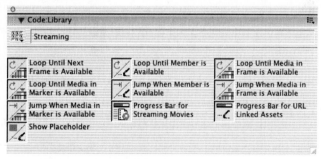

Media Behaviors

The Media category consists of Flash, QuickTime, and Sound behaviors. These behaviors can be used with Flash files, QuickTime files, or sound files, respectively. They are used to enhance the quality and control of these various third-party file types:

- **Media Flash Behaviors**. The Media Flash behaviors work only on graphics that were created using Macromedia's Flash software. Unless you are working with Flash graphics, you needn't worry about this category.

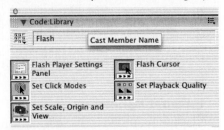

- **Media QuickTime Behaviors**. Media QuickTime behaviors work only on Apple's QuickTime files. From this category, you can choose to show the QuickTime controls and/or slider with any QuickTime video.

- **Media Sound Behaviors**. Using the Media Sound behaviors, you can play, pause, or stop a sound file, make your computer beep when you click the mouse on a graphic, add volume, or pan sliders for better control.

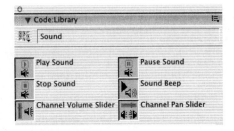

Navigation Behaviors

The Navigation category contains behaviors that allow you to navigate through the different frames of a Director movie. Some options are Go Previous Button, Go Loop, and Hold on Current Frame.

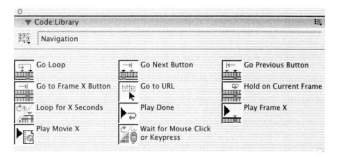

Paintbox Behaviors

The Paintbox behaviors can be attached to sprites to make them act like a canvas — you can use a brush tool to paint on them, among other things.

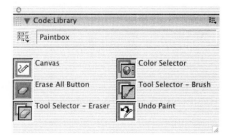

Text Behaviors

The Text behaviors can be used for many things, including creating hyperlinks for the Internet, and adding commas to large numbers so they are easier to read.

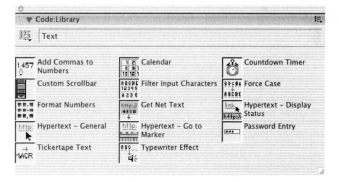

Behavior Inspector

The Behavior Inspector is a palette used to create, track, and modify behaviors. The top section of the palette provides a list of the behaviors applied to the currently selected sprite. To add a new behavior, you can click the "+" button in the top-left corner of the palette. You can use the top window of the palette to change the order of multiple behaviors that are attached to a single sprite.

Switching the order of behaviors is often necessary since Director follows Lingo and behavior instructions in the order they were applied to a sprite. Each script is most likely attempting to do something different, so keeping track of them can quickly become confusing. If you need to switch the order of the behaviors, follow these simple steps:

- Select the sprite in the Score that has multiple behaviors attached to it.
- Open the Behavior Inspector.
- In the top window, select a behavior you want to move, and then click the up or down arrow in the top-right corner of the Behavior Inspector to move the behavior in the stacking order. Behaviors at the top of the window execute first.

The middle section of the palette allows you to set the time frame for when a new behavior is triggered, as well as what action is applied. The bottom section displays the descriptions of the behaviors that have been applied.

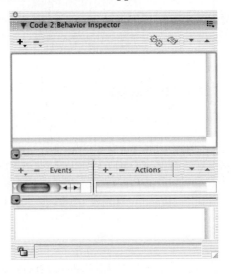

Apply Behaviors

1. Launch Director if it is not already running. If you want to preview a completed version of the movie developed in this exercise, select **finbehaviors.dir** from the **RF_Director** folder and play it. To begin the exercise, open **behaviors.dir** from the **RF_Director** folder. Click the Loop button at the bottom of the Stage, or access the Control panel (Window>Control Panel) and adjust the setting there, to ensure your movie is set to Loop.

2. All the sprites in this file are already in the Score and on the Stage. Let's add behaviors to several of them and set the parameters for their behaviors. To begin, highlight the clownfish sprite in the Score.

3. Select Window>Library Palette to display the Library palette. From the drop-down menu in the top-left corner, select Animation>Interactive. From the list of icons, find the Turn Towards Mouse icon. You are going to set the clownfish so it turns toward the mouse cursor.

4. Drag a copy of this icon on top of the clownfish sprite in the Score. The Parameters dialog box appears. Change the parameters to match the dialog box below. Click OK.

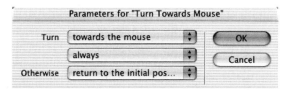

5. Highlight the bigseahorse sprite in the Score. Select Animation>Automatic>FadeIn/Out from the Library palette. Drag a copy of this icon on top of the bigseahorse sprite in the Score. Change the parameters in the Fade In/Out dialog box to match the settings shown below, and then click OK. Attaching this behavior makes the bigseahorse sprite fade out as it swims away, making it a more realistic disappearance.

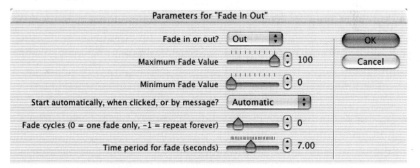

6. Highlight the urchin sprite in your Score. Return to the Animation>Interactive section of the Library palette. At the top, locate the Avoid Mouse behavior. Drag a copy of this behavior onto the urchin sprite in the Score. Change the parameters to match the dialog box below, and then click OK.

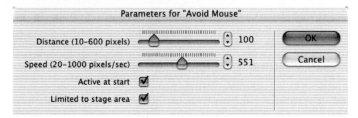

7. Each behavior was placed in your Cast as a cast member. That means they can be highlighted one at a time and their scripts can be accessed. To give you an idea of the time you save when you use behaviors, a small portion of the script for the Avoid Mouse behavior is shown below.

8. Let's tell the biggerfry sprite to follow the mouse cursor around. Select Animation>Interactive and drag a copy of the Sprite Track Mouse behavior on top of the biggerfry sprite in the Score. Change the parameters to match the dialog box below and then click OK.

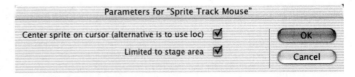

9. The last sprite to receive a behavior is anemone1. In the Animation>Automatic category in the Library palette, locate the Waft behavior. This behavior allows anemone1 to gently waft to the ground. Drag a copy of the Waft behavior on top of the anemone1 sprite in your Score. Change the parameters to match the dialog box shown below and then click OK.

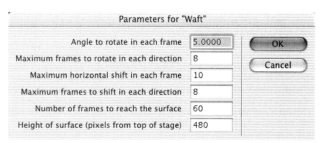

10. The following image displays a copy of the finished Cast. Note that it doesn't matter if the order of your behaviors differs from the order in the Cast.

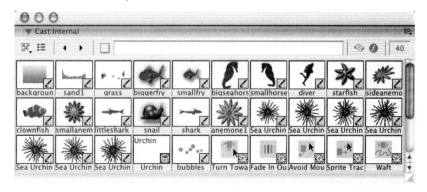

11. Rewind and play your movie. Move your mouse around and watch the biggerfry follow it. Watch the clownfish spin. Try to catch the urchin — you won't be able to. Watch the anemone waft gently to the ground, and see the bigseahorse fade as he swims away.

12. Save the movie, and then close Director.

Chapter Summary

In this chapter, you explored the Library palette. You browsed through the many categories of pre-scripted Lingo contained in the palette. You also learned about the Behavior Inspector and applied some of the behaviors found there. This gave you a taste of their robust capabilities. Experimenting with behaviors in your spare time will help you understand their full potential. You may even learn something by opening their scripts and trying to decipher them. You now see the possibilities that the powerful world of Lingo scripting can bring to your Director presentations.

These are just a few of the many behaviors available in the Library palette. Many more behaviors can be scripted with Lingo as you gain more experience; but for now, these behaviors provide examples of the amazing new effects you can apply with minimal effort.

10 The Cursor

Chapter Objectives:

Oftentimes, we are not consciously aware of the power of suggestion that a cursor change invokes when we are playing a computer game or surfing the Internet. The cursor can let us know that we can "pick up" an item, click on it, or use it in some other fashion.

When planning and creating an interactive project, it is best to plan the use of multiple custom cursors, animated cursors, and rollover cursor changes. Cursors can be used to add a very professional appearance to your projects. When over-used, however, custom cursors can lose some of their effectiveness. In Chapter 10, you will:

- Become familiar with cursors and how to change them.
- Discover how to turn a graphic into a cursor.
- Learn how to modify the hotspot on a cursor.
- Become familiar with creating animated cursors and applying them to a project.
- Learn about the Cursor Properties Editor.

Projects to be Completed:

- Gaenzle Illustration and Design (A)
- Redi-Base (B)
- Digital Portfolio (C)
- Shaw's Portfolio (D)
- ABC's (E)

The Cursor

Cursors are excellent features for any form of interactive media, and are most often used to prompt users to perform an action. There are various cursors built into the Macintosh and Windows operating systems, but you can design custom cursors and add them to your Director movies to create a more personal appearance.

You can associate specific cursors with individual sprites to prompt the user to perform a particular action. You can even hide cursors for situations where the user should not perform any action at all.

Changing a Cursor

There are a few methods you can use to change a cursor. One option is to use Lingo to script the change. Unless you are making a Shockwave movie, however, there are quicker and more efficient alternatives.

The Behavior Inspector is another option. A sprite can be given a specific instruction, such as "while the mouse is in this particular area, use this cursor."

The most efficient way to change a cursor is through the Library palette. The Rollover Cursor Change is a pre-scripted behavior that can be added to a sprite. The behavior is actually attached to the sprite, and when the cursor moves inside the bounds of that sprite, it changes to the specified cursor.

To set the default cursor to something other than the arrow when it isn't rolling over a sprite, you need to create a cast member to use as a background. When the background cast member is dragged to the Score, it becomes a sprite, and the Rollover Cursor Change behavior can then be attached to it and applied to the cursor of choice. This way, the cursor is always gliding over a sprite (the background) with a Rollover Cursor Change behavior attached to it; it never defaults to the arrow.

Cursor Properties Editor

The Cursor Properties Editor, accessed from the Insert>Media Elements menu, offers the ability to select a Bitmap cast member and change it to a Cursor cast member. You can make adjustments to how the cursor displays and behaves.

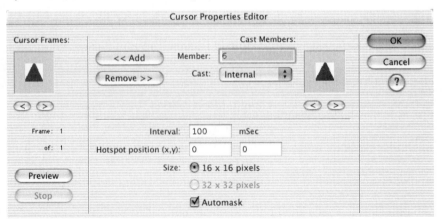

For a cast member to display in the Cast Members box on the top-right side of the Cursor Properties Editor, it must be an 8-bit graphic (also referred to as indexed color or 256 colors). When you create a graphic in the Paint Editor, it usually defaults to a 32-bit graphic. To change the bit depth, you would open the graphic from within the Paint Editor and then select Modify>Transform Bitmap. From this window, you can use the Color Depth setting to change the graphic to 8-bit color.

As you shuffle through the available 8-bit cast members, you can click the Add button when you reach the one you want to turn into a cursor. You can click the Automask check box to change the white around the edges of the graphic to transparent — unless you want to keep the bounding box.

The resulting cursor size on a Macintosh must be 16 pixels × 16 pixels, so it defaults to this size (notice the 32 × 32 option is grayed out). If you are working on the Windows platform, the 32 × 32 pixels option is the default, and the 16 × 16 option is grayed out.

The Hotspot position is the "activation" area of the cursor. An example of an object with a hotspot is a paintbrush — the very tip of the brush is the hotspot or activation area. The hotspot dimensions (in pixels) can't be larger than the size of the graphic. With a 16 × 16-pixel graphic (Macintosh), and the cursor tip placed in the bottom-left corner, the coordinates would be set to X: 0, Y: 16. A 32 × 32-pixel graphic (Windows) has bottom-left corner cursor tip coordinates of X: 0, Y: 32.

Create and Apply a Custom Cursor

1. Launch Director if it is not already open. Choose File>New>Movie. Open the Paint Editor and use the Filled Ellipse tool to paint a small filled circle (fill it with a fairly light color such as medium gray). Name it "Circle".

2. Click the "+" button in the top-left corner of the Paint Editor to display the next available empty cast slot. Use the Filled Rectangle tool to create a small black-filled square. Name it "Square".

3. Select Modify>Transform Bitmap and change "Square" Color Depth to 8-bit. Click Transform. A warning message appears, which says you cannot undo this operation. Click OK. Close the Paint Editor.

4. Drag a copy of Circle from the Cast to the Score and place it in Channel 1, Frames 1-30.

5. Select Insert>Media Element>Cursor. The Cursor Properties Editor appears. Since Square is the only 8-bit graphic you created so far, it immediately displays in the Cast Members box.

6. Click Add to add it to the Cursor Frames box. Make certain Automask is checked. Set the Hotspot position coordinates to 8,8 (Macintosh) or 16,16 (Windows), which is the middle of the graphic. Click OK.

7. In your Cast, name the new cursor "My Cursor".

8. Highlight the Circle sprite in your Score and open the Library palette.

If you run your cursor past the outside edge of the circle (or any other irregular shape), and it still occasionally turns into your custom cursor, highlight the sprite in the Score and select Matte from the Sprite Ink effects drop-down menu. This removes the white (extra hotspot area) around the irregular shape.

9. Select Animation>Interactive in the Library palette, and click the down arrow until you find the Rollover Cursor Change behavior. Drag a copy of it on top of the Circle sprite in the Score.

10. The Parameters box appears. Choose Cursor Member from the Use which type of cursor drop-down menu (top menu). Ignore the Built-in cursor menu (middle menu). Choose My Cursor from the Cursor member drop-down menu (bottom menu) and then click OK.

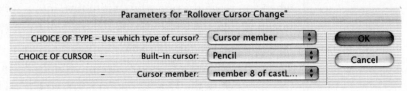

11. Open the Control panel if it's not already open. Make certain the Loop option is turned on.

12. Rewind and play your movie. Move the cursor around the Stage. The cursor is an arrow until it goes over the circle, at which point it turns into the square you created.

13. Save your changes and keep Director open for next exercise.

Animated Cursors

Now that you know how to turn a cast member into a cursor and apply it to a sprite, animating the cursor is a natural progression. The following is a list of the steps in the process:

- Create various cast members to turn into an animation.
- Convert the graphics to 8-bit color depth in Modify>Transform Bitmap.
- Turn each one into a single cursor member by selecting Insert>Media Element>Cursor. Each cast member is added, one at a time, until they are all on the Cursor side of the dialog box.
- Preview the animation and modify it until you are satisfied with the sequence.
- From the Library palette, apply the appropriate behavior — the Rollover Cursor Change — to a sprite the same way you did with the single cursor.

Create Animated Cursors

1. If you want to preview a completed version of this exercise file before you begin, open and play **finshapes.dir** from the **RF_Director** folder. Open **shapes.dir** from the **RF_Director** folder. Your Stage should resemble the image below. This is a mock-up Main menu for an educational game disk.

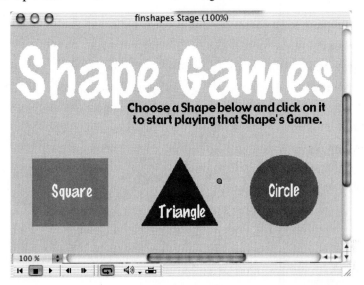

2. Activate the Paint Editor and click the "+" button to choose the next empty cast member slot. Draw a small yellow square.

3. Click the "+" button again to choose the next empty cast member slot. Choose the Onion Skin option from the View menu, click the toggle button to turn it on, and set it to 1 Preceding Cast Member. You should see a hint of the yellow square. If the Onion Skin option is not available, click the Paint Editor to make sure it's active, and then try to access the option again.

4. Create a purple triangle on top of the faint outline of the yellow square. This allows you to make the triangle about the same size as the square.

5. Change the setting in the Onion Skin palette to 2 Preceding Cast Members. Click the "+" sign in the Paint Editor for the next available slot.

6. Draw a light blue circle on top of the other two shapes. Close the Paint Editor and the Onion Skin palette.

7. Navigate to the Cast window and name the new members "Square", "Triangle", and "Circle" in the order you created them.

8. One at a time, select the cursors and then choose Modify>Transform Bitmap to convert them to 8-bit graphics.

9. Select Insert>Media Element>Cursor. Shuffle through the cast members until you find the square, and then click the Add button to add it to the Cursor Frames window. Add the triangle and the circle in the same manner.

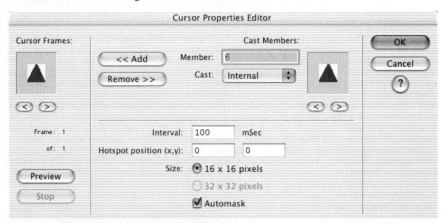

10. Change the Hotspot position to 8,8 (Macintosh) or 16,16 (Windows). Make certain the Size is set to 16 × 16 pixels (Macintosh) or 32 × 32 pixels (Windows). Automask should be checked.

11. Click the Preview button and your cursor begins to animate. The interval should be set to 100, or whatever number you decide looks best. Click Stop and then click OK.

12. Navigate to the Score and highlight the sprite named Square.

13. Open the Library palette. Select Animation>Interactive in the Library palette, and click the down arrow until you find the Rollover Cursor Change behavior. Drag a copy of it on top of the Square sprite in the Score.

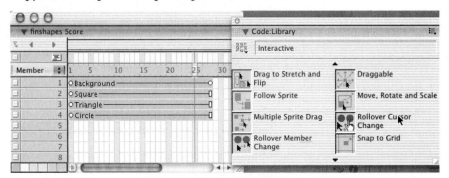

14. In the dialog box that appears, select Cursor Member from the Use which type of cursor drop-down menu. Select the correct cast member from the Cursor member drop-down menu (it should default to the correct one since you've made only one). Ignore the Built-in cursor menu. The box should resemble the image below. Click OK.

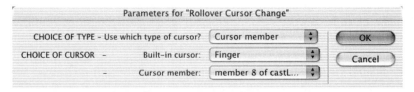

15. Repeat Steps 12-14 for the Triangle and Circle sprites to finish creating the cursor animation.

16. Highlight the Background sprite in the Score. Apply the Rollover Cursor Change behavior to it. Set up the Parameters box a little differently (see the example below). From the Use which type of cursor drop-down menu, select Built-in cursor. Set the Built-in cursor menu to Pencil. Ignore the Cursor member menu. Click OK.

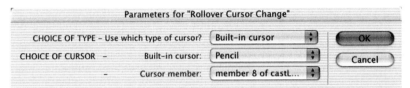

17. Make certain your Control panel is set to Loop.

18. Rewind and play your movie. Move the cursor around. When you glide over the triangle, circle, or square, you should see your animated cursor. When you are over the background, you should see the pencil cursor.

19. Save your changes in the **Work_In_Progress** folder as "shapepractice.dir" and then close Director.

Chapter Summary

In this chapter, you learned how to create a cursor graphic from scratch in the Paint Editor. You then learned how to turn that graphic into a cursor cast member. The next step you learned was how to take that cursor and apply it to a graphic so the cursor changed when the mouse rolled over the graphic.

In addition, you learned how to make your default cursor appear different than the generic arrow. Finally, you learned how to turn multiple cursor graphics into an animated cursor that can capture a user's attention. All of these skills allow you to create user-friendly presentations.

Complete Project D: Shaw's Portfolio

11 Color Settings, Pickers, Palettes, and Cycling

Chapter Objectives:

This chapter is devoted to color and what choices you can make concerning color in Director. The color settings required for your movie or presentation are entirely dependent upon where you will ultimately play the movie. If, for example, the movie will be viewed on the Web and at an interactive kiosk, you must create or configure your colors so they will work in both instances. In Chapter 11, you will:

- Learn about the different types of color palettes available for use.

- Become familiar with the Color Picker and how to use it.

- Discover how different bit depths can affect the playback of a movie.

- Learn how to use Color Cycling to visually animate graphics.

- Become familiar with the Color palette frame properties.

Projects to be Completed:

- Gaenzle Illustration and Design (A)
- Redi-Base (B)
- Digital Portfolio (C)
- Shaw's Portfolio (D)
- ABC's (E)

Color Settings, Pickers, Palettes, and Cycling

Learning about the types of Director color palettes and the different bit depths that can be used is very important because it can affect the playback of your movie. Applying Color Cycling and using color to create special effects can make your graphics appear animated.

You must also be aware of the platform on which the Director movie will be played. Windows machines tend to display most colors darker than Macintosh machines. If you are creating a movie for one platform, you can adjust for this. If you are creating a movie that will be viewed on both platforms, you must preview your work on both platforms and tweak the colors as necessary.

If the movie is to be viewed only on the computer it was created on, you have an advantage; you either already know or can easily find out all of your computer's specifications, including how powerful it is and what kind of monitor is used.

These are only a few of the many issues concerning color that must be considered before creating a Director piece. It is best to plan your project carefully to prevent unwanted color issues when it is viewed.

Color Settings

There are some general color settings you should explore before beginning your project so you are aware of how they are currently set. Then, you can decide if you should leave them alone or change them to better suit your project.

General Preferences

If you are a Macintosh user, you can check the color options in the General Preferences dialog box before you begin a new project. You can press Command-U to access this dialog box. Make certain the Reset Monitor to Movie's Color Depth check box is clicked.

Windows users do not have this option available from within Director. You must go into the Windows Control panel to change this option by selecting Settings>Control Panel>Display.

Windows users must go into the Windows Control panel to access the General Preferences dialog box to change their color options (select Settings>Control Panel>Display).

This option resets the monitor to match the movie's color depth so the colors are not skewed or modified. For instance, if you were to produce your movie using thousands of colors, and the monitor used to view it is set to only 256 colors, your movie's wide range of colors would be converted to 256 and would look quite different.

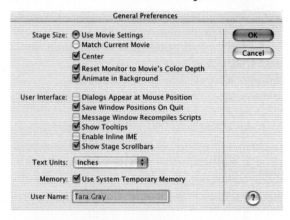

Movie Properties

A movie's color settings can be found on the Movie tab of the Property Inspector.

You have two choices for color mode: RGB (Red, Green, Blue) and Palette Index. Director typically defaults to RGB color mode. When RGB is chosen, a two-digit number or letter combination is assigned for each of the red, green, and blue values that make up the color. These are called *hexadecimal values*. The result is a six-digit number that provides consistent and accurate color.

When you choose Palette Index, the number in the list within the palette provides the name for the color. If it is the fifth color in the first row, it is color #5. Choosing the Palette Index option is perfectly acceptable as long as you move this particular color palette with your work and don't disturb the order of the colors. If color #5 is blue, and later, you rearrange the colors to make #5 olive green, anything assigned #5 becomes olive green.

Palette Index colors are still RGB colors, but there are only 256 of them available in the Index palette at any one time, unlike when you choose the RGB option, where millions of colors are available.

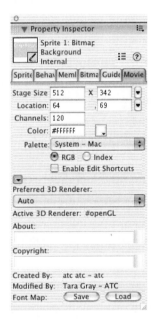

You can set your default Color palette. For productions being displayed on a single workstation, the System-Mac or System-Win color selection is acceptable, depending on which platform you are using. These options offer 256 RGB colors on either platform and ensure consistent presentations on both.

If your presentation is destined for the Internet, and you want to be absolutely sure that everything remains exactly the same no matter what machine is used to view it, select the Web 216 palette. These 216 colors are made up of 216 RBG colors that the Macintosh and Windows system palettes share from the 256 system colors. They are called the "Web-Safe colors" because no matter what type of machine used to view them, they always look the same, albeit darker on Windows and lighter on Macintosh. The Web-Safe palette also helps keep file sizes to a minimum, keeping download time more reasonable for the average user.

Color Pickers

The Macintosh version of Director contains different color pickers, which are used to choose new colors. This section shows you the preferred color pickers and ways to access and manipulate them.

Different color pickers are not available in the Windows version of Director. What Windows users see when they open the Color palette window is the standard Windows Color Picker that has nothing to do with the Director software.

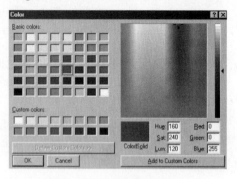

Standard Windows Color Picker

Favorite Colors

Although we have been working with the Paint Editor and its many available options, it contains a few areas related to customizing your Color palette that we have not yet discussed. When a new color is selected, either the hexadecimal equivalent or a Palette Index number at the top of the Color palette is provided. This is helpful for those times when you require a color to precisely match one that was previously used.

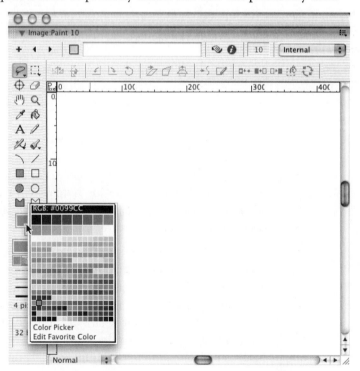

At the top of the Color palette is a series of 16 colored squares, referred to as "Favorite Colors." These colors can be changed in the Edit Favorite Colors window, which can be opened by selecting Edit Favorite Colors from the bottom of the Color palette. In this window, you must first select the Favorite Color you want to change. Then you can either click the Color Picker button to display the Color Picker dialog box, enter the exact hexadecimal color value or Palette Index number, and then click OK.

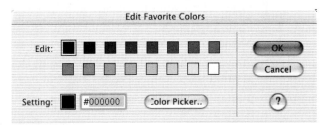

Color Picker Box

Selecting Color Picker from the bottom of the Color palette opens a window where you can change colors and create custom palettes (custom palettes will be explained later in this chapter).

If you opened the Color Picker dialog box (Macintosh only), you would see a large Color Picker with some icons across the top of the window:

- The first icon is the Color Picker icon; clicking it displays the Color Picker.
- The second icon is for the various color sliders. You can use color sliders similar to those found in Adobe Photoshop and other paint programs. The sliders available are Grayscale, RGB, CMYK, and HSB.
- The third icon is the Color Palettes icon that contains various palettes.
- The fourth icon is the Image Palettes icon. If you import images that carry custom color palettes with them, you can access those palettes in this area.
- The fifth icon is a shortcut to the Crayons Color palette.

Remember, Windows users will not see a box similar to this from which they can select different types of color pickers. Instead, when they click the Color Picker button, the Windows Color Picker opens.

Suitable Color Pickers

There are two color pickers most commonly used with Director. The first is the RGB picker. Here, you can create colors by moving the Red, Green, and Blue sliders back and forth. RGB is the best option for productions that will be previewed on both the Macintosh and Windows platforms. It is rapidly becoming the preferred color mode because of higher Internet bandwidths, faster modems, and advanced computer capabilities.

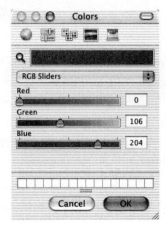

RGB color comes in three bit depths: 8, 16, and 32. The bit depth you chose can significantly alter the file size of an image. Try to use the lowest possible bit depth for each image to keep it as small as possible without sacrificing image quality. The bit depth of Bitmap cast members can be altered in the Modify>Transform Bitmap dialog box.

The second commonly used color-picking technique is to use the CMYK (Cyan, Magenta, Yellow, and Black) sliders. They can be helpful in cases where you created a project for print production and then the client decides to create an interactive piece that matches their specific company's colors. Using the CMYK sliders, you can input the exact percentages used in the original work to create the same colors for additional deliverables.

Color Palettes Window

When you select Color Palettes from the Window menu, you can open a moveable, independent window that contains many pre-created color palettes.

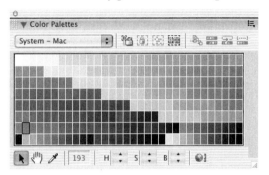

You can select a specific color palette from the drop-down menu to meet your specific needs. Among the most commonly used (besides the system palettes) are the Rainbow and Web 216 palettes. There are also collections of pastels and vivid colors available for use.

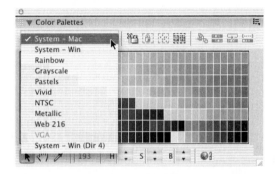

Director includes an Eyedropper tool that works similar to eyedropper tools in other drawing and painting programs. The Eyedropper tool can be used to sample a color from an image and place it in the Color palette for use elsewhere. To do this, you would simply highlight the desired location in the Color palette, select the Eyedropper tool, and click the color you want to reference.

From left to right, the Arrow, Hand, and Eyedropper tools.

Custom Color Palettes

To change any of the colors in a palette, or to make a custom palette, you would highlight the color using the selection (Arrow) tool located at the bottom left of the palette, or simply click the color you want to change. Then you would click the Color Picker button. A dialog box would appear, asking you to name the new palette.

The Color Picker button.

The controls for adjusting the hue, saturation, and brightness are identified with the corresponding "H," "S," and "B" boxes at the bottom of the Color palette. Adjust the arrows up or down to quickly alter and preview your color changes.

The order of the colors within the palette can be altered at any time using the Hand tool, located next to the Arrow tool. You can simply drag the colors around to rearrange or duplicate them. When you are done with your changes, the new palette appears in the Cast.

Color Palette Channel

The Color Palette channel is located in the Special Channels section of your Score directly below the Tempo channel. You load different color palettes in this channel. Each frame of a movie can run off a different color palette. A color palette, similar to any other sprite, can be extended to cover several frames.

You might import an image that has different colors than the movie you created. Upon import, this image brings its own custom color palette that contains the colors used to create it. When you place the image in your Score, you will notice that Director automatically places the image's custom color palette in the Color Palette channel starting on the same frame as the image.

To make different frames use different color palettes, you can highlight the frame in the Color Palette channel and select Modify>Frame>Palette to choose the palette you want to apply to that frame.

Create a Custom Palette

1. With Director running, select Window>Color Palettes.

2. Click any color you want to change. Select Color Picker from the bottom-right corner of the Color palette. Save the new palette as "New Palette" and then click OK.

3. The Color Picker window should display. At the top of this window, click the second icon from the left — this is the Sliders icon. Choose the RGB sliders and manipulate the sliders to create a different color (Windows users: the color slider is on the right side of this window. Slide the small black triangle button to change the colors in the large swatch within the Windows Color Picker). Click OK. Notice that the new color replaced the old. It now appears in the Cast as shown below.

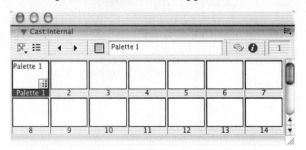

You cannot make your new Color palette appear in the Paint Editor unless you first paint something in the window. This is a minor inconvenience, as you can quickly paint a stroke with a paintbrush and erase it later.

4. Pick another color in the Color palette to alter and repeat the process. Keep an eye on the positions of your new colors in the Color palette. You need to refer to their locations later.

5. Using the Color Picker (the first icon from the left at the top of the window), alter two more colors (Windows users, alter two more colors from the Windows Color Picker). Now you have four new colors.

6. Use the Hand tool (at the bottom left of the Color palettes window) to click each new color, one at a time, and drag it to the top-left corner of the Color palette. When you are finished, all four new colors should be in positions 1-4 of the Color palette. Close the Color palette.

7. To force your new Color palette to appear in the Paint Editor, open the Paint Editor, draw a shape of any kind, and then select Modify>Transform Bitmap. Set the Color Depth to 8 Bits. Now you can select New Palette from the Palette drop-down menu. Click Transform, and then click OK. Notice how New Palette is now available in the Paint Editor, ready to use. Click the Foreground and Background Color boxes to verify this.

8. Close Director without saving your changes.

Color Cycling

Color Cycling is a Color palette special effect. A series of colors taken from the current Color palette can be displayed quickly to show a range of colors in a sequence. You can set the sprites to cycle through the colors, making them appear animated. For example, Color Cycling could be used to make blinking lights around a spaceship. Color Cycling can be applied through the Color Palette channel's frame properties or through a behavior from the Library palette, both of which are discussed below.

Palette Channel Frame Properties

To apply Color Cycling to an entire frame or multiple frames, you can double-click in a frame in the Color Palette channel. The frame you choose must contain a graphic. In addition, your monitor should be set to 256 colors to ensure this method works successfully.

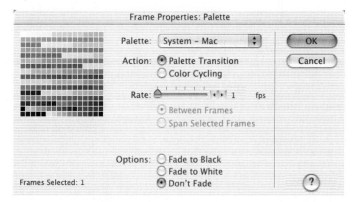

Then, you can pick a color palette, set the action to Color Cycling, set the rate at which you want it to cycle, set the number of cycles you want it to complete, and choose whether you want the frame to loop or auto reverse when it reaches the end of each color cycle.

To select the colors you want to cycle, drag across the colors in the Color Swatch box in the top left of the dialog box. They become outlined in black when they are selected. You must select the actual color of the graphic among the colors you want to cycle.

Color Cycling affects anything in a frame that contains the selected color or colors. If you select greens and blues, then greens and blues are the only colors that cycle on your graphic. You will practice this effect in the next exercise.

Additional adjustments can be made to your Color Cycling selection in the Color Palettes window. To display your Color Cycling palette in this window, you can double-click it from the Cast. There are four buttons in the top-right section of the Color Palettes window to help you select or alter the colors.

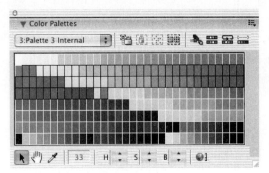

These four buttons do not become active unless more than one color in the palette is selected:

- The first button allows you to sort your selected colors based on hue, saturation, or brightness.
- The second button offers you the flexibility to reverse the order of the colors you selected.
- The third button shifts the colors back one space, making what *was* the first color the *last*.
- The fourth button is used to create animated gradient/blend effects. Clicking it takes the first and last colors you selected and blends the two across the color spaces between them.

Library Palette

The second way to apply Color Cycling is to use the Color Cycling behavior in the Library palette. Similar to other behaviors, the Color Cycling behavior can be attached to a sprite by selecting the behavior and dragging it onto the sprite in the Score.

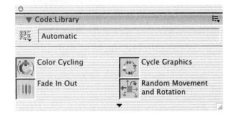

After you have applied the behavior to the sprite, a Parameters dialog box appears.

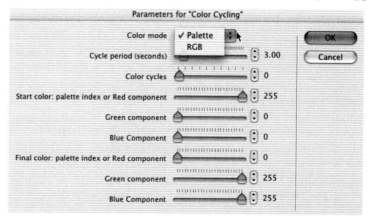

If you choose the Palette color mode from this dialog box, you must set your monitor to 256 colors. If you choose the RGB color mode, you do not need to alter your monitor settings.

Use Color Cycling

1. Open **color.dir** from the **RF_Director** folder.

2. Switch your monitor's color depth to 256 colors. Most monitors default to thousands or millions of colors. The following method of applying Color Cycling does not work if your monitor is not set to 256 colors:

   • If you are using Mac OS X, go to the Apple menu and choose System Preferences. In the dialog box that appears, click Displays, and then change the colors to 256.

   • If you have a relatively new Apple computer, you can change your monitor's setting from the Control Strip.

   • If your computer is older, you may not have a Control Strip. You can go into the Control Panels folder located inside your System folder and double-click the Monitors or Monitors and Sound Control panel. Adjust the setting to 256.

   • If you are running Windows, go to the lower left corner of your desktop and select Start>Settings>Control Panel>Display>Settings>Color Palette Menu. Adjust the setting to 256 colors.

3. Navigate to the Color Palette channel in the Special Channels section of the Score. Double-click Frame 1. It should display the Frame Properties dialog box.

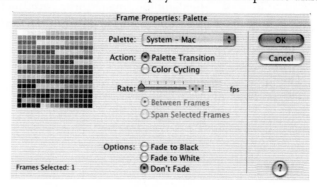

4. Click the Color Cycling radio button, next to Action. This allows you to access the colors in the Swatch box.

5. Highlight the first 12 colors in the top row. Make certain your palette is set to System-Mac or System-Win, depending on your system.

6. Double-check that the rest of the options match the previous image and then click OK.

7. Extend the sprite in the Color Palette channel of your Score to cover Frames 1-10.

   If you rewind and play the movie at this point, you'll notice the background cycles through the colors (yellows, pinks, and oranges), but the shapes do not. This is because we selected a portion of the Color palette that contains the same color as the background — yellow. If we had picked a portion containing the same green as the circle, it would have cycled instead. If we had picked the whole palette, all the sprites would have cycled.

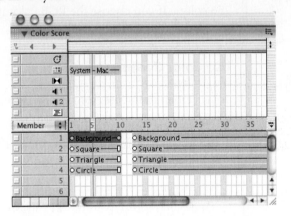

8. In the section of the Score containing sprites (Frames 13-40), make the three individual shapes cycle. First, open the Library palette by selecting Window>Library Palette. Choose Animation>Automatic from the drop-down menu.

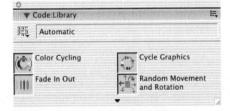

9. Highlight the Square sprite covering Frames 13-40 in the Score. Drag a copy of the Color Cycling behavior from the top left of the Library palette onto the sprite in the Score.

10. The Parameters dialog box appears. Match the settings to those in the following image if they don't already match, and then click OK.

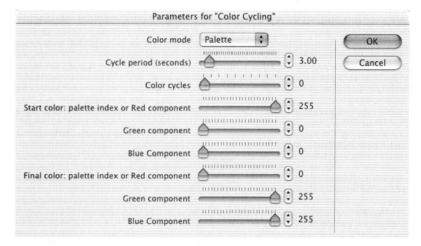

We could have chosen RGB instead of Palette for the color mode, allowing you to run Color Cycling without your monitor set to 256 colors. Since the monitor was already set to 256 in a previous step, we decided to leave the setting alone.

11. Highlight the Triangle sprite covering Frames 13-40 in the Score. Drag a copy of the Color Cycling behavior from the top left of the Library palette onto the sprite in the Score.

12. Match the settings shown in the Parameters dialog box below, and then click OK.

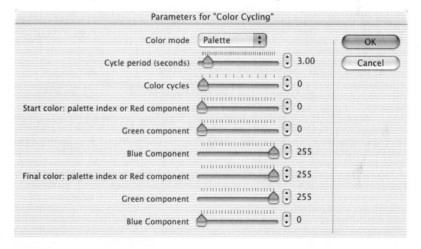

13. Highlight the Circle sprite covering Frames 13-40 in the Score. Drag a copy of the Color Cycling behavior from the top left of the Library palette onto the sprite in the Score.

14. Match the settings shown in the Parameters dialog box below, and then click OK.

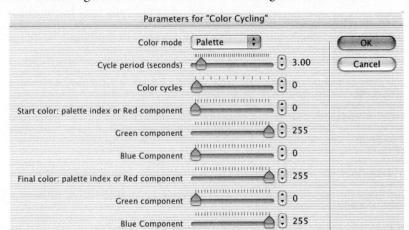

The parameters were set differently for the shapes to ensure they retained their color. For example, you can choose a Start and End Color for each sprite. You can set the parameters so the Start Color of each sprite is its screen color. The red square had a Start Color of 255 in the Red component (100% Red) and 0% in the Green and Blue components.

15. Rewind and play your movie. Your background cycles first, followed by the shapes.

16. Close Director without saving your changes.

Chapter Summary

In this chapter, you explored the many variations of color. You now know what types of color pickers Director has to offer, as well as what types of pre-created palettes are available for use. You learned the difference between applying Color Cycling using a behavior in the Library palette (which is sprite-based) or via the Color Palette channel in the Score (which is frame-based). You also learned some tips that will help to keep your file sizes down to accommodate Internet viewers.

12 *Lingo Basics*

Chapter Objectives:

This chapter is devoted to teaching you the basics of the Lingo scripting language. Lingo is an amazing tool that allows you to instruct Director to do virtually anything. It is a very robust scripting language that is constantly being upgraded and improved, keeping it ahead of the technology curve. In Chapter 12, you will:

- Learn about the different types of scripts you can write using Lingo.

- Become familiar with the hierarchy of various types of Lingo scripts.

- Discover how to troubleshoot basic scripting errors.

- Practice using the Message and Debugging windows.

- Find out where to go to find large sections of pre-scripted Lingo.

Projects to be Completed:

- Gaenzle Illustration and Design (A)

- Redi-Base (B)

- Digital Portfolio (C)

- Shaw's Portfolio (D)

- ABC's (E)

Lingo Basics

Lingo, Director's scripting language, allows you to provide Director with specific instructions to meet your precise needs. Using Lingo is an easy way to customize a production and add interesting features that would otherwise require a much more in-depth knowledge of programming to accomplish.

Scripts

Each set of instructions written for Director is called a *script*. Multiple instructions, also called *commands*, may be placed in each script by listing them in the order you want them to be executed. To avoid confusing those who are new to programming and scripting, we limit each practice script in this chapter to only one instruction.

There are four types of scripts that can be written: Cast Member, Score (or Behavior), Movie, and Parent scripts.

Cast Member Scripts

A script can be attached to a cast member. In the example below, a script is attached to Cast Member 2 that says "continue." This type of script typically starts with the *on mouseUp* handler, which indicates that the task should be initiated when the mouse-click comes back up after a user clicks on the cast member. When a user clicks the cast member, the movie starts to play. These scripts are also known as "Button scripts" when you use the scripts to turn graphics into buttons.

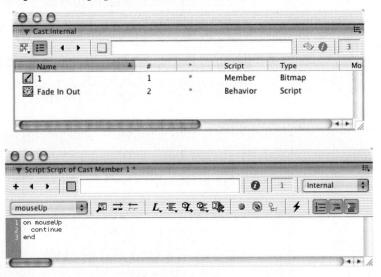

Score Scripts

There are two types of scripts that can be in the Score — Frame scripts and Sprite scripts. Score scripts are also known as "Behavior scripts." You can assign the behavior as many times as you want, to as many scripts as you prefer. As you create these scripts/behaviors, they are immediately added to the Behaviors drop-down menu on the top-left side of the Score. You can choose from this list and apply the scripts as needed.

Frame Scripts

Frame scripts are placed in the Script channel (the bottom channel in the Special Channels section). Double-clicking any frame in the Script channel displays the Script dialog box. The following is an example of a Frame script, which is located in Frame 1 of the movie. Frame scripts start with *on exitFrame me*, telling Director that as soon as the Playback Head starts to leave this frame, follow these instructions - in this case, go to Frame 28.

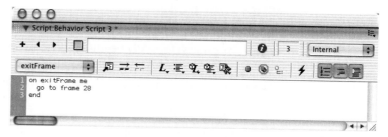

Sprite Scripts

Sprite scripts can be attached to any sprite in the Score. They can be created in the Behavior Inspector or the Library palette to apply an existing behavior to a sprite. You can apply multiple scripts or behaviors to a sprite. Remember, Sprite scripts are attached to a sprite, so they do not affect the original cast member.

Movie Scripts

Scripts that contain instructions that apply to an entire production are called Movie scripts. An example might be a scenario where you want the movie to begin only after the user has met certain criteria. Director keeps processing the instructions until they are complete, and then the Playback Head begins. To access a Movie script, you can select Window>Script or press Command/Control-0 (the number zero), and a new Script window opens. To designate it as a Movie script, you can go to the Property Inspector, click the Script tab, and select Movie from the Type drop-down menu.

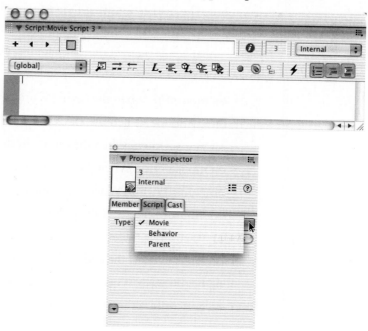

Parent Scripts

Parent scripts are complex and require a solid knowledge of object-oriented programming to effectively use them. Parent scripts are not covered in this book. If you want to learn more about Parent scripts, there is an abundance of Lingo dictionaries that you can purchase. O'Reilly & Associates publishes *Lingo in a Nutshell,* which is a helpful book, however the *Lingo Dictionary,* available from the Help menu, is also a good place to start.

Script Hierarchy

Director processes Scripts in a definite order as the Playback Head moves through a movie. The process typically begins with small Sprite scripts and works up to Movie scripts. As the Playback Head rolls onto Frame 1, Director looks for Sprite scripts and then executes and/or continues to look for any Cast Member scripts. The general order is:

A. Sprite script

B. Cast Member script

C. Frame script

D. Movie script

It is important to have a general idea of the order in which scripts are executed so you are certain to place the correct instructions in the appropriate type of script.

Script Anatomy

Lingo scripts are built similar to a gift: The gift itself — the script's instructions — is nestled inside a box that describes the gift in detail with a nametag on it. In a Lingo script, the box and nametag are known as *event handlers.*

Event Handlers

On mouseUp and *end mouseUp* are examples of event handlers. Event handlers always travel in pairs, with a starting and ending statement. They trigger Director to watch for instructions. The instructions that Director should follow must be written between these two statements.

Director understands many different event handlers. A few of the more common event handlers are listed below:

- **on mouseUp**. When the mouse is on its way back up from being clicked.
- **on exitFrame**. When the Playback Head prepares to leave the current frame.
- **on mouseDown**. When the mouse button is clicked.
- **on mouseEnter**. When the mouse pointer enters a sprite's boundaries.
- **on mouseWithin**. While the pointer is still within a sprite's boundaries.
- **on mouseLeave**. After the pointer leaves a sprite's boundaries.
- **on startMovie**. Before the Playback Head starts to move.
- **on endMovie**. At the end of the movie (after the Playback Head stops).
- **on beginsprite**. When the Playback Head reaches the first frame of a sprite.
- **on endsprite**. When the Playback Head leaves the last frame of a sprite.

When a Score or Cast Member script is opened, Director displays a default event handler. The default is set to whichever handler is used most frequently in that type of script. The cursor appears where you are to type your instructions.

Often, a script pops up with no handler; instead, the word "Global" appears at the top of the dialog box. Other times, you may want to change the handler. To access Lingo code, simply click the italic "L" menu button in the center of the second row of buttons; this is the Alphabetical Lingo button. The drop-down menu that appears contains the different Lingo handlers and instructions, listed alphabetically. If you are looking for *on mouseUp*, as shown below, you would go to the Mo to Move section, and then choose the appropriate handler from the list. A space appears between the event handlers in the Script window where you can type your commands.

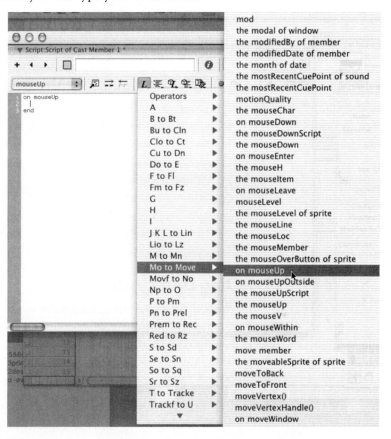

The button to the right of the "L" menu button (the Categorized Lingo button) displays a drop-down menu that lists Lingo in various categories. If you know what you want Director to do, but don't know the name of the command, you can go to the appropriate category. You will most likely find what you are looking for.

If you already know the type of Lingo you want to use, you can delete the default words and type in what you want, rather than looking it up.

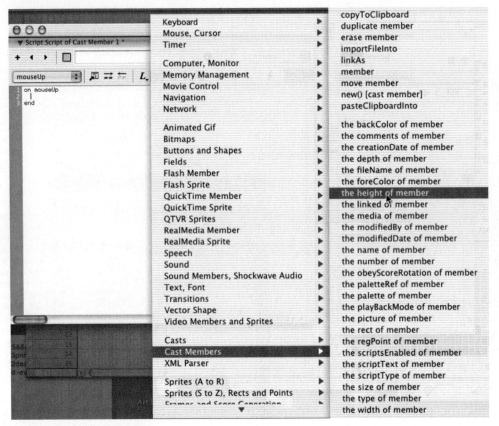

Dissecting Lingo Instructions

Lingo is made up of many parts. It's similar to the English language. In English, sentences can be comprised of nouns, verbs, pronouns, adverbs, prepositions, conjunctions, and adjectives. Lingo can be comprised of commands, keywords, operators, functions, constants, and properties. Below is a brief explanation, along with a few examples, of each component:

- **Commands (*continue, pause, quit, halt, go*).** Commands tell Director to do something.
- **Keywords (*the, on, end*).** Certain words that have a special meaning in Director. For instance, *on* means "instructions are coming." This means that a property comes next.
- **Operators (>, <, +, -).** Operators are ways to manipulate values (numbers). Director can perform basic mathematical calculations.
- **Functions (*date, time, key*).** These are questions that Director is prepared to answer. If you use *date*, Director displays the current date (as per the computer's clock). If you use *key*, Director can display which key or combination of keys was last pressed.

- **Constants (*return, true, empty, false*).** Constants never change; they always mean the same thing within Director. *True* and *false* are used often in Lingo to determine if a condition is met within "If, Then, Else" statements (if a condition is true, then do this; otherwise, do that).

- **Properties (*locV, locH, width*).** Properties are the attributes of an object. Italic and 12 pt. are attributes of type. They help describe or define the object. *LocV* is vertical location; *locH* is horizontal location.

At this point, it is important for you to have a general understanding that Lingo instructions are combinations of the parts listed above. It is not important that you memorize everything mentioned. Lingo is quite complicated; we cannot discuss it in full in the confines of this book. As stated under the Parent Scripts section, there are many other books that are devoted solely to Lingo, including *Lingo in a Nutshell* by O'Reilly & Associates, and Macromedia's own *Lingo Dictionary*.

Script Window Preferences

Director has a Script Window Preferences box you can use to assign different colors to different parts of your Lingo scripts. This should make Lingo a little easier to understand. Here, you can set some standards and even choose the font in which your scripts appear. Select Director>Preferences>Script (Macintosh) or Edit>Preferences>Script (Windows) to access this dialog box.

Director MX includes some new additions to the Script Window Preferences box. You now have the ability to color-code your scripts to make them easier to read and dissect. The lines of code are numbered so they are easier to reference and it is easier to locate items. Formatting is also available. These items are automated; you must turn them off if you don't want to use them.

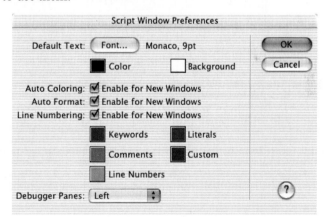

Script Errors

If you don't clearly formulate your instructions, a warning box appears.

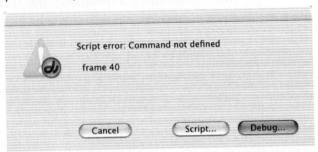

The warning box shown above tells you the command was not defined. The instruction in the script says *frame 40*; it should say *go to frame 40*.

You have the option to cancel the warning box, but canceling won't solve the problem. The Script button takes you straight to the offending script. This is the perfect solution if you know what is wrong and how to resolve the problem. If it is a long Script or you don't know where the problem is, you can press the Debug button to display the Debugger window.

There are times when the Debug button is not available. If it isn't, the script is more than likely incomplete.

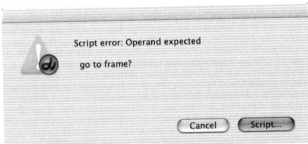

Debugger

The Debugger identifies the offending line of code so it can be fixed. In the example below, you can see the arrow is pointing to the error in the script. After the problem has been identified, you can make changes directly in the script. For long and complex scripts, the Debugger utility is incredibly valuable. As stated above, the Debugger can be accessed when there is a script error and the error box displays with the Debug option.

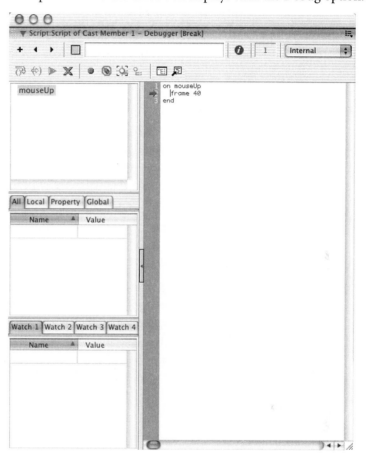

Message Window

The Message window allows you to see how Director works and processes scripts on a step-by-step basis. Director refers to dispatching steps as "sending messages" to different areas within the program. You can use this window to test scripts and verify they are running as intended.

Work with the Message Window

1. With Director open, select Window>Message (or press Command/Control-M) to display the Message window. It displays "Welcome to Director" at the top of the window.

2. There are 10 buttons across the top. Click the Trace button, which is the sixth button from the left. It keeps a running list of all the messages it sends.

3. Your cursor will be in the top window under the Welcome phrase. Type the phrase *beep (2)* and press the Return/Enter key. You should hear two beeps. It is the system beep on your machine. You wrote a script, minus the handlers, and ran it to test it. Let's try another command.

4. Type *put the date* and press the Return/Enter key. The current date, as per your computer's clock, is displayed in the bottom window. Examine the steps. The first line is your instruction in the top window, the second and third lines are the message as it was executed and the result.

5. If you want the result to appear in the Message window as shown below Step 6, you must type the word "put" before your Lingo instructions. Without this extra word, Director might still execute the instruction, but you have no way of confirming it is working correctly.

6. Type *put 5+5* and press the Return/Enter key. You should see the line where it sends the message and then the line containing the answer, 10, in the bottom window. Compare your Message window with the one below. They should look identical.

7. Close the Message window.

8. Keep Director open for the next exercise, but do not save this movie.

Menu Commands

There are several commands that refer to scripting in the Control menu. For now, let's focus only on the Disable Scripts option. As you gain experience and begin to generate long scripts in several places to accomplish different functions, the scripts become confusing. There may be times when you set up conditions in such a way that you can never see one of the alternative endings play out in real time unless you disable the scripts.

Work with Lingo

1. Select File>New Movie. Make certain the Special Channels section of the Score is open. If it is not, click the Hide/Show effects channels button on the right edge of the Score to open it.

2. Double-click in Frame 40 of the Script channel to display the Frame (or Behavior) script. Your cursor should be blinking between the *on exitFrame me* and *end* event handlers. Type *go to frame 1* and then close the Script window.

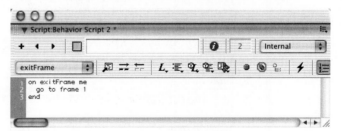

3. Open the Paint Editor and use the Filled Ellipse tool to draw a filled oval. Create the phrase "Click Me!" with the Text tool. Select the text and drag it on top of the oval. You created a Click Me! button. Let's add a script to make it work.

4. While you are still in the Paint Editor, or from the Cast, click the Script button to open the script of Cast Member 2. The script should have the *on mouseUp* and *end* event handlers showing, and the cursor should be blinking between them. Type *go to frame 40*. Close the Script window and Paint Editor.

5. Select Window>Message to open the Message window. Make certain the Trace button is pressed.

6. From the Cast, drag a copy of Cast Member 2 into Channel 1, Frames 1-28 of the Score. Open the Control panel (Window>Control Panel) and set your Frames per Second to 5.

7. Make sure your Score is visible. While watching your Message window, rewind, turn off loop, and play your movie. Quickly click the Click Me! button, making the movie jump to Frame 40, and then it should automatically go to Frame 1. Stop the movie. The Message window should resemble the following example.

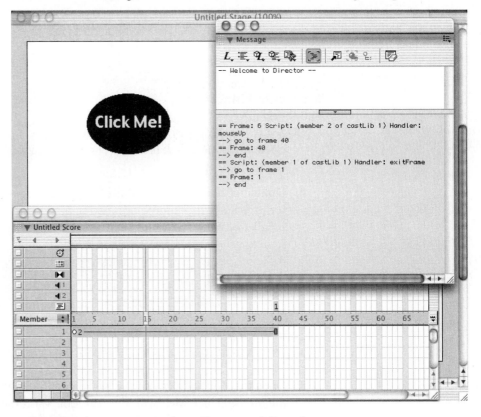

Examine the messages and see if you can follow them.

8. Let's ruin a script on purpose. Return to the Cast Member script attached to the Click Me! button. Delete the words *go to* so the instruction reads *frame 40.* Close the window and play your movie. Click the Click Me! button on the Stage. An error message should appear.

9. Click the Debug button to open the Debugger window. The offending script line is displayed in the right window with an arrow pointing to it.

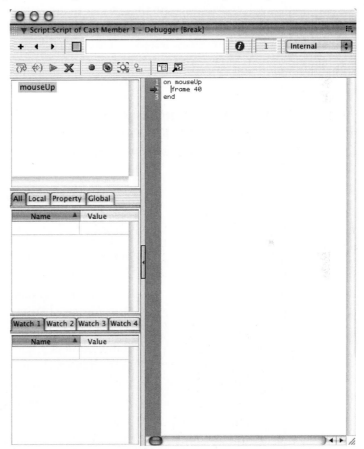

10. Fix the script so it says *go to frame 40,* and then close the Debugger window. Rewind and play the movie to make certain it works.

11. Close Director without saving the movie.

Lingo Tips

Here are some tips for working with Lingo:

- Lingo instructions and messages must be surrounded by event handlers.

- Watch out for typos. Director doesn't respond to words it doesn't understand, and that includes misspelled words. If you aren't good at spelling, carry a dictionary and double-check everything. You can ask someone else to proofread your scripts as a backup plan.

- Use the Copy and Paste commands to reduce your workload. When you have to create many similar scripts, type the script once and then copy and paste it. Make small, individual changes to minimize the possibility of errors creeping in. Another option is to use the drop-down lists that contain Lingo in chunks — allow Director to write the scripts for you.

- Keep an eye on your Message window if something is not working correctly.

- Make certain that proper names, such as a marker name or the name of a file, are placed within quotation marks and spelled correctly. Watch the uppercase and lowercase letters — Director is case-sensitive.

- If you are going to do a lot of scripting, customize your script colors so they are soothing to your eyes.

Frequently Used Lingo Scripts

The following is a list of frequently used scripts that will help get you started with Lingo. Most of these can work with many different event handlers.

Instruction	Definition
pause	Pauses a Director movie
continue	Continues a paused movie
quit	Stops the movie and closes Director
halt	Stops the movie on its current frame but doesn't quit Director
beep	Makes a system beep
alert "message"	Displays an alert dialog box with your message on it — type your message between the quotes
go to frame	Allows you to jump to a specified frame number or replace the frame number
go to the frame	Loops Director continually on the current frame
go to "nameofmarker"	Allows you to jump to markers — fill in name of marker between the quotes (case-sensitive)
go to movie "name.dir"	Allows you to jump to another Director movie — type the file name in between the quotes
go loop	Jumps the Playback Head to the first marker to the left

Chapter Summary

In this chapter, you learned some basic Lingo grammar and the different types of scripts you can create with it. The Debugger window and Message window were discussed, and you received some practice using them. The boundaries of Lingo are seemingly limitless, so an in-depth understanding of Lingo is not for the faint of heart. It requires time, practice, and patience, but it can be extremely rewarding.

13 Working with Lingo

Chapter Objectives:

As you already know, using Lingo can expand the capabilities of the Director program. Lingo allows you to create many different effects in Director that cannot be done with the Score alone. Scripts can be created at different levels of the hierarchy and executed at different times within a Director movie. In Chapter 13, you will:

- Understand how Lingo is constructed.
- Learn about the different elements of Lingo.
- Become more familiar with the Script window.
- Understand how to use the different levels of scripts.
- Learn about dot syntax, and how and where it is used.
- Learn to use the Object Inspector.

Projects to be Completed:

- Gaenzle Illustration and Design (A)
- Redi-Base (B)
- Digital Portfolio (C)
- Shaw's Portfolio (D)
- ABC's (E)

A special "thank you" to Michele Ebert, a freelance multimedia designer and colleague at Allentown Business School, who graciously took the time to write this chapter.

Working with Lingo

You already learned that Lingo can enhance the interactivity of your projects, but Lingo can also do much more. For instance, Lingo can be used to animate a sprite and change the properties of a sprite without using the Score. Before you can apply these types of interactivity, you must learn how Lingo is constructed, and understand dot syntax.

Lingo can be intimidating if you are not familiar with programming. To ease any uncertainty you might have, we'll approach Lingo slowly and provide all the background information you need to create Lingo scripts.

Before you begin to write Lingo, there are a few rules to follow that will help you write more effective code:

- Write Lingo one command at a time. Commands are terms that instruct Director to do something while the movie is playing.

- Test each command as you write it. This makes it easier to debug the code if something does not work correctly.

- Put comments after each set of code that explain what you are trying to do. This helps when you need to go back to the code or if you are working on the code with someone else.

- Double-check your scripts to make sure you're using the correct syntax. Director has a Lingo menu (shown below) and a built-in Lingo Dictionary to assist you.

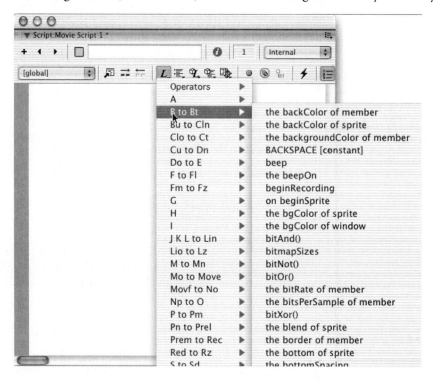

Lingo Dictionary

The Lingo Dictionary is a built-in dictionary that contains information about almost every piece of Lingo code known to Macromedia. It can be found on the Main menu bar under the Help menu.

When you are in the Lingo Dictionary, you can enter the Lingo command you are looking for. You can type the command under the Index or Search tab.

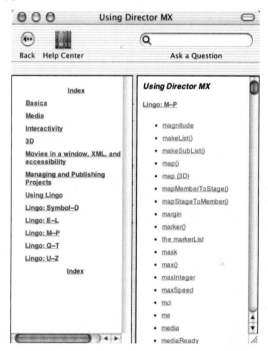

Lingo Elements

There are a few elements that are used when creating scripts. While we explore these elements, we are also going to examine variables, handlers, and if/then/else statements. There are several other elements that are beyond the scope of this chapter.

Variables

Variables contain *values* that represent data that will be used later in a script. Every time you use the variable name, you receive the data it represents. The beauty of this method is that you can repeatedly use variables without having to rewrite the same data.

For example, we might write the script *set myName to "Michele"*. This means that every time we use the Lingo term *myName*, it means Michele. *MyName* is the variable and "*Michele*" is the value of that variable.

Notice that the value "*Michele*" is placed in quotes. We place quotes around values because they are applied word for word and letter by letter. The exact value should display on the screen when the variable is used. When the program reads Lingo data inside quotes, it takes the data literally, and knows there is a name inside the quotes, not code.

As discussed in the previous chapter, the Message window is an excellent place to test your scripts. Let's test a short script in the Message window.

Variable Practice

1. Launch Director if it is not already running. Select Window>Message to open the Message window.

2. In the Message window, enter the following, exactly as shown:

   ```
   set myName to "Michele"
   put myName
   ```

3. Press the Return/Enter key. As you can see in the output part of the Message window, Michele is displayed exactly as you wrote it, inside the quotes.

4. Close the Message window. Keep the document open for the next exercise.

Variable Rules

There are a few important rules you must follow when using variables:

- A variable can be up to 256 characters long. The shorter the name (variable), however, the easier it is to use.

- The variable must start with a letter.

- After the first letter, you can use numbers.

- Variables can only be one word in length (they cannot contain spaces).

There are many different types of variables that can be used. In the test code, you used a *string variable*, which means the variable contains letters, called *characters*. Numbers are also considered characters until you use them as data to add/subtract/multiply/divide. Referring to the rules above, numbers can be used only after a letter when you use numbers in a variable.

Handlers

Another term you should become familiar with is *handler*. As discussed in the previous chapter, event handlers describe when an event will take place. For example, *on mouseUp* refers to when the mouse is in the up position — this usually means the resting state of the mouse. There are many pre-made handlers in Director. They can't control everything you want to do, however, so Director provides the tools you need to create your own handlers using Lingo.

For example, if you want to hide cast members throughout your movie, you could set the visibility of the cast member to False (turn it off). If you had to repeat this task throughout the entire movie, it would become a chore and waste a significant amount of time. There is, however, an easier way to accomplish the same result — you can create a handler.

You can define a new handler in a movie script, and then whenever you need to use it, you can call it up by typing it inside the handlers of whatever Sprite script you choose. Let's create a handler in the following exercise.

Create a Custom Handler

1. Open **creative.dir** from the **RF_Director** folder. If you want to view the finished version of this file for comparison, it is called **fincreative.dir** and is located in the **RF_Director** folder.

2. Next, let's create a Movie script. Select any open slot in the Cast. Open the Script window (Window>Script). In the Property Inspector, make sure Movie is chosen as the Type of Script (under the Script tab). Name this script "hideSprites".

3. In the Script window, type in the following:

```
on hideSprites
    sprite(2).visible = 0
    sprite(3).visible = 0
end
```

On hideSprites is the new handler you are creating. The next three lines of code tell the handler what to do. Next, we need to tell the movie when to use this handler. Close the Script window.

4. Open the script in the Cast called *hide button_script* by highlighting this cast member and clicking the Script button in the Cast window. (If you want to create the script from scratch, you can Control/right-click the actual hide button sprite in the Score, and then choose Script from the drop-down menu shown below).

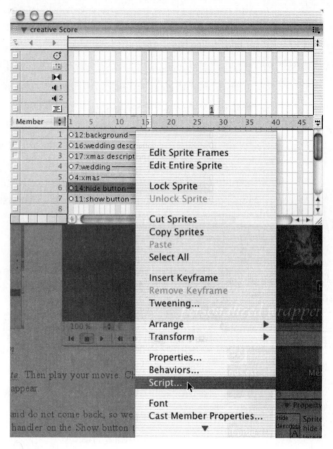

5. Change the *mouseUp* handler to say *on mouseDown*.

6. In between the handlers (on Line 2), enter *hidesprites*. Close the window. Rewind and play your movie. Click the Hide descriptions button and watch the descriptions disappear. You may have to scroll down to see them. Notice that they do not come back, so we need to create a second handler for the Show descriptions button to make the descriptions reappear.

7. Create a new Movie script and name it "showSprite".

8. We are going to name this handler "showSprites".

9. In the Script window, enter the following and then close the Script window:

```
on showSprites
   sprite(2).visible = 1
   sprite(3).visible = 1
end
```

10. Now let's write a script for the Show button. In the Cast, open the script cast member named *show button_script*.

In this example we used 1 and 0 to hide and show the sprites. In programming, 1=true and 0=false.

11. Change the event handler from *on mouseUp* to *on mouseDown*. Type in the *showSprites* handler we created, and then close the Script window.

```
on mouseDown
    showSprites
end
```

12. Play your movie. Click the Show descriptions and Hide descriptions buttons on the Stage to make the descriptions appear and disappear. Do not save your changes, but keep Director open for the next exercise.

If, Then, Else Statements

Other programming terms you will hear and use are "if" statements and "else" statements. These are called *conditionals*. Each statement is a condition on what the user decides.

Conditionals can be broken down into three parts:

- First, the "if" statement performs a test. You are trying to discover if the test's answer is true or false.
- The "then" section is what you want to happen if the result of the test in the "if" statement is true.
- An optional section is the "else" statement, which contains what you want to happen if the result of the test in the "if" statement is false.
- You can also refer to the test as a question that is being asked.

You can reduce the if/then/else statement to: If "X" event happens, then do "Y", or else do "Z." For example:

If (you are tired) then (lie down).

If (you are tired) then (lie down) else (keep working).

Exercise Setup

In this exercise, we will create an object that continues to move across the stage. When it reaches the edge of the stage, it returns to the opposite side and continues to move across the stage again.

Use an If, Then, Else Statement

1. If you want to view the finished version of this file for comparison, it is called **fincar.dir** and is located in the **RF_Director** folder. To start this exercise, open **car.dir** from the **RF_Director** folder and play the movie to see what happens. Stop the movie.

2. Open the Script window for the car sprite. Control/right-click the car cast member and choose Script from the drop-down menu. Name this script "pspeed".

3. First, we are going to determine the property value that will represent the movement of the sprite. We will use the property *pspeed*. The "5" in our script determines how far the object moves (in pixels) each time it moves. Delete any handlers currently in the Script window, and then type the following in the Script window:

```
property pspeed
on beginSprite me
    pspeed = 5
end
```

4. Next, let's tell Director when to execute the Lingo script by using the *on exitFrame* handler (continue to use the same Script window from Step 3). Then we will tell the sprite that when it reaches the edge of the screen (position 640), it should start over (Lines 2 and 3 of the script). If it is not at the end of the screen, we tell it to keep moving in increments of 5 pixels (Line 4 of the script). On the next line in the Script window, type the following:

```
on exitFrame me
    if sprite(2).loch > 640 then
        sprite(2).loch = 0
    else
        sprite(2).loch = sprite(2).loch + pspeed
    end if
end
```

*In this example, we used a custom property of a sprite — **pspeed**. You will learn more about custom properties in the next section.*

5. Save your movie as "carpractice.dir" in your **Work_In_Progress** folder, and then test it. Keep Director open for the next exercise.

Dot Syntax

Up to this point in the book, you have worked with Movie scripts and Sprite scripts. In the previous chapter, you learned about the hierarchy of scripting. Next, let's talk about how scripts are written.

You can use dot syntax to express the properties or functions related to an object. A *dot syntax expression* begins with the name of the object, followed by a period (dot), and then the property (function) you want to specify. The dot syntax simply means you are using a "." to signal that you are referring to something different. The dot is a virtual divider. Dot syntax is a generic programming method, and can be found in many different programming languages including Flash Action scripting, JavaScript, ASP, and many others. An everyday example of dot syntax is a Web address (www.againsttheclock.com).

Whenever you work with dot syntax (and Lingo in general), you work with *objects*. Anything that is tangible in the Director environment is an object. For example, graphics are objects, text members are objects, sprites are objects, and behaviors are objects. The characteristics of these objects are referred to as *properties*. (Properties will be discussed in further detail later in this chapter).

For example, the visible sprite property indicates a sprite's visibility on the Stage. The expression *sprite(3).visible* refers to the visible property of Sprite 3.

Dot syntax is considered the shorthand version of code. The main rule it follows is *object.property*. With dot syntax, you put the object first and the property last, separated by a dot.

Here is an example of the longhand code:

```
on mouseUp me
    set the visibility of sprite 1 to FALSE
end
```

Here is a dot syntax version of the same code:

```
on mouseUp me
    sprite (1).visible = 0
end
```

You will often notice *me* being used after the event handler. It is a generic reference to whatever the behavior is attached to. When you use *me* instead of the specific name of the object to which the behavior is attached, you can reuse the script. For example, if Sprite 1 and Sprite 2 use the same event handler (*on mouseUp*), when Sprite 1 is executed, *me* will stand for Sprite 1; when Sprite 2 is executed, *me* will stand for Sprite 2.

Let's dissect a line of code so you can better understand the concept of *me*:

on mouseEnter me	(When the mouse enters the parameters of the sprite determined in the next line.)
sprite(5).visible = 0	(The number 5 represents the channel where the sprite is located. Visible is the property of the object sprite in channel 5. 0 is the value of the property. 0= false 1=true.)
end	(This ends the statement and is absolutely necessary.)

You may have heard the term **on mouseOver** if you have scripted in other languages. **On mouseEnter** and **on mouseOver** are essentially the same. **On mouseEnter** is used in Director and **on mouseOver** is used in other languages such as Flash Action scripting.

In this exercise, we are going to practice using the dot syntax method. We are going to create a simple rollover button using different cast members.

Create a Rollover Effect

1. If you want to view the finished version of this file for comparison, it is called **finrollover.dir** and it is located in the **RF_Director** folder. To start the exercise, open **rollover.dir** from the **RF_Director** folder. You see three different button cast members in the Cast:

   • Cast Member 4 is the Up state of the button (before you click the mouse).

   • Cast Member 3 is the Over state of the button (when your cursor glides over the sprite or enters the sprite's boundaries).

   • Cast Member 2 is the Down state of the button (when you click the mouse).

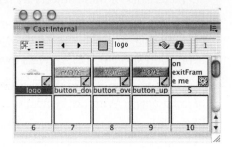

2. Drag the Up state of the button to your Stage. This cast member is called button_up. Place it anywhere on the Stage. The finished project shows it in the lower center of the Stage. Place button_up into Channel 1, Frames 1-28.

3. Highlight the button_up sprite in the Score. Control/right-click to display the Script window for this sprite. Do not script the cast member. Make sure it is a Behavior script attached to the sprite. Delete the default script and type in the following script:

   on mouseEnter me   (This is when the mouse enters the sprite.)
       sprite(1).member = "button_over" (We are telling the sprite what cast member to display when the mouse rolls over or enters the original sprite's boundaries.)

   end

   on mouseLeave me   (This is when the mouse leaves the sprite.)
       sprite(1).member = "button_up"   (We are telling it to display the Up state of the button.)

   end

   on mouseDown me   (We are going to tell it what cast member to display when the user clicks the button.)

       sprite(1).member = "button_down"

   end

```
        on mouseUp me
```

(This is the original state of the button when the movie is executed until the user interacts with the button.)

```
    sprite(1).member = "button_up"

end
```

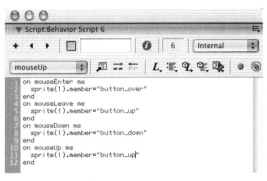

4. Close the Script window. Rewind and play your movie, and then try rolling over the button and clicking it. Next, we will make a rollover using the Rollover Member Change behavior in the Behavior library. Then, we will compare the code.

5. Drag another copy of the button_up cast member to the Stage and place it anywhere next to the other button.

6. Open the Library palette (Window>Library Palette). Choose Animation>Interactive from the drop-down menu on the left side of the palette.

7. Scroll down until you find the Rollover Member Change behavior.

8. Drag this behavior onto your second button sprite in the Score.

9. Choose the button_over cast member as your rollover member. Rewind and play your movie. Click on both buttons to see what happens. You will see that they both perform the same function.

10. Highlight the Rollover Member Change cast member in your Cast, and display the Script window for this cast member (Window>Script). Examine the pre-scripted Lingo behavior.

11. Save your movie and keep Director open for the next exercise.

You will notice that this script is much longer and more confusing than the script we created earlier in this chapter. Behaviors are an excellent way to add Lingo to your Score when you don't know much about Lingo code. Please note that pre-scripted Lingo code (which is found in the Behaviors section of the Library palette) should not be altered to create different effects. You would need to understand what the programmer had written before you could copy the script and change it.

Properties

When we discussed the rule for dot syntax, we mentioned properties. Properties are the characteristics of objects that can be changed through Lingo scripting. Take, for example, an 8-oz. round green ball. Round, green, and 8-oz. are properties of the ball; the ball is the object. Think of properties as adjectives that describe the object (noun).

Sprites and cast members have their own built-in properties, but you can also create your own. Below is a list of some of the built-in sprite properties that can be set with Lingo.

You can declare which properties in a Movie script will be available to the entire Director movie, and you can declare properties directly before the handler in the Sprite member script. Properties can be used throughout the movie to achieve the same result without having to repeatedly rewrite a script.

PROPERTY	DESCRIPTION
blend	Changes the opacity of a sprite.
cursor	Changes the cursor of a sprite.
locH	Determines and sets the horizontal location of a sprite.
locV	Determines and sets the vertical location of a sprite.
member	Assigns or alters the member of a sprite.
visible	Toggles the visibility of a sprite.
height	Determines or changes the height of a sprite.
width	Determines or changes the width of a sprite.
volume	Determines or changes the volume of a sprite.
ink	Determines or changes the Ink blend of a sprite.

These are a few of the more commonly used properties. There are many that pertain specifically to sprites, cast members, digital video, system properties, or movie properties.

Exercise Setup

In the next exercise, you create a movie that allows you to move a sprite to the left or right by clicking a button.

Change Properties

1. If you want to view the finished version of this file for comparison, it is called **finufo.dir** and is located in the **RF_Director** folder. To start this exercise, open **ufo.dir** located in the **RF_Director** folder. You see a UFO on the Stage. It is placed in Channel 2.

2. Control/right-click the sprite to display the Behavior script window for Sprite 2 (ufo) and select the Script option. Name this script "movement".

   We are going to create a property. We will name the property "move" and put a "p" in front of it that will stand for "property". Next you will place the property *pmove* before the handler. This is because we created our new property and we need to declare it before the handler executes. We must also assign a value to the property and tell it when to execute.

3. Delete the default script and type in the following:

   ```
   property pmove
   on beginsprite me
       pmove = 5          (This is setting the property of pmove to 5 pixels.)
   end
   ```

4. Next, let's take the current location of Sprite 2 and add the property *pmove* to it (this moves the sprite five pixels to the right). Then we are going to loop it on the frame so the movie continues to play. Press Return/Enter to advance to the next line, and then type:

```
on exitFrame me
    sprite(2).locH = sprite(2).locH + pmove
    go to the frame        (this loops on the frame)
end
```

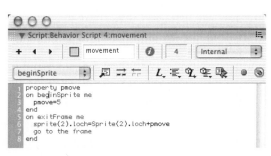

5. Save your movie as "ufopractice.dir" in your **Work_In_Progress** folder. Rewind and play the movie to test it.

6. Notice that the UFO continually moves to the right, and then moves off the stage. You need to add a toggle button that moves it to the left or the right. If the sprite is moving to the right and you click the button, the sprite will change direction and move to the left. If the sprite is moving to the left and you click the button, the sprite will change direction and move to the right.

7. From the Cast, drag the button (toggle_btn) into Frame 1 of Channel 3. Make it the same length as the UFO sprite. Let's script this button.

8. Control/right-click the sprite and choose Script to open the Script window for this button.

9. As you enter the next script, notice that we reference the property we created in the last script. Type the following script in the Script window:

```
on mouseUp me
    sprite (2).pmove = sprite(2).pmove * -1
end
```

In line 2, we take the current location of the sprite and multiply it times –1. This moves it to the left or to the right, depending on whether the location number is positive or negative.

10. Save your changes and test the movie by rewinding and playing it. Keep the file open for the next exercise.

Object Inspector

The Object Inspector allows you to add variables or objects to the Inspector and view their values. After an object has been added to the Object Inspector, you can see all the variables and values the object contains. This allows you to track specific properties of the object. For example, if you want to identify the location of a sprite, you could add the sprite to the Object Inspector and then find its location at any time within the movie.

When you multiply a negative number times a positive number, the result is a negative number. When you click the button again, you would multiply a negative number times a negative number, which would result in a positive number.

The Object Inspector is session-based, not movie-based. When you enter an object or variable in the Object Inspector, it remains there until you close Director. For example, if you were to close Movie1 and open Movie2, the objects from Movie1 would still be in the Object Inspector. On the other hand, if you were to close Director, restart the program, and then open Movie1, the objects would no longer be in the Object Inspector. When you end a Director session, the Object Inspector is emptied.

Find the Location Using the Object Inspector

1. Continue working in the open ufopractice.dir. If you closed the file, open it from your Work_In_Progress folder.

2. Select Window>Object Inspector to open the Object Inspector. (You might find this window already open on the right side of your screen, grouped with windows that contain other utilities.)

3. Drag a copy of the ufo sprite from the Score and drop it on the Object Inspector window. It puts the word sprite in the name column.

4. Click the arrow to the left of the sprite name. It opens a large list of that particular sprite's characteristics.

Name	Value
▼ sprite(2)	
spriteNum	2
member	(member 2 of castLib 1)
startFrame	1
endFrame	28
editable	0
visible	1
▶ color	paletteIndex(255)
▶ bgColor	paletteIndex(0)
blend	100
ink	0
▶ loc	point(205, 240)
width	144
height	38
rotation	0.0000
skew	0.0000
flipH	0

▼ Code 2:Object Inspector

5. Play the movie and watch the loc property change as the object (Sprite 2) moves across the screen. You can press the Move the UFO button on the Stage to watch the coordinates change in the Object Inspector as Sprite 2 moves from left to right. As you can see, the Object Inspector can be used to monitor the properties of objects in Director movies.

6. Close the movie without saving your changes, and then close Director.

Chapter Summary

In this chapter, you learned about some of the elements of the Lingo scripting language. You learned how to use them to create animation and special effects. You learned about dot syntax, and discovered how to build Lingo scripts using this method. Finally, you learned about the Lingo Dictionary and the Object Inspector and how to access each.

Complete Project E: ABC's

14   3-D and Director

Chapter Objectives:

Director is designed to manage 3-D objects in two ways. The first, using Lingo, is the preferred method, offering sophisticated results. The alternative is to use basic 3-D behaviors to manipulate objects. This method produces acceptable results, but they are not unique. This chapter focuses primarily on using 3-D behaviors, because they are easy to learn, and easy to apply. We also sample some of the remarkable 3-D effects you can create with Lingo. In Chapter 14, you will:

- Learn about different 3-D file formats that can be imported into Director MX.

- Discover how to create a 3-D object from scratch using Lingo.

- Become familiar with the Shockwave 3-D Viewer.

- Explore the various properties of a 3-D object.

- Learn to create 3-D type with Director.

3-D and Director

Designing for the 3-D world is not always easy. Working in three dimensions is much more difficult than working in two. Many users master 3-D design quickly; for others, the task proves much more difficult. There is usually a long learning curve before a user is fully 3-D-capable. Given proper time and patience, you, too, can learn to effectively use 3-D tools to create impressive results.

Importing 3-D Objects

Let's begin with learning how to import 3-D objects. This operation is very similar to importing any other object into Director. The only difference lies in the file types that are accepted into Director. The two acceptable file types are W3-D and OBJ.

W3-D Objects

Director's newest file format is W3-D. To create a W3-D file and export it to Director, you must have a translator for the original 3-D-modeling application. Macromedia is working diligently to ensure that all of the major 3-D-modeling programs provide translators for their software, allowing users to export their 3-D models with ease. 3-DS Max (3-D Studio Max) and LightWave have translators, among others.

OBJ Objects

OBJ is a well-known 3-D file format that has been in use for many years. Most 3-D-modeling programs employ this format for saving files. Based on this fact, Macromedia developed a converter that translates OBJ files into W3-D files, which can then be imported into Director. This converter can be found on Macromedia's Web site. It is called 3-D Speedport. It is a Director Xtra that must be placed in Director's Xtras folder to operate correctly. After installation and computer restart, the converter displays in the Xtras menu for easy access and use.

Import a 3-D File

1. Launch Director if it is not already running. If you want to view the finished version of this file before beginning the exercise, open **finpda.dir** from the **RF_Director** folder. Your Cast should be in Thumbnail view for this exercise.

2. Select File>Import to display the Import Files window. Navigate to **pda.w3d** in the **RF_Director** folder. Click the Import button to import the file into Director. It should display in your Cast similar to the image below.

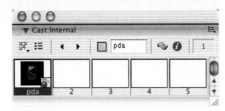

3. Click on the Stage (not on a sprite). Select the Movie tab of the Property Inspector and ensure the movie Size is set to 640 × 480 pixels.

4. Save the file in your **Work_In_Progress** folder and name it "pdapractice.dir". Keep the file open for the next exercise.

Thank you to Steve Skrzenski, a fellow instructor at Allentown Business School, for creating the 3-D object we used in the exercises in this chapter.

Shockwave 3-D Viewer

The Shockwave 3-D Viewer is a window inside Director that is used to view and manipulate 3-D objects. It serves the same function as a QuickTime window, where you can view QuickTime files. The illustration below shows the window with a 3-D object in it. The top of the window is the same as all Director windows. It provides an area to name your cast members and offers access to the scripts and property information. It also provides the ability to step forward and backward through your Cast, or create a blank window when necessary.

You can access the Shockwave 3-D Viewer from the Window menu, or click the shortcut button at the top of the menu bar.

The Shockwave 3-D Viewer shortcut button.

The window has the typical step-backward and step-forward controls, as well as the Stop, Play, Rewind, and Loop controls. Since you can now control Director in real time, a clock is also displayed so you can keep track of the length of an animation.

The four icons across the top, from left to right, are Reset Camera Transform, Set Camera Transform, Root Lock, and Reset World. The five icons down the side, from top to bottom, are Dolly Camera, Rotate Camera, Pan Camera, Camera Y-Up, and Camera Z-Up.

The Viewer allows you to manipulate the cameras surrounding your 3-D object. It also provides some information at the bottom of the window, such as how many lights are on the object, and how many cameras, models, and polygons you have.

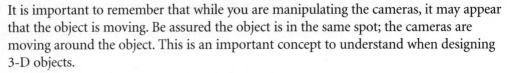

It is important to remember that while you are manipulating the cameras, it may appear that the object is moving. Be assured the object is in the same spot; the cameras are moving around the object. This is an important concept to understand when designing 3-D objects.

It is important to remember that while you are manipulating the cameras, it may appear that the object is moving. Be assured the object is in the same spot; the cameras are moving around the object. This is an important concept to understand when designing 3-D objects.

The Dolly Camera button is the top camera button. In the traditional movie industry, dolly cameras are placed on carts, and follow along beside the actors during filming, allowing the camera to smoothly zoom-in on the action.

The Rotate Camera button allows the camera to rotate around the object so the object appears to be spinning. This camera works together with the Camera Y-Up and Camera Z-Up buttons. When you select the Rotate Camera button, one of these other two cameras (Y-Up or Z-Up) is automatically selected. This occurs because when a camera rotates, it is either rotating around the Y-axis or the Z-axis. The action (or reaction) of these cameras largely depends upon the orientation of your object.

The Pan Camera pans across the screen in a straight line, moving from Point A to Point B.

The Reset Camera Transform button resembles a house. It can be found in the top-left corner of new icons. Any camera manipulations in the Shockwave 3-D Viewer window can be reset to their original position, at any time, by clicking this button. The only instance when your cameras will not reset with this button is when you select the Set Camera Transform button. This button sets the cameras somewhat permanently into new positions. Even when you take this action, there are ways to undo the transformation, such as re-importing the file, or using the Reset World button. Until you click the Set Camera Transform button, you will not see any changes to your sprite (if you have one) on the Stage.

The Root Lock button works with full 3-D animations. It keeps the animations in one spot while they are playing. For instance, if you have an animation of a dog running, he would run in one spot, rather than run across the window.

The Reset World button resets all of the lighting, cameras, textures, and animations associated with the original W3-D file of the object. It does not, however, reset the cast member properties, such as those listed in the Property Inspector.

Now that we have discussed the various cameras and controls for the 3-D Shockwave Viewer window, let's experiment with them in the following exercise.

3-D Shockwave Viewer

1. In the open pdapractice.dir, double-click the pda cast member to open it in the 3-D Shockwave Viewer.

2. Choose the Dolly Camera button on the left side of the screen. To select the correct icon, refer to the previous illustration, or hover your cursor over the buttons until the tool tip names show up. Notice that your cursor changes to a unique upward arrow. Click the bottom of the pda image and drag up toward the top of the window. This enlarges the pda so its screen resembles the one shown in Step 10.

3. Select the Rotate Camera button, located directly below the Dolly Camera button. Then choose the Camera Y-Up button (it should already be selected). Click the pda image, and drag the cursor around the screen. Experiment until you are comfortable manipulating the pda. This rotates the camera on the Y-axis.

Remember, the cameras are moving around the object. The object itself is not moving.

4. Now click the Camera Z-Up button, and repeat Step 3 until you are comfortable using Camera Z-Up (keep the Rotate Camera button selected). This rotates the camera on the Z-axis.

5. Drag a copy of the pda cast member to the Score, and place it into Frame 1, Channel 1. Return to the 3-D Shockwave Viewer window. Keep the Stage uncluttered so you can see it for the next few steps.

6. Click the Rotate Camera button. Notice the cursor changed again. Make sure the Property Inspector is open, and the 3-D Model tab is selected. Note the rotation numbers — they should all read "0".

7. Rotate the pda until you are satisfied with the result. Notice that the image on the Stage is still the old version, and the numbers in the Property Inspector have not changed to reflect your movements.

8. Click the Set Camera Transform button in the 3-D Shockwave Viewer to set the changes. Notice that now both the Property Inspector and the Stage reflect your changes.

9. Click the Reset World button in the Shockwave Viewer. You find that it cannot reset the rotation because the Set Transform button was clicked. At this point, the best way to reset the rotation (if you need/want to) is to click the Revert to World Defaults button in the Property Inspector. It resets all of the properties to their original positions.

10. Move the model around using a combination of cameras until you reach something similar to the image below.

11. Save your changes and close the 3-D Shockwave Viewer window. Keep the file open for the next exercise.

Property Inspector

As 3-D file types are imported into Director, accommodations must be made within the Property Inspector to display their unique properties. A 3-D tab contains the 3-D properties, and additional 3-D-related properties can be found in the Movie tab.

3-D Model Tab

The Property Inspector has a 3-D tab to accommodate the properties of 3-D files. The 3-D Model tab is present in the Property Inspector whenever a 3-D cast member is highlighted in the Cast. This tab contains the camera position and rotation angles on the X-, Y-, and Z-axes. It also has a Direct to Stage option similar to the QuickTime Properties tab. Some lighting options and shading textures are available as well.

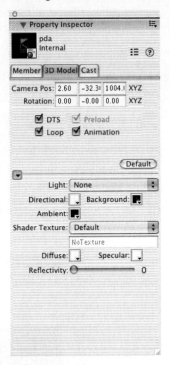

The image shown below is the 3-D Model tab set to List view. Here you can view more precise information, including the exact hexadecimal value of your colors (Ambient light, background colors).

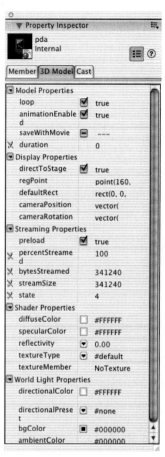

Movie Tab

The Movie tab includes 3-D options in its menu. It is the first drop-down menu on the bottom half of the tab. It allows you to set the 3-D rendering engine for the Director movie. It defaults to Auto, which means it will search the user's computer and choose the most suitable option from the search results. If it can't find a hardware-rendering engine (such as DirectX or openGL), it reverts to the software-rendering engine that was created by NxView for this precise purpose.

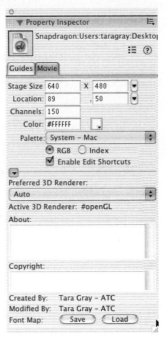

Below you can see the various rendering options from which you can choose.

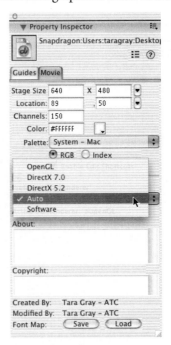

3-D Properties

1. Continue working in the open pdapractice.dir. Make sure the pda sprite extends from Frame 1 to Frame 30.

2. Click the first keyframe and drag the pda off the right edge of the Stage.

3. Insert a keyframe at Frame 10. Click the keyframe to highlight it and then drag the pda back to its original position on the Stage.

4. Play your movie. The pda should start off the right side of the Stage, slide in, and then stop at Frame 10 where it should stay until Frame 30.

5. Click the Movie tab and make sure the background of your movie is set to black.

6. Click the 3-D Model tab. Click the Ambient color swatch, and choose some different colors. Watch the Stage to see what happens. You can either leave it on the color of your choice or reset it to black.

7. Click the Background Color swatch and choose some different colors. Again, watch the Stage to see what happens. Reset it to black when you are finished.

8. Close the 3-D Shockwave Viewer, save your changes and keep the file open for the next exercise.

3-DPI

Even though 3-DPI is not part of the Property Inspector, it contains properties. 3-DPI is a third-party utility created by Ullala. 3-DPI makes 3-D editing an easier task. It is a .dcr file and must be placed in Director's Xtras folder. After installation, the computer must be restarted; 3-DPI then displays under the Xtras menu as shown below.

This utility can be found at www.3dpi-director.com. As of this writing, a new version was recently released for Mac OS X. Windows versions also exist. The utility is shareware that costs $50 to purchase — a very low price for all the options it offers. If you are planning to undertake 3-D Lingo programming, you might consider purchasing this program. As is it shareware, it is legal to download a copy of the program and try it free of charge before making the decision to purchase your own license.

We do not go into detail on this utility at this time, as not everyone will want to delve deeply into Lingo programming. For the benefit of those who may be interested, however, we wanted to mention it. 3-DPI is a very complete utility that has the potential to greatly enhance your productivity.

3-D Behaviors

There is a section called Three-D in the Behavior library. It contains two sub-categories — Actions and Triggers. They typically work in conjunction with each other. For every action, there is usually a trigger of some kind.

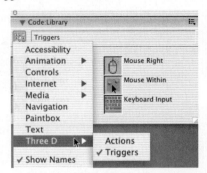

Actions

Actions are behaviors that 3-D models (objects) and animations can make, or they can be events that happen to the models and animations. Typically, a trigger must be attached to the action in order for it to take place. There are three types of actions — local, public, and independent.

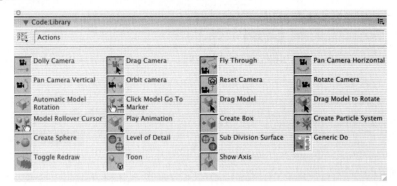

Local

Local actions, similar to all actions and triggers, are attached to 3-D sprites using the typical drag-and-drop method. Local actions, however, require that the trigger to which you want the action to respond must be attached to the same 3-D sprite or there will be no resultant action.

The following is a list of the available local actions and their descriptions. Each action occurs when a trigger is initiated:

- **Create Box**. Adds boxes to your 3-D world.
- **Create Particle System**. Creates a particle system (like snow or rain) based on your input.
- **Create Sphere**. Adds spheres to your 3-D world.
- **Drag Camera**. Allows users to control the cameras.
- **Drag Model**. Allows users to drag the 3-D model anywhere they choose.
- **Drag Model to Rotate**. Allows the model to rotate around the specified axis.

- **Fly Through**. Allows the user to fly through the 3-D space with a camera.
- **Go to Marker**. Jumps the Playback Head to a certain marker.
- **Orbit Camera**. The camera orbits the 3-D model.
- **Play Animation**. Plays an animation (doesn't work with 3-D text).

Public

Public actions are attached to 3-D sprites, and require a trigger to initiate the action. The triggers for these actions can be assigned to any sprite; this has no effect on the resultant action. Below is a list of public actions:

- **Dolly Camera**. Zooms the camera in or out (requires separate triggers).
- **Generic Do.** Creates custom Lingo handlers and assigns regular triggers.
- **Pan Camera Horizontal**. Slides the camera along the horizontal axis.
- **Pan Camera Vertical**. Slides the camera along the vertical axis.
- **Reset Camera**. Resets the camera to its starting point.
- **Rotate Camera**. Rotates the camera on the Z-axis.
- **Toggle Redraw**. Creates the effect of the Trails button on 3-D objects.

Independent

Independent actions do not require triggers. You apply them to a sprite, and they automatically engage in an ongoing fashion:

- **Automatic Model Rotation**. Automatically rotates the model around an axis.
- **Level of Detail**. Reduces the number of detail polygons (3-D objects are made up of many polygons) used as an image goes farther away from the camera, reducing the amount of memory required.
- **Model Rollover Cursor**. Changes the cursor upon rollover.
- **Show Axis**. Used in debugging, displays on the Stage using colored lines to distinguish one from another.
- **Subdivision Surfaces**. Used to smooth curves on a sprite.
- **Toon**. Changes the 3-D model so it resembles a cartoon.

Triggers

Triggers initiate actions. Both local and public actions require triggers before an action will take place. Triggers can be anything from a mouse click, to pressing a certain key on the keyboard:

- **Mouse Left**. Initiates an action when the user clicks the left mouse button.
- **Mouse Right**. Initiates an action when the user clicks the right mouse button (Windows only).
- **Mouse Within**. Initiates an action when the user's mouse moves inside the boundaries of the 3-D model.
- **Mouse Enter**. Initiates an action when the user's mouse enters the boundaries of a 3-D model.

- **Mouse Leave**. Initiates an action when the user's mouse leaves the boundaries of a 3-D model.
- **Keyboard Input**. Initiates an action when the user presses a specific key on the keyboard.

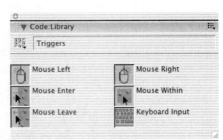

Combining Actions and Triggers

To combine actions and triggers, you must apply the action first and set its parameters. Then you can choose the trigger you want to accompany it and apply it to the sprite. Next, you can set the parameters for the trigger. You can play the movie to test the settings.

Actions and Triggers

1. Continue working in the open pdapractice.dir.

2. Open the Library palette and select 3-D>Actions.

3. Double-click the Script channel in Frame 30 and enter a *go to the frame* script. When the Playback Head reaches Frame 30, it loops on that frame.

4. From the Library palette, drag a copy of the Automatic Model Rotation action onto the pda sprite. Choose "13" as the speed and "Y" as the axis from the Parameters dialog box. As this is an independent action, it does not require a trigger. It works automatically.

5. Play your movie and you find the pda rotates into the scene, stops moving forward, but continues to rotate as if on display.

6. Now let's add some fireworks. Drag a copy of the Create Particle System action onto the pda sprite. From the Parameters dialog box, set How Many Particles to 70, Starting Size to 4.0, Final Size to 1.0, and Gaussian distribution. For the Colors to Use, choose How Should the Colors be Selected. You may choose whatever Start and End Colors you prefer. If you aren't sure what colors to use, start as white and end as a red. Click OK.

7. This action requires a trigger. From the Library palette, select 3-D>Triggers. Drag a copy of Mouse Within onto the pda sprite. Make sure the Parameters dialog box says, Group Unassigned! - Create Particles. Play the movie. You see that whenever the mouse is on top of the pda sprite or within the pda sprite's bounding box, sparks fly and follow the mouse as it moves.

8. Your Cast and Stage should now resemble the images below (as the image is rotating). Save your changes and keep the file open for the next exercise.

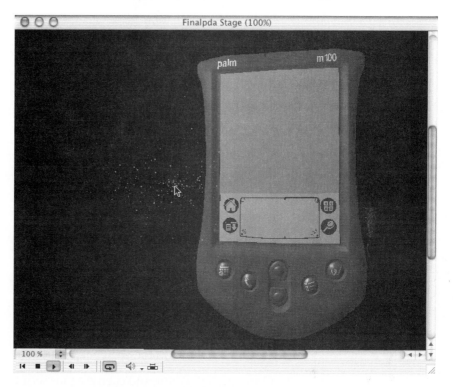

3-D Text

Director now has the ability to create 3-D text. To do this, you would create 2-D text in the Text Editor, go to the Text tab in the Property Inspector, and select 3-D Mode from the Display drop-down menu at the top of the tab. After the 3-D conversion, you would find a new property tab in the Property Inspector called 3-D Extruder, which you can use to make adjustments.

3-D Extruder

The 3-D Extruder tab has many options you can use to manipulate 3-D text. You can set the camera position and rotation, control the tunnel depth (the depth of the extrude), decide which faces are shown (front or back), and set the smoothness of the extrude.

The type of bevel and its amount are fully adjustable, as are the various forms of lighting. There is Directional lighting (you choose the direction), Ambient lighting, and Background lighting. The color can be adjusted on all of these lighting settings.

Shaders and textures may also be used. You can use the default settings or create your own textures in the Paint Editor.

The Shader lights can be adjusted. Diffused and Specular lighting colors can be changed. There is also a Reflectivity slider that adjusts the amount of reflectivity shown on your object.

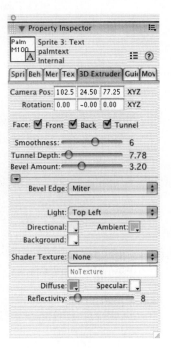

Create 3-D Text

1. Continue working in the open pdapractice.dir.

2. Open the Text Editor, and choose a sans serif font (no tails on the letters) that is relatively chunky, such as Helvetica or Arial. We chose the Macintosh system font Charcoal for the example below. Choose 36-pt. Size, and Bold it if the font is too thin for your preference. Type "Palm M100" as shown below. Close the Text Editor.

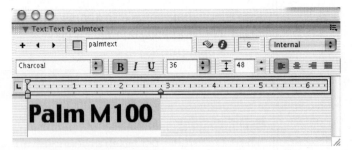

3. Open the Cast and highlight the new 2-D cast member. Select the Property Inspector and click the Text tab.

4. Choose 3-D Mode from the Display drop-down menu.

5. Drag a copy of your text sprite to the Stage. Place it in the upper-left corner, aligned with the top of the pda's screen. Make sure the sprite is in Channel 3, Frames 1–30. Name the cast member "palmtext".

6. Choose the 3-D Extruder tab, where you can edit the 3-D text. If you prefer, you can use the numbers shown below as a guide. Each typeface needs different amounts of these properties, so don't be surprised if you get something different than the result shown. For the lights, we chose light pink for the Ambient, dark pink for the Diffuse, yellow for the Directional, and white for the Background and Specular lighting. Don't forget to set it to Background Transparent in the Property Inspector.

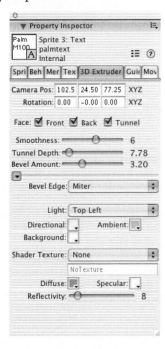

7. Highlight the first keyframe of the text sprite and drag it off the left edge of your Stage.

8. Insert a keyframe into Frame 10 of your text sprite. Highlight this new keyframe.

9. Drag the text to its original place to the left of the pda, aligned with the top of the pda screen.

10. Save your changes and keep the file open for the next exercise.

3-D Objects

Next, we are going to use Lingo to create a simple 3-D object. Explaining every new term presented in this section is not possible; instead, as each section of code is presented, we include layman's terms to describe its functionality.

Use Lingo to Create a Box

1. Continue working in the open pdapractice.dir.

2. Open the Shockwave 3-D Viewer (Window>Shockwave 3-D). It displays as a black, empty screen. Click the Set Camera Transform button. This tells Director you will be creating something in this empty window, and to keep it.

3. Name the new 3-D Shockwave cast member "pdaBox" It will be a small sample box in which the pda is packaged.

4. Select the Window menu, and choose the Script option. A new Movie Script window appears. Click the capital "L" drop-down menu and choose the Prem to Rec alphabetized section. Select *on prepareMovie* as your handler.

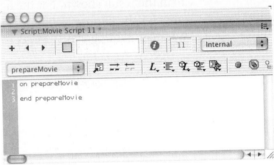

5. The first line of text you will enter between the handlers is the text that tells Director you are making a new 3-D resource — a box. Enter the following between the *prepareMovie* handlers:

    mr1 = member("pdaBox"). newModelResource("myBox", #box, #front)

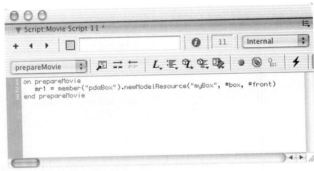

6. Determine the object's size by setting its properties. Type the following three lines (underneath the first line you typed) to determine the box's length, width, and height:

    mr1.length = 50
    mr1.width = 25
    mr1.height = 150

7. Instruct Director to create the model and give it a resource name by entering the following:

```
md1 = member ("pdaBox").newModel("myBoxModel")
md1.resource = member("pdaBox").modelResource("myBox")
```

8. The last step is to return to the top, underneath the *on prepareMovie* handler, and enter a line of type that ensures this is the only item called "pdaBox". This resets the world for that box so everything is set to zero. Your Cast and Movie script should resemble the two examples below:

```
member("pdaBox").resetWorld()
```

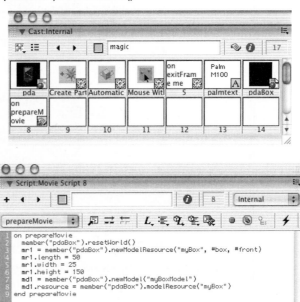

9. Close the Movie Script window. We must add a camera and lighting so we can view the script. If you rewind and play the Director movie (so the new Movie script registers), you should see the box pop up in the 3-D Shockwave Viewer. You must select that particular cast member. The box should appear similar to the one shown below.

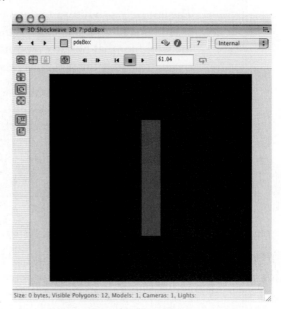

10. Click the Dolly Camera button in the 3-D Shockwave Viewer window, and drag to make the box smaller (about half its current size).

11. Choose the 3-D Model tab in the Property Inspector and click the Ambient lighting color picker. Choose white. Set the Directional lighting to Top-Right.

12. Click the Rotate Camera button. Make sure the Camera Y-Up button is chosen. Click the box and drag to the left so the box's corner is closest to you, and you see the front and side views as shown below.

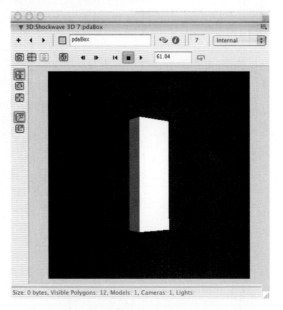

13. Open the Paint Editor. Select the Air Brush and pick a color (we used gray so it would be acceptable in grayscale). Choose a fairly large-sized dot, and a lot of flow and diameter. Spray the entire paint canvas. Cover as much as you can with dots of color. Name the cast member "boxtexture". Refer to the following graphic for a small sample of the Paint Editor.

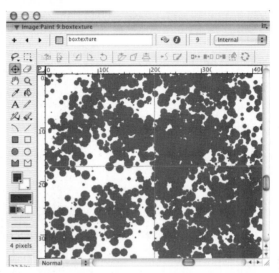

14. Click the pdaBox cast member. Choose the 3-D Model tab in the Property Inspector. At the bottom of the Property Inspector, choose Member from the Shader texture drop-down menu. Enter the name "boxtexture" into the empty box below the Shader texture drop-down menu.

15. Save the movie. Rewind and play the movie. The box should display with its new texture, similar to the one shown below. If it doesn't display, start the movie again.

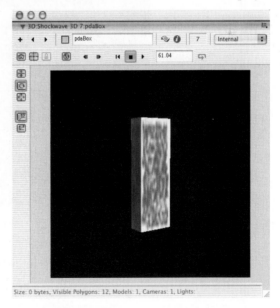

16. Drag a copy of the pdaBox cast member to the Stage and position it to the middle-left of the pda. Put it into Channel 2, Frames 1–30.

17. Insert a keyframe at Frame 10.

18. Click the first keyframe, and drag the pdaBox sprite off the left edge of your screen.

19. Open the Text Editor and type the words, "Magic in a Box!" Center-align the words and place two words on each line as indicated below. Choose a color that coordinates well with the colors in your Palm M100 logo. Name the cast member "magic".

20. Place the magic cast member into Channel 4, Frames 10-30. Choose Background Transparent from the Property Inspector. Insert keyframes at Frames 15, 20, and 25.

21. Set the Opacity of Keyframes 15 and 25 to 10%. This produces a slow, pulsing effect. Save the movie, rewind, and then play it. Keep the file open for the next exercise.

In the next section, you will publish the movie to the Web where you can see it run — if you have the Shockwave 3-D plug-in installed. If you don't, you can download a copy of it from www.macromedia.com.

Publishing to the Web

Macromedia added a new HTML template to Director's Publish Settings dialog box. It is called the 3-D Content Loader. Until you master Director's 3-D functions, it is a good idea to use the 3-D Content Loader when publishing 3-D content to the Web.

Publish to the Web

1. Continue working in the open pdapractice.dir.

2. Select File>Publish Settings. The front page should match the sample below. The rest of the tabs can be left at their defaults. Click OK.

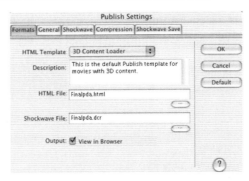

3. Select File>Publish. Director creates the necessary .dcr and .html files for you. It automatically previews the file in your default browser if you checked the View in Browser option on the Publish Settings dialog box, and you have the Shockwave 3-D plug-in. If it is operating correctly, the file should resemble the image below. If you do not have the Shockwave plug-in, you can download a free copy from www.Shockwave.com (navigate to the download area and choose the appropriate operating system).

4. Save your changes and quit Director.

Chapter Summary

In this chapter, you learned which 3-D file formats can be imported into Director, and you imported one file for practice. You discovered how to script a 3-D object from scratch using Lingo, and wrap it with a custom-made texture. Various properties available for use with 3-D objects were explored.

In addition, you learned how to put together an action and a trigger in order to manipulate 3-D objects. Finally, you learned how to make a presentation play in an Internet browser for all to see.

15 *Preparation and Delivery*

Chapter Objectives:

Preparation and delivery of your files are very important topics, as they can literally make or break your project. Choosing the appropriate method of delivery is dependent upon your audience and the type of hardware used to view it. This chapter shows you a variety of ways to deliver a project and compare the resultant file sizes. In this chapter, you will:

- Learn different ways to deliver your projects.

- Discover and practice how to create different types of projectors.

- Become familiar with the options available for creating projectors.

- Explore the file sizes created by the different types of projectors.

- Learn about and practice publishing a file for the Internet.

- Learn to print parts of your presentation from Director.

Preparation and Delivery

There are two different ways you can deliver a finished Director project. The first is to create a self-contained version of your project called a *projector* for distribution via CD or disk. The viewers do not need to have a copy of Director on their computer to run a projector.

The Internet is an alternative distribution method for a Director project. To prepare a final project for the Web, it must be saved as a Shockwave movie (Director refers to this as "publishing" your movie). Through the Publish settings, Director automatically generates an HTML page where your Shockwave movie can reside on the Web. The Shockwave file is saved as a .dcr file. The Director movie can then be viewed in many standard Web browsers, such as Microsoft Internet Explorer and Netscape Navigator, as long as they have the Shockwave plug-in loaded into their Plug-ins folders. Newer versions of the most commonly used browsers include this plug-in, so the odds are in your favor that users have it.

It is important to do everything you can to make your movie file as lean as possible before you finalize the production for distribution. The following list identifies a few ways to streamline your file:

- Use Background Transparent only when necessary. Use Matte instead.
- Delete any unused cast members and linked files from your Score.
- Keep your Bitmap cast members as small as possible. Select Transform Bitmap to reduce them to 8-bit images if possible. Make a copy of the image and test the transform on the copy — in case you aren't satisfied with the 8-bit result. Remember, you cannot undo a Transform Bitmap command.
- Use vector images whenever possible. Bitmaps may be re-created as vector images in the Vector Shape window.
- For distribution on the Web, keep the Stage size at less than 640 × 480 pixels (500 × 440 works well) since the Internet browser takes up a lot of room at the top and the left and right sides of the monitor.
- For projects that won't be viewed on the Web, work with 640 × 480 pixels unless you know for certain your viewers have large monitors and fast machines.
- Audio and video created in other software applications should be compressed using a format such as Cinepak. Make these files as compact as possible. Refer to the software manuals for the software used to create them for help in compressing these files.
- Keep your usage of video and sound files to a minimum for Shockwave movies that are destined for the Internet. While the speed and capacity of the Internet is starting to better accommodate sound files, video files still don't stream very well.

Projectors

As stated earlier, projectors are self-contained versions of Director movies. The viewer simply double-clicks the movie's icon, and the movie opens and plays. A copy of the Director software does not have to be loaded on the viewer's machine.

Since projectors are self-contained, they need to incorporate some system-specific resources. For instance, if you create your projector on a Macintosh, it can run only on a Macintosh. If you want a projector that runs on a Windows computer, you must take your original .dir file and open it on a Windows machine and create a projector from there.

Macromedia offers the projector at no cost for distribution purposes. Each time a projector file is opened or closed, a "Made with Macromedia" splash screen appears.

For specifics about the projector-distribution agreements, locate the Made with Macromedia folder inside your Director folder. Here, you will find a Read Me document that explains all the details.

When you are ready to make your projector, you can select File>Create Projector.

A dialog box appears that is similar to the Import dialog box. You can find your project in the box on the left and then add it so it appears in the box on the right. If your project contains multiple movies linked together, be certain to add all of them.

After you have added the necessary movie(s), you can click the Options button to adjust your projector's settings. The Projector Options dialog box is shown in the following image. Here is a brief explanation of each option:

- There are two playback options. Play Every Movie is relevant if your project is made up of more than one Director movie. Animate in Background allows your movie to continue to play even if two files are open at one time.

- Full Screen fills the monitor with the same color as the background of the movie. Show Title Bar allows the Title bar to show across the top of your Stage.

- Stage Size offers several options. The Use Movie Settings option uses whatever movie settings you specified for each Director movie. Match First Movie makes all the movies in your project match the settings of the first one that plays. Center ensures your Stage is centered on the monitor, no matter what size monitor is used to play it. Reset Monitor to Match Movie's Color Depth automatically resets any monitor to match the movie's color depth, whether it is 256 colors or millions of colors, assuming the monitor can handle that many colors.

- Media allows you to compress your movie as a whole using the Shockwave format. This decreases file size.

- The Player section allows you to choose from three types of players (how the player code is included in the projector). A Standard player uses no compression, allowing it to be the fastest but largest file. A Compressed player compresses the player code, but not the file as a whole, as the Media Compression option does. Shockwave instructs the Director movie to play through the Shockwave Player. It does not, however, include Shockwave Player in the projector file. Viewers must have a copy of this plug-in installed on their system. If they try to play a Shockwave projector and do not have the plug-in, they will be asked whether they want to download it (for free) from Macromedia's Web site, www.macromedia.com.

- Target is a Macintosh-only option that allows you to choose whether you want this projector to run on OS X or in Classic (prior to OS X) mode.
- Use System Temporary Memory is a Macintosh-only option that allows Director to borrow memory from the Macintosh system when necessary.

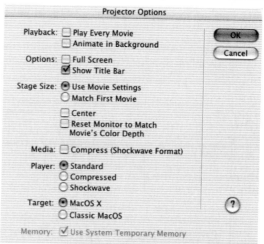

When all of your selections are in place, you can click OK. Then, you can click the Create button to make the projector. Next, a Save dialog box would appears. You can name the file, put it where you want it, and click Save.

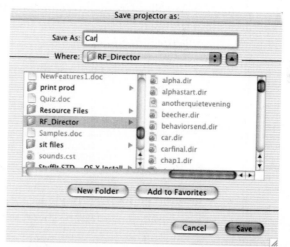

While the projector is being made, a Creating Projector dialog box with a status bar appears. The status bar shows which file it is adding and how long the process will take to complete.

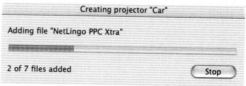

The projector, when shown in icon form, is in the shape of a circle with the Director colors and logo on it, similar to the Car icon shown below.

When viewed in a list, the projector resembles an application. Under the Kind heading, it is called an Application Program, as seen below.

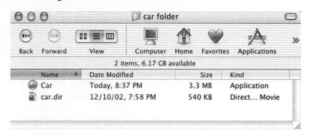

Create Different Types of Projectors

1. Create a new folder in your **Work_In_Progress** folder and name it "Theatre".

2. Open **fintheatre.dir** from the **RF_Director** folder.

3. Select File>Create Projector. Find **fintheatre.dir** in the list and click Add so the file displays in the box in the middle of the screen. (Windows users might see a slightly different setup.)

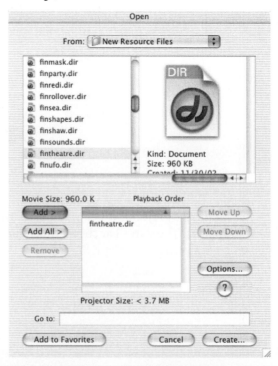

Some of the file sizes generated in this exercise may not be exactly the same as the ones shown in images. This is because of all the different computer configurations that are available. Instead of using these numbers verbatim, use them as general estimates to scrutinize the relationship between the different types of projectors and the file sizes they create.

The first type of projector you are going to make is a Compressed projector (a projector in Shockwave format, not a projector that requires the Shockwave Player).

4. Click the Options button. Match your options to those in the following example and then click OK.

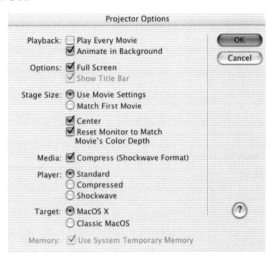

5. Click Create. A Save As dialog box appears. Open the **Theatre** folder you just created. Name the projector "Theatre1" and click Save (in the **Theatre** folder).

6. The second projector you are going to create is uncompressed. Select File>Create Projector and add fintheatre.dir again. In the Projector Options dialog box, uncheck the Media Compress (Shockwave Format) option, and then click OK.

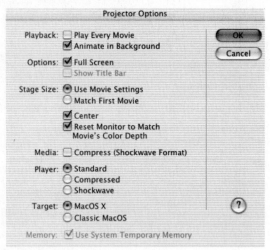

7. Click the Create button to create the projector.

8. Save it as "Theatre2" and place it in the **Theatre** folder.

9. Stop for a moment and take a quick look at the folder that contains your projectors. Choose View>List to see them in List view. Notice the small size of the compressed projector. It is about 4.2MB; the uncompressed projector is 4.8MB.

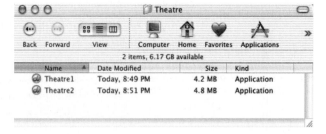

10. The third projector you are going to create is an uncompressed projector that runs off the Shockwave Player, not its own resources. It requires the Shockwave Player to run. Select File>Create Projector, add fintheatre.dir, and click the Options button. Select the Shockwave option in the Player section. Match the rest of the options to the following example. Match the target to that of your computer as necessary.

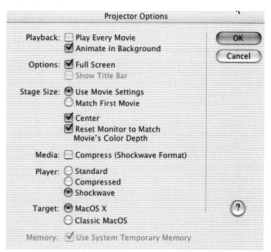

11. Click OK and then click the Create button. Name it "Theatre3" and place it in the **Theatre** folder.

12. The next projector you are going to create is a compressed projector that requires the Shockwave Player to run. Select File>Create Projector, add finheatre.dir, and click the Options button. Check the Compress (Shockwave Format) option and match the rest of the options to those shown below.

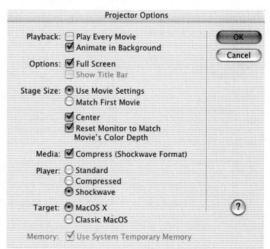

13. Click OK and then click the Create button. Name the projector "Theatre4" and save it in the **Theatre** folder. (Windows users can skip the last projector in the next two steps, and go straight to Step 16).

14. The last projector you are going to create is a projector identical to the first one (Theatre1) except we are going to set the Target to Classic MacOS. Select File>Create Projector, add fintheatre.dir, and click the Options button. Match the options to those shown below.

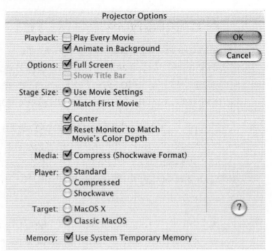

15. Click OK and then click the Create button. Name the projector "Theatre5" and save it in the **Theatre** folder.

16. Go to the **Theatre** folder and look at all five projectors (four for Windows users). Notice that projectors made to run through the Shockwave Player are smaller files. This is because Director doesn't need to save the entire projector inside the file. The projector may be accessed on both the Macintosh and Windows platforms. For Macintosh users, notice that the projector (Theatre5) created in Classic MacOS is labeled as a Classic Application.

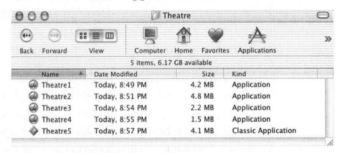

17. One at a time, double-click the projectors and make certain they work. The last two projectors, unless you have Shockwave Player installed on your computer or you clicked the Web Download if Needed option, cause an error message to appear when selected.

The first two projectors are application programs, but the last two require Shockwave Player. If you have a fast Internet connection, download a copy of Shockwave Player and play the last two projectors.

18. Don't forget to take your video clips — in this case, Sol and Emily — with you in the same folder wherever you go. A projector does not embed video clips. You need the originals for your movie to play correctly. Don't save your changes, and close Director.

About Shockwave Movies

Shockwave movies are not projectors and are not self-contained. They are compressed using the Shockwave compression scheme, and at the same time, they generate the HTML code necessary to play the movie on the Web. The extension .dcr is applied to a new Shockwave file. A separate .html file containing the HTML code is generated as well.

A browser with the Shockwave plug-in is necessary to view Shockwave files on the Web. The first versions of Internet Explorer to contain the Shockwave plug-in are version 3.0 for Windows and version 4.01 for Macintosh. The first version of Netscape Navigator to contain the plug-in is version 3.0 for both platforms. Newer versions of these applications include the plug-in.

If your browser is newer than the above-mentioned versions but didn't come with the plug-in, go to Macromedia's Web site, www.macromedia.com, and download a free copy.

You can also view Shockwave movies with Macromedia's Shockwave Player. A free copy of the application can be downloaded from the Macromedia Web site.

Shockwave files cannot be edited. If changes are required, the edits must be made to the original Director movie, and the Shockwave file must be re-created. This type of file offers you the flexibility to distribute Shockwave movies over the Internet without the concern of anyone altering your work.

It is not recommended that you use video clips in a Shockwave movie because they are not reliable across platforms. If you choose to do so, however, be certain to place all the video files in one folder within the same folder as your projector and name it "dswmedia". This instructs the Shockwave plug-in or player where to find these files when it runs on Windows workstations.

Streaming Shockwave Movies

There are a couple of steps you must complete to correctly set up your files for the Internet. The first step would be to select Modify>Movie>Playback and be certain to check the Play Movie While Downloading option. You would set the Frames to Download Before Playing to 5, causing five frames of the movie to be preloaded into the receiving computer's memory so the movie is ready ahead of time. This is known as *streaming* a movie. When a movie is streamed, each part is loaded just before it is needed. You would match the rest of the settings to those shown in the image below.

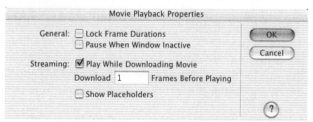

The next area to check is the Publish Settings dialog box, which can be accessed from the File menu. The dialog box has five tabs. The Formats tab shows you the .html and Shockwave files the Publish command creates.

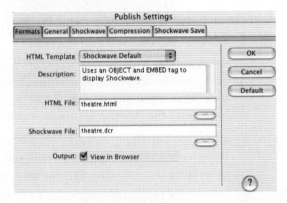

The General tab shows the dimensions of the movie when it opens in the browser window. It also allows you to pick a background color for the Web page in case your movie doesn't fill the entire browser window.

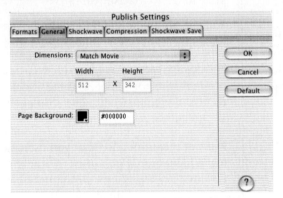

On the Shockwave tab, the default options are fine for most users.

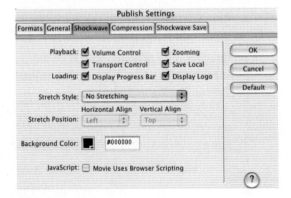

On the Compression tab, you can set an overall JPEG compression level for your Shockwave movie by choosing JPEG and adjusting the slider. The higher the number, the better the image quality, and the larger the file size.

Shockwave Audio compression is also available on this tab. You can choose Compression Enabled and select a speed. There is a Convert Stereo to Mono option that reduces audio file sizes when selected. Typically, Mono is used only for voice-overs.

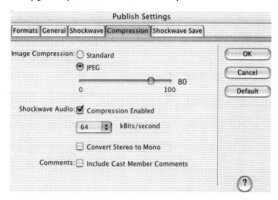

The final tab contains the Shockwave Save settings. These settings need to be adjusted only when creating a file for playback with Macromedia's Shockmachine. Here, you can give your movie a category and a title, among other things.

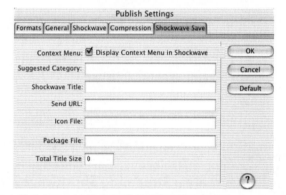

After you checked the options on these tabs, you would be ready to create a Shockwave movie. The Publish command can be accessed from the File menu.

In the example below, you can view how both the Shockwave file (theatre.dcr) and the HTML file (theatre.html) appear as icons.

When viewed in a list, you can see from the following image that they are just documents. The Shockwave file is listed as a Shockwave Movie, and the HTML file is listed as an HTML document.

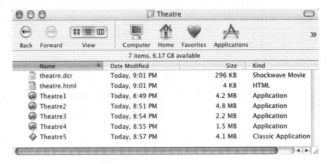

Create a Streaming Shockwave Movie

1. If you didn't do so in the previous exercise, locate fintheatre.dir in the RF_Director folder. Save a copy of this file in the Theatre folder and name it "theatre.dir".

2. Open the theatre.dir movie you just created.

3. Ensure the Shockwave Audio settings are correct, because this movie contains sounds. Select File>Publish Settings>Compression and match the settings to those shown below.

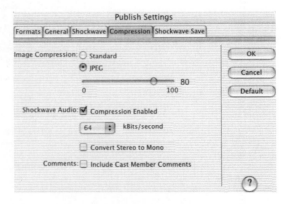

4. Select File>Publish, and Director automatically generates the .html and .dcr files for you.

5. After the files are created, navigate to the **Theatre** folder, and you see the Shockwave .dcr file and the .html file. If you have the Shockwave plug-in included in your browser, feel free to double-click on the .html file and view it in the browser. If you do not have the newest Shockwave plug-in, you can go to www.macromedia.com and download a copy for free. Keep in mind that it will take 15–20 minutes to download at 28.8KBs.

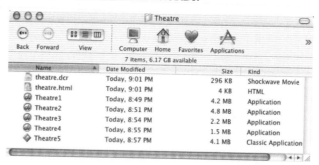

6. Keep Director open for the next exercise.

Printing Screens

On occasion, it might be necessary to print various portions of your production. You might need to show a client new art at various stages, pin up thumbnails of your cast members, or print your screens to keep a running storyboard.

Director provides numerous printing options. You can print the Stage, cast members, scripts, or other movie components. You can even choose to print parts of the Score or certain frames, such as those with artwork changes only, or those with markers only.

The image below shows all the available options when you choose the Print Stage option from the Print dialog box.

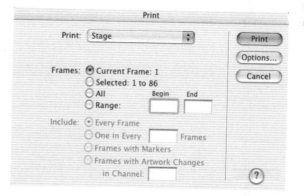

The next image shows all the available Print categories. Notice that some of the available options change when the category is changed.

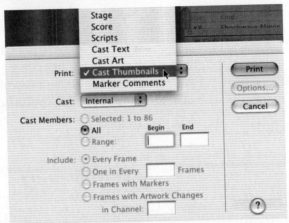

Other options can be found by clicking the Options button. These include the ability to scale your output and to choose whether you want certain identifying marks to show on each of your pages.

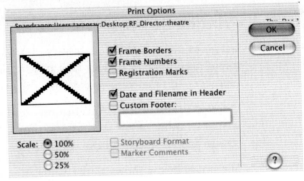

Print Parts of Your Presentation

1. Open **finparty.dir** located in the **RF_Director** folder.

2. Select File>Print, choose the Stage category, and then print Frames 80-85 at 50% with Frame Numbers and Registration Marks turned on.

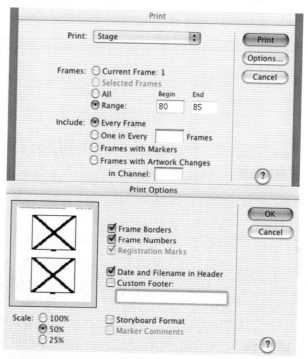

3. Choose the Cast Thumbnails category and print the entire Cast as thumbnails.

4. Choose the Scripts category and print the scripts for Cast Members 4-6.

5. Select File>Quit and close Director.

Chapter Summary

In this final chapter of the book, you learned about various preparation and delivery methods available for Director projects. You learned how to keep your file size down and make your files play faster. Many projectors were introduced and compared to provide a better understanding of their differing file sizes and requirements.

Publishing files to the Internet was also introduced and practiced, as this is a very common delivery method. Finally, you learned how to print various parts of your project to show clients, colleagues, or instructors.

Free-Form Project #2

Assignment

Your local Director-users group is sponsoring a contest. The first prize is a three-day, all-expenses-paid trip to the Macromedia Developers Conference in San Francisco. The winner of the prize is the one who develops the best game in 10 days or less.

Your assignment is to create a game that requires the user to hit a moving target. If you've ever been to a carnival or seashore amusement park, you've probably tried one of these skill games — the fishing game with the little magnet on the end of the fishing pole, or the flip-the-frog game where you try to get the frog onto the moving lilypad. In its most basic form, the game would be good practice for someone who needed to polish her eye-hand-mouse coordination.

Applying Your Skills

To develop the game, use the following features, functions, and methods:

- Create an introductory splash screen with an animation to introduce the game.

- Use the Paint window to develop an eye-catching background for the target items (such as the lilypads or fish pond).

- Create a custom cursor that resembles the frog you are going to throw (or the ping pong ball), and make certain it's active all the time.

- Create cast members to aim for. Use any combination of the Paint, Text, or Vector Shape windows. You can have different targets that move faster or slower depending on their type.

- Use film loops in at least two of your animations.

- Mix and match behaviors, making certain you apply at least four different behaviors to keep the game interesting.

Specifications

Stage Size: 640 × 480 pixels

Required Sections: Introduction, Rules, Game Body, Tally, Reward

Required Components: custom cursor, lilypads or other targets, credits, background, Rollover Cursor behavior, Frame scripts, Cast Member scripts

Construct the game around a central theme. We designed a sample project using an under-the-sea theme. To view it, open skillgame.dir from the Resource CD-ROM in the **RF_FreeForm_DirectorMX** folder.

Create an introduction, complete with an animation and rules on how to play. Then create animated objects and different levels (advance to Level 2 after you successfully complete Level 1, and then move to Level 3, and so on). Divise a scoring method. Show some type of a "You Win!" screen at the end of the game.

Included Files

We did not supply a starter file for this project. You need to create cast members based upon your original theme. Our finished sample is skillgame.dir in the **RF_FreeForm_DirectorMX** folder on the Resource CD-ROM. If you are very short of time, you can use the cast members from this file as a starting point for your project.

Publisher's Comments

This is an excellent opportunity to show off your Director skills and use your imagination to create an entertaining game. Try to create a new game — one that might someday become a prototype for a new arcade game. This project is all about having fun.

Be certain to test the game and verify that when you click, the target changes. In some games, if you make a less-than-direct hit, the target only partially changes. You can accomplish this in a variety of ways. For example, make two hotspots on each target, one that results in full points being awarded, and another that only results in half.

Review #2

Chapters 9 through 15

In the second half of the book, you discovered more about the Lingo scripting language, and how to use it to apply behaviors to sprites. You learned the value of custom cursors, and how to develop special cursors to meet specific needs. The various color palettes were discussed, and you learned why certain colors are used for presentations delivered on the Web. You delved deeper into Lingo scripting, learned how to create Director commands using Lingo code, and found out about dot syntax. You explored the world of 3-D animation, discovered how to apply 3-D behaviors to existing objects, and learned how create 3-D objects using Lingo scripting. And finally, you learned how to deliver your Director files in a variety of different ways to reach many diverse audiences. Through this series of discussions, exercises, and projects you should:

- Be familiar with how to apply behaviors to sprites, and know how to access behaviors from the Library palette.

- Know how to create custom cursors to add a personal touch to a Director presentation.

- Understand why certain color palettes must be used when delivering presentations over the Web, and know how to use the Color Picker.

- Be comfortable using the Lingo scripting language, and know how to locate and correct errors in your code.

- Understand dot syntax and be able to apply it in basic Lingo code.

- Be familiar with applying 3-D behaviors to existing objects, creating original 3-D objects using Lingo code, and importing 3-D objects from other programs.

- Know how to successfully prepare and deliver your presentations in various ways, including to CD and the Web, and know how to print portions of your movie when necessary.

Project A: Gaenzle Illustration and Design

This project was originally created as a class project. Later, it was repurposed as a promotional CD for an illustration and design company.

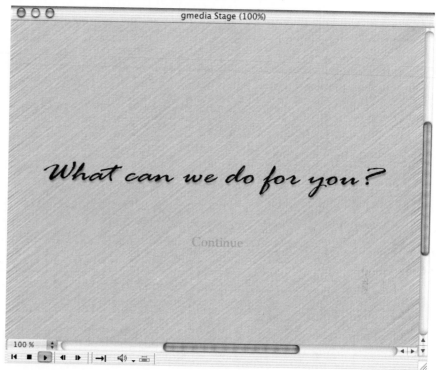

The purpose of this project is to familiarize you with a working Director file. This particular production makes use of sound effects, animations, various graphics, and pieces of artwork. Although you will not be creating this movie, it is important to browse around to become familiar with the Director interface and learn how the movie was created.

Getting Started

1. Navigate to the **gmedia.dir** file in your **RF_Director** folder and drag a copy into your **Work_In_Progress** folder. Work from the copy for the remainder of the project.

2. Using the Control bar at the bottom of the Stage, click the Play button to start the Director production.

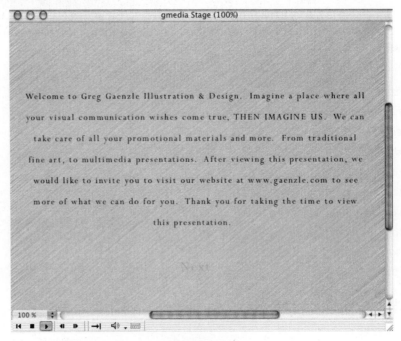

The Introduction.

3. Work your way through each of the five pages (Home, What We Do, Clients, Portfolio, Contact Us) using the appropriate buttons (along the top gray bar) to familiarize yourself with the project and how to navigate through it. Make certain you explore all the buttons except the Quit button.

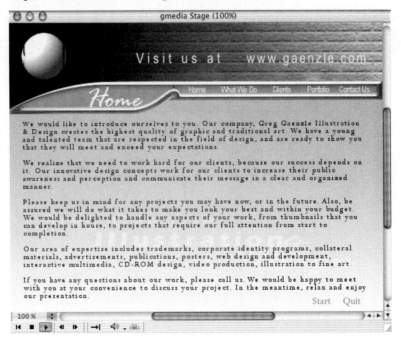

Home page.

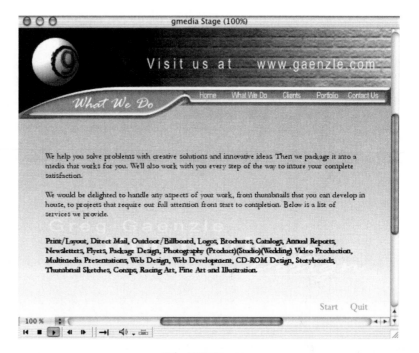

What We Do page.

Clients page.

Portfolio page.

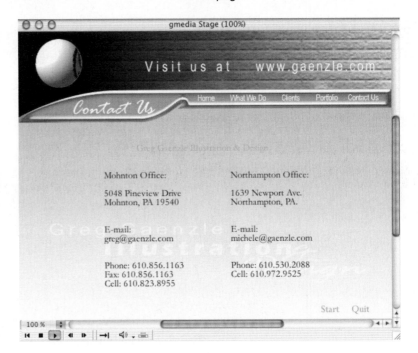

Contact Us page.

4. Select Window>Cast to open the Cast. Scroll down through the cast members and examine all of them.

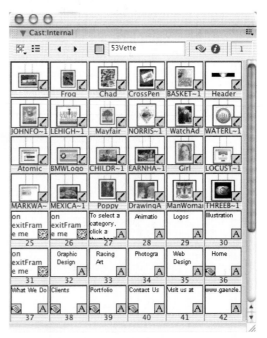

The Cast.

5. Open the Score (Window>Score). Scroll to the right and look at the names of the sprites and where they are placed. See if you can figure out what is going to happen in the movie by looking at the Score.

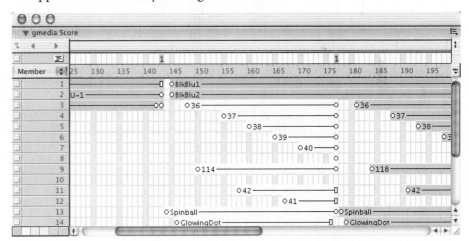

The Score.

6. Drag the red Playback Head to the section of yellow sprites; they make up the Home page. The orange sprites make up the What We Do page. The light-blue sprites make up the Clients page. The pink sprites make up the Contact Us page. The green sprites make up the large Portfolio page.

7. Click any sprite that is currently located under the Playback Head. Notice that the image of the sprite is highlighted on the Stage.

8. Click another object on the Stage and take note that the corresponding sprite in the Score is highlighted, allowing you to easily identify which image belongs with which sprite.

9. Scroll to Frame 242 (after the yellow section) and double-click the single sprite in the Script channel (the channel located directly above the frame numbers). You see a Script appear that contain the words *go to the frame* in it. This script is telling the movie to stop on Frame 242 until something else happens.

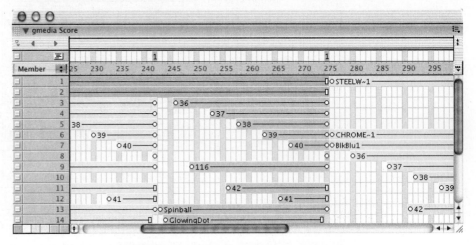

Notice that there are buttons on the Stage (Home, What We Do, Clients, Portfolio, and Contact Us) in the navigation bar. Each of these buttons has a script attached to it, so when the button is clicked, Director reads and executes the script. Click the Portfolio button and you advance to Frame 276. Frame 276 is the first frame in the green section.

10. While in the Portfolio section, you see that it asks you to click one of the thumb-nails that run across the screen in a horizontal line. Click through each of the thumbnails to see the variety of artwork this studio can provide. Click the second item from the right to see something similar to the images below.

11. Drag the Playback Head to Frame 242. With the Score open so you can see Frame 276, click Play on the Control bar at the bottom of the Stage to resume playing the movie from that point. Next, click the Portfolio button and watch the Playback Head jump to Frame 276.

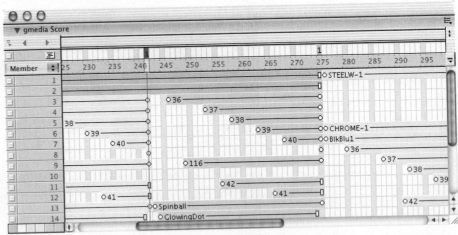

Director works in a linear fashion, one frame after another. You do, however, have the option to interrupt a movie and provide alternative instructions through the Lingo scripting language, which was done here.

12. Press Command/Control-. (period) to stop the Director movie. Take as much additional time as you prefer to work with this file. There are many functions you can test: move sprites around, double-click cast members, add more sprites to the Score, rearrange the pages in the Score, and change the graphic layout of the pages on the Stage to name a few. Try performing all of the above tasks at least once. Have fun and explore. The more you use the Director software, the more familiar you become with it.

It might be good practice for readers to record a synopsis of what they observed and learned from exploring this Director movie.

Project B: Redi-Base

Redi-Base, a new food product, will be featured and sampled at an upcoming food festival. Your job is to create a presentation that could be used by sales representatives to market the product. The ability to work with keyframes and use Director's frame-based timeline are critical elements to successfully accomplishing this project. You will also practice moving and extending sprites.

If you want to watch the finished version of this project before you begin the tutorial, access **finredi.dir** from the **RF_Director** folder.

Getting Started

1. Launch Director and open **redibase.dir** from your **RF_Director** folder. Choose File>Save As and save a copy of the file in your **Work_In_Progress** folder. Name the copy "redibase.dir," and work with it for the remainder of the project.

2. Familiarize yourself with the items in the Cast. First, you must label your cast members, which makes it easier to read your Score.

Thank you to Sally Behler, who created the movie used in this project for her own home business. At the time of this printing, it was a working Web site.

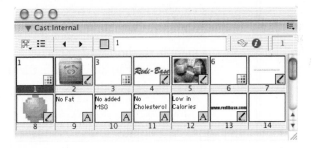

Name Cast Members

1. Starting with Cast Member 1, highlight each cast member, one at a time, and then name each member by single-clicking in the Name area at the top of the Cast, and entering the members' names as shown below. It doesn't matter if the names are uppercase, lowercase, or initial capped.

#1 Jar Palette	#2 Jar	#3 Logo Palette
#4 Logo	#5 Photo	#6 Slogan2
#7 Slogan	#8 Button	#9 No Fat
#10 No Added	#11 No	#12 Low
#13 Website		

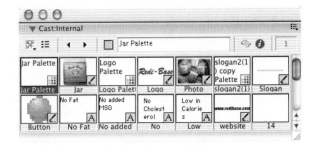

Create the Animated Introduction

1. Drag a copy of the Logo cast Member to the Score and place it in Frame 1, Channel 1. As images are placed in the Score, each automatically brings along its own Color palette, which is placed in the Palette channel. The palettes appear in the Cast because these cast members, are made from their own special colors that may not be included in the current color palette.

2. Logo should already be horizontally centered on the Stage. Place it about one-third of the way down from the top.

3. Use one of the following options to extend the sprite so it covers Frames 1-166. If your sprite is only one frame long, hold down the Option/Alt key and drag the right side of the sprite until you reach Frame 166; if your sprite is more than one frame long, drag the right side of the sprite until it reaches Frame 166. This sprite, which is the product's logo, should remain on the Stage throughout the presentation.

4. Drag a copy of the Slogan cast member to the Stage and center it beneath the logo. In the Score, it should have been automatically placed in Channel 2. Extend Slogan so it covers Frames 1-166, using the appropriate method from Step 3.

5. Shift-click to highlight both sprites in the Score, and then click the light yellow square in the bottom-left corner of the Score. Changing the sprites' color to yellow makes it easier to differentiate them from other changes that occur throughout the movie. Save your changes.

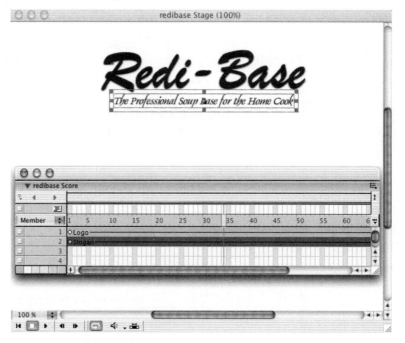

6. For the first 30 frames, we are going to display a jar of the product so people can see its container size, type, and contents. Drag a copy of the Jar cast member to the Stage and center it beneath the slogan. Leave about 1-1/2 in. (guess on the distance or compare to the finished project or images shown below) between the top of the jar and the bottom of the slogan. Make certain the Jar sprite is in Channel 3, and then extend it to cover Frames 1-30. Leave the Jar sprite colored blue.

Create Animated Bullet Points

After you complete the next few steps, the following should happen: When Jar reaches Frame 30, four bullet points (Button cast members) appear beneath the Slogan and replace the Jar. One by one, words begin to slide in from the right side and stop next to the bullet points.

1. Drag Button to Channel 5, Frames 31-135 of the Score. Move the Button on the Stage so it is about 1 in. below the slogan. Align it with the left edge of the "d" in the Redi-Base logo.

2. Drag another copy of the Button cast member to Channel 7, Frames 31-135 of the Score, and place it about 1 in. below the first Button on the Stage.

3. Drag another copy of the Button cast member to Channel 9, Frames 31-135 of the Score, and place it about 1 in. below the second button on the Stage.

4. Finally, drag a fourth copy of the Button cast member to Channel 11, Frames 31-135 of the Score, and place it about 1 in. below the third button. Save your changes.

5. Hold down the Shift key, highlight all four Button sprites in the Score, and change their color to pink so it is easy to identify them.

6. You may want to use the Align palette (located under the Window menu), turn on the grid overlay, or use guides (both grids and guides are located in the Property Inspector under the Guides tab) to help you accurately align the rest of the buttons.

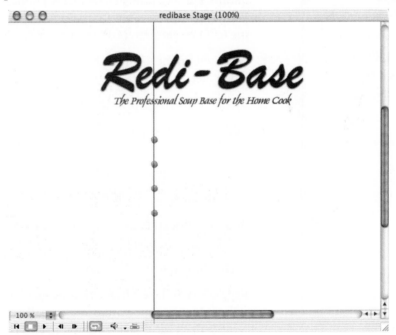

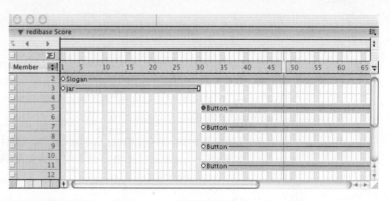

Now let's work with keyframes so the text slides into place.

7. Select the No Fat cast member and place it next to the first button on the Stage. Put it in Channel 4, Frames 31-135 of the Score.

8. Insert a keyframe at Frame 46 (highlight Channel 4, Frame 46, and then choose Insert>Keyframe). Now you have three keyframes: one at the beginning, one at the end, and one at Frame 46.

In Step 9, you told the first keyframe to start off the right side of the Stage. When the Playback Head reaches the second keyframe (Frame 46), the text phrase should be next to the bullet. When the Playback Head reaches Frame 136, it should disappear.

9. Highlight the first keyframe by single-clicking it. Then, while holding down the Shift key, drag the text off the right side of the Stage. The Shift key makes certain the animation path stays straight.

10. Add the next text phrase, No Added. Place it on the Stage next to the second button. Put the sprite in Channel 6, Frames 46-135. This text phrase starts at Frame 46 because you want the second phrase to start moving onto the Stage as the first one gets into position next to the button.

11. Highlight Frame 62 of the No Added cast member and insert a keyframe as you did in Step 8.

12. Repeat Step 9. Save your changes.

13. Add the third text phrase, the No cast member. Place it next to the third button. Put the sprite in Channel 8, Frames 62-135 in the Score.

14. Highlight Frame 78 of the No cast member and insert a keyframe.

15. Repeat Step 9.

16. Add the last text phrase, the Low cast member. Place it next to the fourth button. Put the sprite in Channel 10, Frames 78-135 of the Score.

17. Highlight Frame 94 of the Low cast member and insert a keyframe.

18. Repeat Step 9. Take a moment to rewind and play your movie. You see that the text slides into place, one phrase at a time. If you have any trouble with this, you might want to open the finished version to check your progress and identify mistakes you might have made. As stated in the beginning, the finished version is called **finredi.dir** and is located in the **RF_Director** folder.

19. One at a time, highlight the four text-phrase sprites in the Score and change their color to green to identify them as text sprites.

Create the Ending

1. The last section of the production displays a photo and the company's Web site address. First, drag a copy of the Photo cast member into Channel 3, Frames 136-166. Center it horizontally. Vertically, it should start 1-2 in. below the baseline of the slogan — whatever looks visually appealing to you.

2. Now drag a copy of the Website cast member to the Stage and center it about 1 in. beneath the photo. Place it in Channel 4, Frames 136-166. Save your changes.

3. Highlight Frame 150 of the Website sprite and create a keyframe.

4. Highlight the first keyframe of the Website sprite. Hold down the Shift key, and drag a corner of the selection box on the Stage to reduce it (drag your arrow toward the center of the sprite) until it is the size of a small dot. Then, while the first keyframe is still highlighted, use the Arrow keys to center it beneath the photo.

    Reducing the Website sprite in the first keyframe, and leaving it the correct size in the last keyframe, tells it to start as a small dot and zoom in until it is back to its original size at Frame 150.

5. Highlight the Photo and Website sprites in the Score and change their color to orange.

6. You are finished with your presentation. The final Stage and Score sections should resemble the examples provided below. Rewind and play the production.

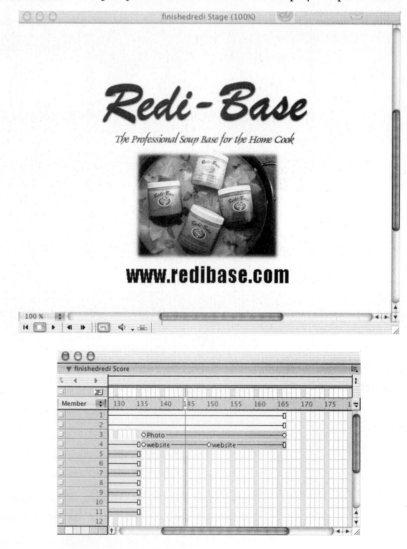

7. Save your changes and close Director.

Project C: Digital Portfolio

One of the most important aspects of a designer's career path is to create and compile a dramatic, compelling portfolio of artwork. This project — designed for a kiosk — was selected from such a portfolio. This is a fun and colorful project. To complete it, you will add sections on Web Design and Fine Art.

Getting Started

Elizabeth Beecher, a student from Allentown Business School, was kind enough to contribute some of her work for this project.

To view this work, you should install QuickTime on your machine. If you don't, you will receive a warning message when you try to view the QuickTime video on the front page of this presentation. You can ignore this warning if you prefer.

1. Locate **beecher.dir** and **x.mov** in your **RF_Director** folder and move them to the **Work_In_Progress** folder. Open **beecher.dir**. (It runs much faster from your hard drive.)

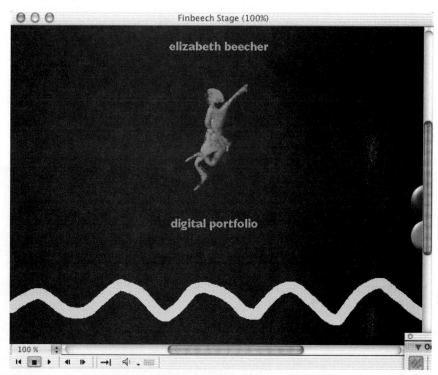

2. Use the Control bar at the bottom of the Stage to play the movie. It runs through an introduction and stops on the Main menu, which offers some options. Browse and experiment with these features to see how they work.

Add Buttons to the Main Menu

1. Use the Control bar to stop the movie. Let's place a few additional buttons that direct the user to the Web Design and Fine Art areas of the electronic portfolio. Open the Score and scroll until you can see Frames 30-70.

2. Open the Cast and drag a copy of eliza port button (Cast Member 1) to the Score. Place it in Channel 2, Frames 36-63. Position it on the Stage so it is horizontally even with the graphic art button and on the right side of the icon in the center.

3. Drag a copy of fine art text (Cast Member 36) to the Score and place it in Channel 6, Frames 36-63. Go to the Stage and drag the text so it is placed to the right of the white button and even with the graphic art text on the left.

4. Drag a copy of purple button (Cast Member 4) to the Score. Place it in Channel 5, Frames 36-63. Position it on the Stage so it is horizontally even with the animation button and on the right side of the image in the center.

5. Drag a copy of web design text (Cast Member 46) to the Score and place it in Channel 9, Frames 36-63. Go to the Stage and drag the text so it is to the right of the purple button and even with the animation type. Your menu should resemble the image below.

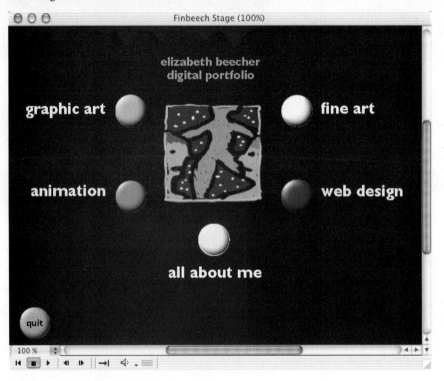

6. Save your changes, and keep the file open.

Make the Buttons Work

It's time to activate the buttons. The fine art button must jump the viewer to Frame 64 in the Score.

1. Go to the Cast. Highlight the eliza port button (Cast Member 1) and click the Script button in the top-right corner of the Cast window. The script for that Cast member should appear and your cursor should show up between *on mouseUp* and *end* or *end mouseUp*. Type *go to frame 64*. Close the Script window.

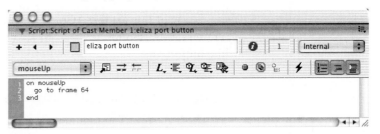

2. Return to the Cast window. Highlight the purple button (Cast Member 4). Click the Script button and type *go to frame 375*. Close the Script window, and then rewind and play the movie. Click the buttons and watch the Score to make sure they jump the movie to Frames 64 and 375 respectively. Don't forget to stop the movie when you are finished.

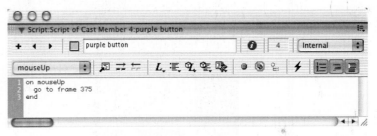

Create the Web Section

1. Go to Frame 375. Let's build the Web Design page first since it has only one example of work. The page will have two buttons on it when you open it — a Main Menu button and a Quit button.

2. To activate the Quit button, go to the Cast window and highlight the orange button (Cast Member 53). Click the Script button, type *quit* in the Script window, and then close the Script window. Don't test this button until you are completely finished with this project because it will quit the Director application. The word *halt* may be substituted in the script for *quit* if you prefer Director to stop rather than quit. Every Quit button in this project in now active because they are all sprites generated from Cast Member 53.

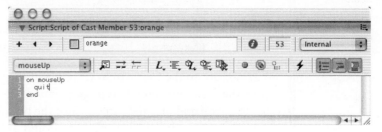

3. The Main Menu button already works, so let's put the artwork in place. Go to the Cast and drag a copy of the web page Cast Member (120) to the Score and place it in Channel 1, Frames 375-380. Place it in the top-right corner of the Stage (it should be to the right of the red button).

4. Next, add a transition so the switch from the Main menu to this page is not so abrupt. Go to the Score and open the Special Channels section (click the small button at the top-right edge of the Score with the up and down arrows on it — Windows versions will show two vertical plus (+) signs). Go to the Transition channel of Frame 375 and double-click it to bring up the Transition options. Choose Center Out, Square. Leave the Duration set to 2 seconds for this and all the remaining transitions. Make certain the Changing Area Only option is selected, and then click OK to close the Transition dialog box.

5. Let's add a way to stop the movie in this area so viewers can browse at their leisure. For this exercise, let's use the *pause* script. Go to the Score and double-click the Frame Script channel of Frame 375. The Frame Script channel is the channel directly above the frame numbers where the Playback Head is located. Type *pause* and then close the window.

6. Return to the Main menu and play this section of the project. Make sure the transition and the Pause command work correctly.

7. Save your changes.

Create the Fine Art Section

1. For the Fine Art section, go to Frame 64 in the Score.

2. Add a *pause* script in the Frame script of Frame 64.

3. This section has a splash of color and a painting on each page. Go to the Cast and drag a copy of red shape (Cast Member 57) to Channel 1, Frames 64-91. Move the shape so it extends off three sides of the Stage — the top, right, and bottom. If necessary, enlarge the shape by grabbing the corners of the sprite on the Stage and pulling them.

4. Highlight the sprite in the Score and choose Matte from the Ink Effects menu in the Property Inspector to apply the Matte Ink effect to the sprite.

5. Go to the Cast and drag a copy of beachgirls (Cast Member 7) to the Score. Place it in Channel 2, Frames 64-91. Move the painting on top of the red shape so the top-right edge of the painting abuts the top-right edge of the Stage.

The **pause** script is not always the script to use to temporarily stop a movie; but in this particular exercise, it works better than some of the other alternatives.

6. A description of the painting needs to be placed on the Stage. Go to the Cast and drag a copy of b girls (Cast Member 80) to Channel 9, Frames 64-91. On the Stage, move it to the bottom-left corner of the painting so a little bit of it is on the painting, but most of it is on the red shape. Set the Ink effect of this sprite to Background Transparent.

7. Put a Cover Down Right transition in Frame 64 (double-click the Transition channel in Frame 64). Save your changes.

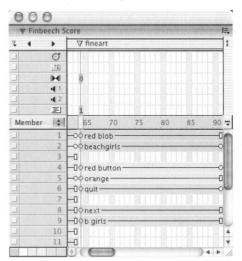

8. Look at the red button (Cast Member 54). This button doesn't work yet. You need to activate this button before going on to the next page of artwork. To do this, go to the Cast, highlight Cast Member 54, and click the Script button. Type *go to frame 92* and then close the Script window. This button takes the viewer to the next page of artwork.

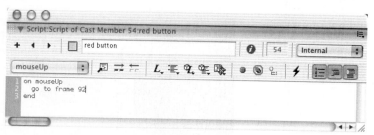

To make sure it works, drag the Playback Head to Frame 62 and play the movie. Click the red Next button. The Playback Head should go to Frame 92 in the Score. The Playback Head should keep going because we haven't added a *pause* script yet. Stop the movie and drag the Playback Head to Frame 92 for the next step.

9. Add a *go to the frame* script in the Frame script of Frame 92.

10. This time, the splash of color is purple. Go to the Cast and drag a copy of purple shape (Cast Member 62) to Channel 1, Frames 92-119. On the Stage, move the shape so it extends off three sides of the Stage — the top, right, and bottom. Set the Ink effect of this sprite to Matte.

11. Put the painting on the purple shape. Go to the Cast and drag a copy of leg (Cast Member 6) to the Score and place it in Channel 2, Frames 92-119. On the Stage, move the painting so the top-right edge of the painting abuts the top-right edge of the Stage. If necessary, resize by holding down the Shift key (to maintain proportions) and drag toward the center of the painting.

12. For the description of the painting, go to the Cast and drag a copy of leg type (Cast Member 8) to Channel 9, Frames 91-119. On the Stage, move it to directly below the bottom-left corner of the painting. Set the Ink effect of this sprite to Background Transparent.

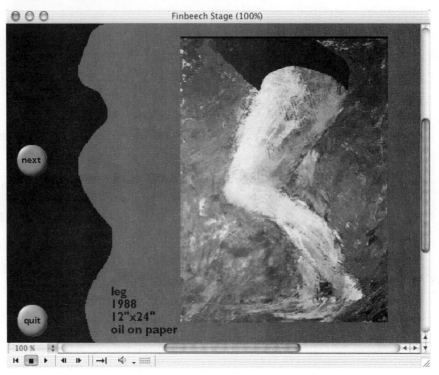

13. Add a Dissolve Patterns transition in Frame 92. Save your changes.

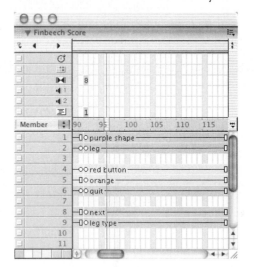

14. Go to the Cast, highlight Cast Member 93, and click the Script button. Type *go to frame 120* in the Script window, and then close the Script window. This button should take the viewer to the next page of artwork.

15. The third piece of art needs a *pause* script placed in the Frame script of Frame 120.

16. This time the color is green. Go to the Cast and drag a copy of green shape (Cast Member 66) to Channel 1, Frames 120-147. On the Stage, move the shape so it extends off three sides of the stage — the top, right, and bottom. Set the Ink effect of this sprite to Matte.

17. Put the painting on the green shape. Go to the Cast and drag a copy of the clique (Cast Member 29) to the Score and place it in Channel 2, Frames 120-147. On the Stage, move the painting so the top-right edge of the painting abuts the top-right edge of the Stage.

18. For the description of the painting, go to the Cast and drag a copy of clique type (Cast Member 67) to Channel 9, Frames 120-147. On the Stage, move it to the bottom-left corner of the painting so it matches the following image. Set the Ink effect of this sprite to Background Transparent.

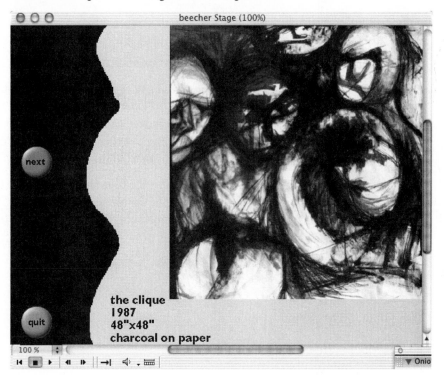

19. Add a Wipe Left transition in Frame 120.

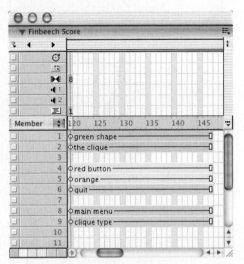

20. Go to the Cast, highlight Cast Member 104, and click the Script button. Type *go to frame 148* and close the Script window. This button should jump the movie to the next page of artwork.

21. The last piece of art needs a *pause* script in the Frame script of Frame 148.

22. This time the splash of color is blue. Go to the Cast and drag a copy of blue shape (Cast Member 60) to Channel 1, Frames 148-175. On the Stage, move the shape so it extends off three sides of the stage — the top, right, and bottom. If necessary, enlarge it by grabbing the corners of the sprite on the Stage and pulling. Set the Ink effect of this sprite to Matte.

23. Place the painting on the blue shape. Go to the Cast and drag a copy of sunbathing (Cast Member 40) to the Score and place it in Channel 2, Frames 148-175. On the Stage, move the painting so the top-right edge of the painting abuts the top-right edge of the Stage.

24. For the description of the painting, go to the Cast and drag a copy of sunbather type (Cast Member 65) to Channel 9, Frames 148-175. On the Stage, move it to the bottom-left corner of the painting so it matches the following image. Set the Ink effect of this sprite to Background Transparent.

25. Add a Random Columns transition in Frame 204.

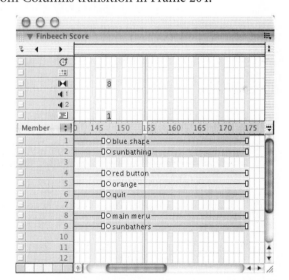

26. The red Main Menu button already works because it is the same Main Menu button you used in the Web Design section.

27. Rewind the movie and play it. Note how your changes enhanced the movie. To compare your work with our completed version, refer to **finbeecher.dir** in the **RF_Director** folder.

28. Save the file and quit Director.

Project D: Shaw's Portfolio

The basis for this project is an interactive portfolio. Although we provide images, video, and sound files, you can choose to use your own components to complete the production. This is an advanced project that merely guides you through the steps as you create the portfolio. It is perfectly acceptable to refer to the chapters and exercises in this book if you need a refresher on how to perform certain tasks.

The specifications for the project call for an introduction, and then a Main menu that contains buttons that link to the other areas of the portfolio. The organization of the artwork is entirely up to you. The final production should include an intriguing but simple introduction, and contain graphic consistency between screens.

If you choose to use Mr. Shaw's artwork, you can include as many or as few pieces as you prefer. We also provide some sound samples and one of Mr. Shaw's videos.

The information below will allow you to accurately categorize each cast member:

- Members 1 and 2 are examples of billboards for Crayola.
- Members 3-7 are examples of two book covers for *The War of the Worlds*.
- Members 8 and 9 are examples of aspirin boxes and an ad showing the boxes.
- Members 10-13 are examples of pages from a catalog with original photography.
- Members 14-19 are examples of an original board game.
- Members 20-24 are examples of a series of perfume ads with original photography.
- Members 25-28 are examples of a series of Frank Lloyd Wright exhibition posters.
- Members 29-34 are examples of three different series of postage stamps with original artwork.
- Members 35-39 are examples of two T-shirt designs for John Coltrane on tour.
- Members 40-42 are examples of full-page, half-page, and quarter-page ads for United Airlines utilizing the Three Stooges with original art.

Thanks to Christopher Shaw, you can utilize many excellent design projects as the pieces in this portfolio. We highly recommend you view Mr. Shaw's finished portfolio at **RF_Director>shaw.dir** *before you start your work.*

If you want to view Mr. Shaw's work, you need QuickTime installed on your machine. If you don't, you will receive a warning message. If you ignore this warning, the QuickTime video that is included in Mr. Shaw's presentation will not display correctly.

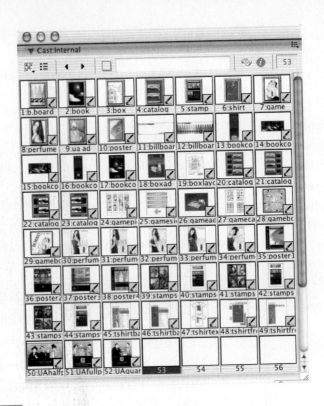

Getting Started

1. Locate shaw.dir and anotherquietevening.mov in the RF_Director folder, and copy them to your Work_In_Progress folder. Open the shaw.dir file and browse around to see what is in the Cast and what you have to work with.

2. Since you moved the files from their original location, you must relink the movie. Highlight the anotherquietevening.mov QuickTime video (Cast Member 49 — the last cast member) and select File>Import. Navigate to your **Work_In_Progress** folder, highlight the video, click Add, and then click Import. This re-establishes the link.

Create the Introduction

1. Create a catchy but simple introduction. Use the Vector Shape, Paint, and Text Editors, to create an introduction with simple animation. The name of the portfolio's owner should appear somewhere during the intro. The following images are two of the introductory screens.

Mr. Shaw creates very strong artwork, so he uses a simplistic and clean approach to his portfolio.

Create the Main Menu

1. Create the Main menu with buttons. It should contain buttons that take you to each category or project, depending on your preferences. In addition, create an Exit button that contains a *quit* script, and a Video button we will script later.

2. Below is Mr. Shaw's example. He chose not to label the buttons, but rather, make them visually interesting and allow them to speak for themselves. There is no right or wrong method, rather what works best overall for your presentation.

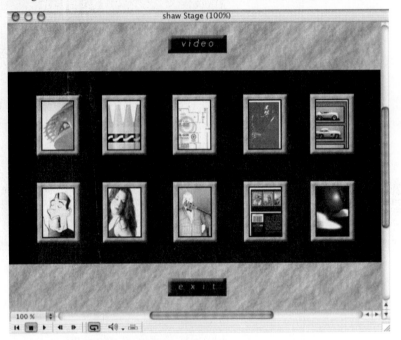

3. Apply a script to each of your buttons that sends viewers to the frame in the Score where each section starts. Starting each section about 20 frames apart should provide plenty of room. If your intro finishes on Frame 25, you can start the first section on Frame 45, the next section on Frame 65, and so on. You can complete this step now or, if you prefer, complete it after the sections — but don't forget to make your buttons work.

4. Save your changes.

Create a Sample Section

1. Create a page or a section to contain a project. For example, below we show the section for the Pain-B-Gone box project in sequence.

2. This is the intro screen to the box project section.

3. This is the first screen in the section. The Continue button takes you to the next screen.

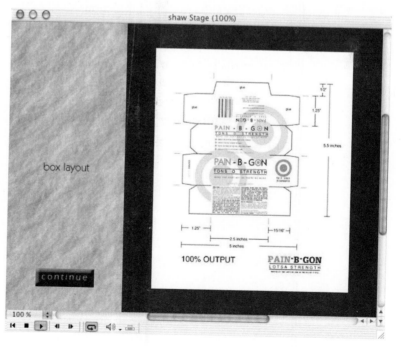

4. This is an ad that was created to better display the box as it would appear when folded to its proper size.

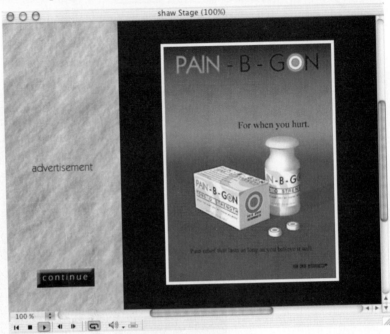

5. Be sure to create buttons that navigate between screens (Next, Back, and Continue) and to the Main menu to ensure users don't get stranded on any page or section.

6. Double-click the Script channel at the end of each screen in the section (as needed) and add a *go to the frame* script. This ensures each screen stops at the end of the sprite and waits for the user to click the Continue or Next button.

7. Create the rest of your sections so all of the Main menu buttons work (except the Video button) and correctly take users to various projects or subject areas.

Add Transitions

1. Add transitions between sections and/or screens. If you use the Transition channel, remember that the transition should be placed in the Transition channel of the first frame of the sprite to which you are transitioning.

2. You may also use the Animation>Sprite Transitions behaviors in the Behavior library to enhance your project. The Fade In/Out transition in the Animation>Automatic section of the Library palette is useful. This is the transition Mr. Shaw used throughout his presentation. The Main menu screen in the sample below is fading in.

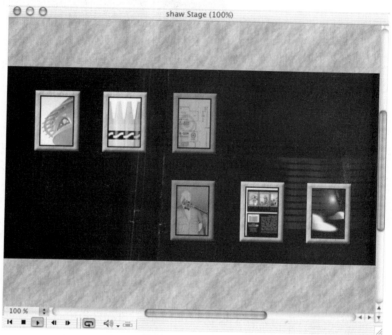

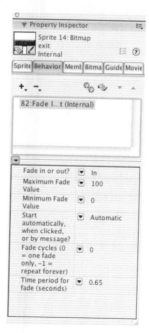

Add Music

1. Add at least one music file, whichever file you prefer. We provide some sounds (the cast members with the megaphone icons on them — Cast Members 43-48) and the intro music used in Mr. Shaw's finished project. Determine exactly where you want to place the sound, drag it to Sound Channel 1 of the Score, and extend it as needed. In the example below, it is placed in the intro area

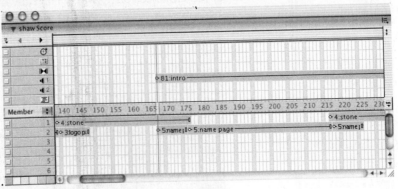

2. Highlight your sound cast member in the Cast and click the Cast Member Properties button to access the Sound tab of the Property Inspector. Examine the options and set them as you prefer.

3. In addition, you can select the Member tab of the Property Inspector to examine a cast member's sound properties. You can also use this tab to listen to the sounds we provided so you can decide if you want to use them, and where to place them.

4. If a sound is too long for a designated area, you can use a cue point to aid with alignment. Navigate to the Tempo channel in the Score. In the Tempo channel, double-click the last frame the sound sprite occupies (the sprite can be any length). The Tempo Frame Properties dialog box appears.

5. Click the Wait for Cue Point radio button. Set the Channel option to Sound1 (name of the sound). Set the Cue Point to End. When the Playback Head reaches that frame, it pauses until the music plays through to the end.

QuickTime must be installed on your machine to complete this section. If you don't have QuickTime and/or don't have access to the Internet to download a copy of QuickTime, you can skip this section.

Add a QuickTime Movie

1. Double-click your movie in the Cast and a QuickTime Player window appears. Preview the movie.

2. Place your movie in its own section in the Score. Arrange it on the Stage.

3. Double-click the Tempo channel and then click the Wait for Cue Point radio button. Set the Cue Point to End.

4. Highlight the movie in the Cast and click the Cast Member Properties button in the top-right corner. Examine the movie's Member properties in the Property Inspector.

5. Select the QuickTime tab in the Property Inspector. The QuickTime Xtra Properties box appears. Choose any options you feel are appropriate for this video.

6. Rewind and play your movie. Tweak it if necessary. Create a thank-you screen if you prefer. If you choose to do this, you must re-script your Quit button so it advances to the thank-you screen before it quits. Then apply a *quit* script to the frame (where this thank-you screen resides).

7. The project is finished. Save your changes and close Director.

Project E: ABC's

The ABC's presentation is an example of using multimedia for educational purposes. In this project, you assemble the various parts of an animation and turn them into film loops. In addition, some fun and playful behaviors are used.

Before starting this project, it is recommended you open and view the finished version. Seeing the end result should greatly enhance your understanding of what you are doing in each section and why you are doing it. The finished presentation is called **finalpha.dir** and is located in the **RF_Director** folder on your Resource CD-ROM.

Create the Introduction

1. Copy **alpha.dir** from the **RF_Director** folder to your **Work_In_Progress** folder. Double-click the copy to open the file.

If you want to see both the number and the name of your sprites in the Score, select Director> Preferences>Cast (Macintosh) or Edit>Preferences>Cast (Windows) and set the Label to show the Number and the Name.

2. Design the introduction screen, which should cover Frames 1-14 (see sidebar). Use Cast Members 21, 22, 23, 25, 26, and 28 to create an image similar to the one shown below. Don't forget to use the Background Transparent option to remove the white halo around the letters.

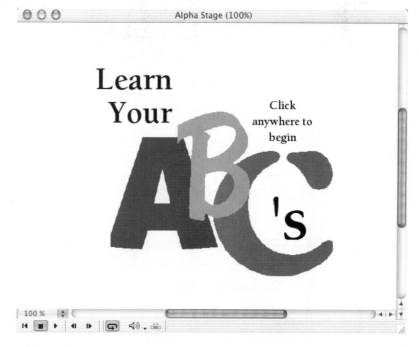

The introduction (and several sections that follow) could be done in one frame each; however, it is recommended to leave the sprites longer so there is more room for their names to be completely spelled out. This will help you to compare your Score to the images in this exercise.

3. Double-click Frame 2 of the Tempo channel and select the Wait for Mouse Click or Key Press command. Click OK.

Create the Main Menu

1. The Main menu should cover Frames 15-42 and contain Cast Members 13-20. Your Main menu should resemble the following image.

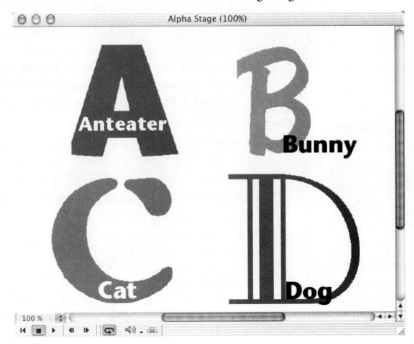

2. One at a time, highlight the B, C, and D letters on the Stage, navigate to the Property Inspector, and click the Highlight check box on the Bitmap tab. This makes each of the buttons become highlighted when they are turned into interactive buttons later in the project.

3. Place a Dissolve, Bits transition in the Transition channel of Frame 15. This allows the introduction to dissolve into the Main menu.

4. Place a marker at Frame 15 and name it "menuA-D".

5. Add a *go to the frame* script in the Frame script (Script channel) of Frame 42 to pause your movie on the Main menu so users can make their choices.

6. Save your changes.

Make the Buttons Work

1. Let's make the letters interactive so they advance the movie to their corresponding page each time they are clicked. (Skip the letter A since it will not be interactive.) In the Cast, highlight B/scr (Cast Member 14), and click the Cast Member Script button. Type *go to* "*bunny*". (Be sure to include the quotes around the word "bunny". Markers are proper names and require quotes. You will be adding a marker named "bunny" later in the project.)

2. Do the same for the letter C (Cast Member 15). The script should read *go to* "*cat*". For the letter D (Cast Member 16), the script should read *go to* "*dog*".

Create the Bunny Section

1. The Bunny page should cover Frames 50-64. First, however, you need to make a somewhat realistic bunny animation, and then turn it into a film loop. First, let's place a couple of bunny heads in different positions in Channel 1. To do this, place Cast Member 1 in Channel 1, Frames 50-51. Place another copy of it in Channel 1, Frames 54-55.

2. Continue with the bunny heads by placing a copy of nose (Cast Member 2) in Channel 1, Frames 52-53 and Frames 56-57. Place a copy of left (Cast Member 3) in Channel 1, Frames 58-60. Place right (Cast Member 4) in Channel 1, Frames 61-64. That completes the head.

3. Let's place a couple of different body positions in Channel 2. Place a copy of arms down (Cast Member 5) in Channel 2, Frames 50-54 and another copy in Frames 60-64. Place a copy of arms up (Cast Member 6) in Channel 2, Frames 55-59. Apply the Ink>Matte effect to all the bunny-part sprites in the Score. Your Score should resemble the following.

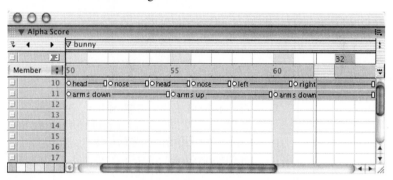

Feel free to experiment with this section of sprites. Make certain you are satisfied with how the bunny animates. Make any changes before going on to the next step.

4. Highlight all the sprites that comprise the bunny. Select Insert>Film Loop. Name the film loop "bunny" and then click OK. Be certain you don't move or rename any of the bunny cast members in the Cast at this point, or the film loop will not work correctly.

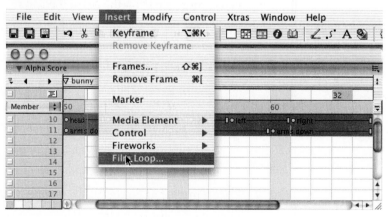

5. Delete the highlighted pieces of the bunny in Channels 1 and 2 in your Score. Navigate to the Cast and drag a copy of the film loop into Channel 3, Frames 50-63. If you need to move the bunny anywhere on Stage, be certain the whole sprite is selected in the Score before you move it.

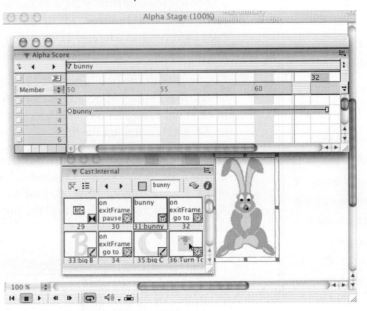

6. The rest of the page should contain Cast Members 22, 18, 33, and 37, and cover Frames 50-63. Cast Member 37 is a Back button, which needs a script that reads *go to "menuA-D"* (don't forget to include the quotes). Cast Member 33 is the big light pink B. Cast Member 18 is the word Bunny. Arrange your image so it resembles the following.

7. Place a marker at Frame 50, and name it "bunny".

8. Place a *go to "bunny"* (include quotes) script in the Frame script (the Script channel) of Frame 63.

Create the Cat Section

1. The next section is the Cat section, which should cover Frames 65-78. One at a time, drag one copy each of Cast Members 11, 19, 23, 35, and 37, and two copies of Cast Member 12 (the cat's eye) to the Score, and place them as shown in the following image. Make certain the cat's eyes have the Matte Ink effect applied to them, and are in front of the cat (use the Modify>Arrange menu item or arrange the sprites in the channels of the Score).

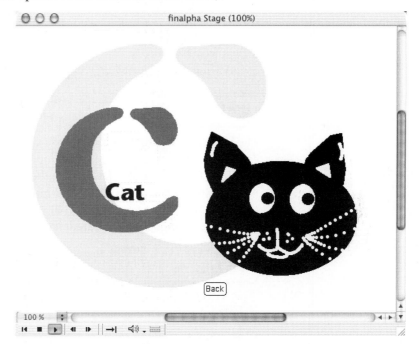

2. Add a *go to "cat"* script into the Frame script of Frame 78.

3. Place a marker at Frame 65 and name it "cat".

4. Let's make the cat's eyes follow the cursor. Place the eyeballs on the cat if they are not already there. Don't worry that the pupils are on the right side of the eyes and not at the bottom; they need to be this way for this Lingo script to work. Select Window>Library Palette.

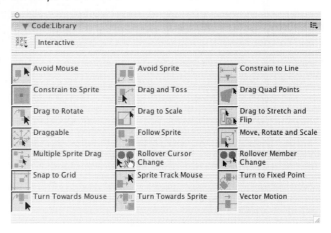

5. Select Animation>Interactive. Scroll down to Turn Towards Mouse and drag a copy of the behavior onto one of the eye sprites in the Cast. In the dialog box that pops up, select Towards the mouse from the Turn menu, select Always from the middle menu, and select Return to the initial position from the Otherwise menu. Click OK.

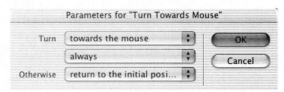

6. Repeat Step 5 for the second eye. The sprites can now spin and create the illusion of following the cursor when you play the movie.

Create the Dog Section

1. The Dog section is the last section you will work on in this project. The dog is easier to animate because he is made up of only one figure. Drag Cast Members 7, 8, 9, and 10 into Channel 1. Cast Member 7 goes into Frames 80-81, Cast Member 8 into Frames 82-83, Cast Member 7 into Frames 84-85, Cast Member 8 into Frames 86-87, Cast Member 9 into Frames 88-89, Cast Member 10 into Frames 90-91, Cast Member 9 into Frames 92-93, and Cast Member 10 into Frames 94-95.

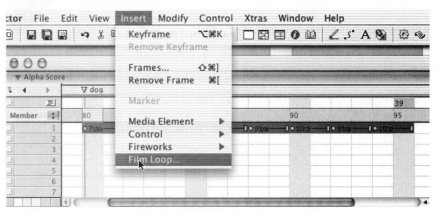

2. Highlight the dog pieces in Channel 1 and then select Insert>Film Loop. Name the film loop whatever you prefer, and then click OK. Delete the original pieces from the Score and replace them with the film loop you just made. Place the loop in Channel 2, Frames 80-95.

3. Place the rest of the elements. Cast Members 20, 24, 37, and 38 should match the image that follows. They should each cover Frames 80-95.

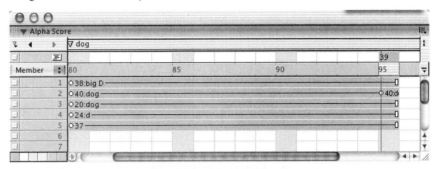

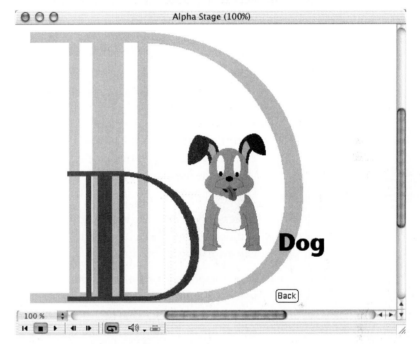

4. Place a *go to "dog"* (include quotes) script into the Frame script of Frame 95.

5. Place a marker at Frame 80 and name it "dog".

Create an Animated Cursor

The next section involves making an animated cursor and applying it to a few sprites using the Rollover Cursor Change behavior from the Library palette.

1. Select Insert>Media Element>Cursor.

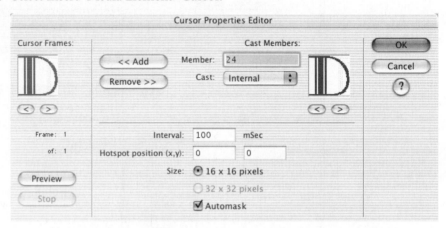

2. Click through the Cast Members section until you reach the letter A (Cast Member 21). Click Add to add Cast Members 21, 22, 23, and 24. Click the Preview button to view the animation. Click OK and it shows up as a cast member with a Cursor icon (green arrow) on it in the Cast.

If your cast members are in different positions than those of the final version of this project, you might need to change the Cursor Member drop-down menu to select the appropriate cursor member.

3. Assign rollovers to the letters A, B, C, and D on the Main menu page. First, select Window>Library Palette. Select Animation>Interactive, and you find the Rollover Cursor Change behavior.

4. Drag the behavior from the Library palette to the Score. Drop it onto one of the letter sprites in the menu section of the Score. Do the same for all four letters. Each time you apply the behavior, the following dialog box appears. In the dialog box, select Cursor member from the Choice of Type menu, select Finger from the Built-in Cursor menu, and select Member 43 of cast from the Cursor member menu. Click OK for each behavior.

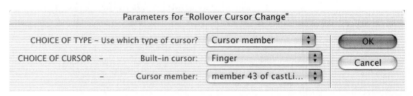

Add Sounds

1. Finally, let's add some music to the cat and dog. One at a time, double-click the cat (Cast Member 42) and dogs (Cast Member 41) sounds in the Cast, and check the Loop option, as shown in the following image.

2. Drag a copy of the cat sound into the Sound channel of Frames 65-78. Drag a copy of the dogs sound into the Sound channel of Frames 80-95.

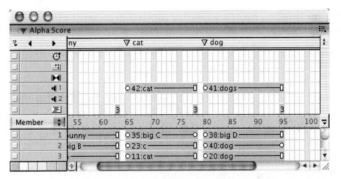

3. Rewind and play your production to view the result. If you have questions, you can refer to the completed version of this production by selecting **RF_Director>finalpha.dir.**

4. Save your changes and close Director.

Accessibility

The ability for a disabled user to use a Web site. Director has pre-scripted behaviors (in the Library Palette) to help make projects accessible for all.

AIFF File

A sound file saved in Audio Interchange File Format. Usually the file extension is .aiff or .aif.

Align Panel

A panel that provides a number of options for aligning objects, relative to each other or to the document.

Alignment

Positioning content to the left, right, center, top, or bottom.

Alpha Channel

An additional channel in an image that defines what parts of the image are transparent or semitransparent. Programs such as Adobe Illustrator, PhotoShop, Premiere, and After Effects use alpha channels to specify transparent regions in an image.

Animation

The technique of simulating movement by creating slight changes to an object or objects over time.

Apple Computer, Inc.

A computer manufacturer based in Cupertino, California. Apple was responsible for the development of the Macintosh computer and the graphical user interface.

Apple QuickTime

A format for providing digital audio, video, and presentations.

Art

Illustrations and photographs in general. All matter other than text that appears in a mechanical.

Audio

The electronic reproduction of audible sound.

AVI

Audio-Visual Interchange. A Windows-based digital video format. The file extension is usually .avi.

Background

A static object or color that lies behind all other objects.

Bandwidth

The transmission capacity, usually measured in bits per second (see BPS), of a network connection.

Behavior

A Lingo script that can be applied to a sprite using the drag-and-drop method.

Bit Depth

A measure of how many colors can be contained in an image. 8-bit color is 256 colors (2 x 2 x 2 x 2 x 2 x 2 x 2 x 2), 16-bit color is 32,768 colors (2 x 2 x 2 x 2 x 2 x 2 x 2 x 2 x 2 x 2 x 2 x 2 x 2 x 2 x 2), and so on.

Bitmap Image

An image constructed from individual dots or pixels set to a grid-like mosaic. The file must contain information about the color and position of each pixel, so the disk space needed for bitmap images can be very large.

Blank Keyframe

A keyframe that causes nothing to appear on the Stage. See also Keyframe.

BMP

A Windows bitmap image format that features low-quality and large file sizes.

Boldface

A heavier, blacker version of a typeface.

Border

A continual line that extends around an element.

Bounding Box

The rectangle area that appears around a sprite when the sprite is selected on the Stage. All sprites, even irregularly shaped ones, are contained within such an area. Ink effects relate to the entire bounding box when they are applied to a sprite.

Button

An element a user can click to cause an effect, such as the submission of a form.

Button State

A visual version of a button. For example, when clicked, the button is in its Down state; when dormant, it is in its Up state. When the mouse is hovered over the button, the button is in its Over state.

Cable Modem

A device connected to your computer that enables you to receive and send information from the Internet over your local cable TV line. The bandwidth of a cable modem far exceeds the bandwidth of the 28.8, 56 Kbps, or ISDN modems.

Cast

A database in which the elements of a Director movie are stored. Graphics, sounds, text fields, digital video, animations, color palettes, and Lingo scripts are all members of the Cast.

Cast Member

Any multimedia element residing in its own slot in the Cast window.

CD-R/CD-RW

A recordable CD disc and drive, also known as a "burner." A CD-R drive can write to a CD-R disc once; afterward, the disc cannot be erased or rewritten. CD-RW allows a CD-RW disc to be erased and rewritten. A CD-RW drive can also "burn" a CD-R disc.

CD-ROM

A device used to store approximately 600 MB of data. Files are permanently stored on the device and can be copied to a disk, but not altered directly.

Channel

A horizontal row of cells in the Score window. By default, there are 150 channels includng the Script channel, Transition channel, Color Palette channel, Tempo channel, and two Sound channels.

Check Box

A square that can be clicked to cause the form to send a name-value pair to the action; a form element that allows a user to choose zero or more choices.

Clip

A small piece of video or audio footage.

Clip Art

Collections of predrawn and digitized graphics.

Clipboard

The portion of computer memory that holds data that has been cut or copied. The next item cut or copied replaces the data already in the clipboard.

Color Picker

A function within a graphics application that assists in selecting or setting a color.

Comment

A line in a piece of programming code that is intended to be read, not executed.

Comp

Comprehensive artwork used to present the general color and layout of a page.

Compression

A technique used to reduce file size by analyzing occurrences of similar data. Compressed files occupy less space, and their use improves digital transmission speeds. Compression can sometimes result in a loss of image quality and/or resolution.

Compression Utility

A software program that reduces a file's size for storage on a disk.

Conditional Statement

An if-then statement.

Confirm Box

A pop-up box similar to an alert box, with both Yes and Cancel buttons.

Contrast

The relationship and degree of difference between the dark and light areas of an image.

Control Panel

The window that contains Director's playback controls and frames per second (fps) information.

Copyright

Ownership of a work. Permits the owner of material to prevent its use without express permission or acknowledgment of the originator. Copyright may be sold, transferred, or given up contractually.

Cursor

A small symbol that can be moved around a video screen. Used to indicate the position where data will be entered or an action taken.

Default

A specification for a mode of computer operation that occurs if no other is selected. The default font size might be 12 point, or a default color for an object might be white with a black border.

Dial-Up

Temporary connection (over a telephone line) to the computer of your ISP in order to establish a connection to the Internet.

Digital Video (DV)

Video information stored on tape or disk in digital format.

Dissolve

A gradual transition from shot to shot, in which the two images overlap.

Down State

A state that occurs when the user clicks a button.

Drop-Down Menu

A select list.

Editable Text

A text element that the user can modify by entering or deleting keystrokes.

Element

The smallest unit of a graphic, or a component of a page layout or design. Any object, text block, or graphic might be referred to as a design element.

Embedded Font

A font that is made part of a document.

Embedding

Including a complete copy of a text file or image within a document, with or without a link. See Linking.

End User

The person or persons who will be viewing and using your designs.

Event

Something that happens in a movie; for example, a user clicking a button or the movie reaching a specific frame.

Fade

The gradual appearance (or disappearance) of a picture, to or from black.

File

A specific collection of information stored on the computer disk, separate from all other information. Can be randomly accessed by the computer.

File Compression

The process of reducing the number of bytes in a file, file compression is usually used when transferring files between computers.

Fill

To add a tone or color to the area inside a closed object in a graphic illustration program.

Film Loop

A sequence of sprites encapsulated into a single cast member. The cast members from which the film loop is derived must also be present in the Cast.

Flat Color

Color that lacks contrast or tonal variation. Also called flat tint.

Flow Chart

A diagram of the structure of an interactive production, documenting the relationship between screens, scenes, and other discrete units.

Font

A font is the complete collection of all the characters (numbers, uppercase and lowercase letters, and in some cases, small caps and symbols) of a given typeface in a specific style; for example, Helvetica Bold.

Frame

An individual column in the Score. Can be referred to by number (Frame 15), or by the marker name attached to it.

Frame Rate

The number of successive images that are displayed in one second, designated fps (frames per second).

Frame Script

A Lingo script attached to an individual frame; placed in the Script channel of the frame.

Frame-by-Frame Animation

Animation using a series of keyframes with no tweening that creates a flip-book type of animation.

Function

A script that can be referenced by name.

GB

Gigabyte. A unit of measure equal to one billion (1,073,741,824) bytes.

GIF

Graphics Interchange Format. A popular graphics format for online clip art and drawn graphics. Graphics in this format are acceptable at low resolution. See JPEG.

Gradient

A gradual transition from one color to another. The shape of the gradient and the proportion of the two colors can be varied. Also known as blends, gradations, graduated fills, and vignettes.

Grayscale

1. An image composed in grays ranging from black to white, usually using 256 different tones. 2. A tint ramp used to measure and control the accuracy of screen percentages. 3. An accessory used to define neutral density in a photographic image.

Grid

A division of a page by horizontal and vertical guides into areas where text or graphics may be placed accurately.

GUI

Graphical User Interface. The basis of the Macintosh and Windows operating systems.

Hit State

The clickable area of a button.

Icon

A small graphic symbol used on the screen to indicate files, folders, or applications, activated by clicking with the mouse or pointing device.

If-Then Statement

A programming construction that executes one section of code if a particular expression is true, and a second section if it is not.

Import

To bring a file generated within one application into another application.

In-Betweening

See Tweening.

Interface

The design with which users interact.

Internet

A global system of interconnected computers.

Jaggies

Visible steps in the curved edge of a graphic or text character that result from enlarging a bitmapped image.

JPEG

A compression algorithm that reduces file size of bitmapped images, named for the Joint Photographic Experts Group, which created the standard. JPEG is "lossy" compression; image quality is reduced in direct proportion to the amount of compression.

Keyframe

An individual frame in a sequence of animation, from which other frames are extrapolated. For instance, a linear movement can be extrapolated from two keyframes, one at the beginning, and one at the end of the movement.

Lasso Tool

A selection tool in graphics applications.

Layer

A function of graphics applications in which elements may be isolated from each other, so a group of elements can be hidden from view, reordered, or otherwise manipulated as a unit, without affecting other elements in the composition.

Leading ("Ledding")

Space added between lines of type. Named after the strips of lead that used to be inserted between lines of metal type. In specifying type, lines of 12-pt. type separated by a 14-pt. space is abbreviated "12/14," or "twelve over fourteen."

Lingo

Macromedia Director's scripting language.

Linking

The act of placing a reference to one file (sound, graphic, or video) into another file. When the referenced file is modified, the placed reference is automatically (or manually, depending on the application) updated.

Looped Sound

A sound file with the Loop option checked in its Properties panel. Unless overridden by an action, it will play again and again.

Looping

The process of continually returning the playback head to a location until another action occurs, such as the movement of the mouse or the selection of a button.

Macromedia Director

A software program used for creating multimedia presentations, such as CD-ROMs and kiosks.

Macromedia Flash

A program used for creating vector-based animations.

Marquee

The blinking lines indicating the area selected with the selection tools. Also called "marching ants".

Masking

A technique used to display certain areas of an image or design; the shape and size of the top-most object or layer defines what is visible on lower layers.

Menu

A list of choices of functions or items, such as fonts.

Menu Bar

The strip across the top of your screen that contains the names of the menus availbale to you.

Movie

Collection if digital video (such as QuickTime) files.

Multimedia

The combination of sound, video images, and text to create an interactive document, program, or presentation.

Onion Skin Tools

Tools that enable you to edit one keyframe while viewing (dimly) other frames before and/or after the current frame.

Online

Currently connected to a computer network.

Opacity

1. The degree to which paper will show print through it. 2. The degree to which images or text below one object, whose opacity has been adjusted, are able to show through.

Operating System (OS)

The software that allows your computer to function. An example of an operating system is Mac OS X or Microsoft Windows.

Operator

A symbol or term used to perform a specific operation. For example, the asterisk (*) multiplies two values; the greater-than symbol (>) compares the first value against the second and decides which is larger.

Over State

A button state that occurs when the user passes the mouse over a button.

Palette

1. As derived from the term in the traditional art world, a collection of selectable colors. 2. Another name for a dialog box or menu of choices.

Pan

1. Horizontal turning of the camera during shooting; the camera base remains stationary. 2. An effect that makes a sound seem to move from left to right (or right to left).

Panel

In Macromedia's workspace, the name given to palettes of tools and options.

Parent

The master element to which secondary "child" elements are related. Can refer to ActionScripts, styles, graphic elements or objects, layers, folders, and Web site frames.

Parent-Child Relationships

The defined hierarchy of a set. For example, a parent job folder can contain individual Font and Image folders (children).

Password

Secret code you must enter after your user ID (login name) in order to log on to a computer.

Password Box

A text box that replaces all characters with a bullet or asterisk to hide their identity.

Pasteboard

In a page-layout program, the desktop area outside the printing-page area.

PDF

Portable Document Format. Developed by Adobe Systems, Inc. (read by Acrobat Reader), this format has become a de facto standard for document transfer across platforms.

PICS

Platform for Internet Content Selection. A method for creating an Internet rating for the Web page.

PICT/PICT2

A common format for defining bitmapped images on the Macintosh. The more recent PICT2 format supports 24-bit color.

Pixel

Picture Element. One of the tiny rectangular areas or dots generated by a computer or output device to constitute images. A greater number of pixels per inch results in higher resolution on screen or in print.

Platform

The type of computer or operating system on which a software application runs. Common platforms are Windows, Macintosh, UNIX and NeXT. When a program can be used on more than one of these platforms, it is termed cross-platform compatible.

Playback

The process of running/viewing a digital movie.

Playback Head

The red line in the score that travels during playback to indicate the currently active frame.

Plug-in

Small piece of software, usually from a third-party developer, that adds new features to another (larger) software application.

PNG

Portable Network Graphics. PNG is a new graphics format similar to GIF. It is a relatively new file format, and is not yet widely supported by most browsers.

Point

A unit of measurement used to specify type size and rule weight, equal to approximately 1/72 inch.

Polygon

A geometric figure, consisting of three or more straight lines enclosing an area. The triangle, square, rectangle, and star are all polygons.

Pop-Up Menu

A menu of choices accessed by clicking and dragging the current choice.

Portrait

Printing from left to right across the narrow side of the page. Portrait orientation on a letter-size page uses a standard 8.5-inch width and 11-inch length.

Preferences

A set of modifiable defaults for an application program.

Preloading

Causing the browser to download images or other items before they are needed, so when they are needed, they are already in the browser cache; improves the speed with which they appear.

Projector

A self-contained, self-running version of a Director movie. A Projector file can run on host systems without the Director application installed.

Property

An aspect or quality of an element.

Publish

The term used to describe a Web page that is made active on the Web.

Pull-Down Menu

A menu that displays additional options.

QuickTime

A standard for digital video. In order to operate QuickTime videos in conjunction with Director, a copy of QuickTime (or QuickTime for Windows) must be installed on the system.

Radio Button

A single round button that can be clicked to cause the form to send a name-value pair to the action.

Radio Group

A group of radio buttons with the same name. Only one radio button may be selected at a time within a radio group.

RAM

Random Access Memory. The "working" memory of a computer that holds files in process. Files in RAM are lost when the computer is turned off, whereas files stored on the hard drive or floppy disks remain available.

Raster Graphics

A class of graphics created and organized in a rectangular array of bitmaps. Often created by paint software or scanners.

Rasterize

The process of converting digital information into pixels. For example, the process used by an imagesetter to translate PostScript files before they are imaged to film or paper.

RealAudio

Client-server software system from RealNetworks enabling online users equipped with conventional multimedia computers and voice-grade telephone lines to browse, select, and play back audio or audio-based multimedia content on demand, in real time.

RealMedia

A term encompassing RealNetworks RealAudio and RealVideo.

RealVideo

A streaming technology developed by RealNetworks for transmitting live video over the Internet. RealVideo uses a variety of data compression techniques and works with both normal IP connections as well as IP Multicast connections.

Registration Point

In Director, the location considered to be the physical center of objects on the Stage. The registration point can be moved using the registration tool in the Paint editor; it does not have to be the actual center of the artwork.

Render

A real-time preview of clips and all effects as your production plays.

Resolution

The density of graphic information expressed in dots per inch (dpi) or pixels per inch (ppi).

RGB

1. The colors of projected light from a computer monitor that, when combined, simulate a subset of the visual spectrum. 2. The color model of most digital artwork. See also CMYK.

Right Alignment

Text having a straight right edge and a ragged or uneven left edge.

Rollover

The act of rolling the cursor over a given element on the screen.

Rotation

Turning an object at some angle to its original axis.

RTF

Rich Text Format. A text format that retains formatting information lost in pure ASCII text.

Ruler

Like a physical ruler, a feature of graphics software used for precise measurement and alignment of objects. See Grid.

Running Time

The duration of a program or a program segment.

Sans Serif

Fonts that do not have serifs. See Serif.

Scaling

The means within a program to reduce or enlarge the amount of space an image occupies by multiplying the data by a factor. Scaling can be proportional, or in one dimension only.

Score

The spreadsheet-like timeline where instructions and information about a Director movie are placed. In order to appear on the Stage during playback, a cast member must first be placed in the Score.

Screen Shot

A printed output or saved file that represents data from a computer monitor.

Scripting

The process of adding programming cababilities to a program (e.g., AppleScript), file (e.g., ActionScript), or Web page (e.g., JavaScript).

Scrub

Advancing or reversing a clip manually. Enables you to precisely identify and mark events.

Selection

The currently active object(s) in a window. Often made by clicking with the mouse or by dragging a marquee around the desired object(s).

Serif

A line or curve projecting from the end of a letterform. Typefaces designed with such projections are called serif faces.

Shareware

Software you can test for a certain amount of time to determine whether or not you want to buy it.

Sharpness

The subjective impression of the density difference between two tones at their boundary, interpreted as fineness of detail.

Shockwave

The technology used to compress, encapsulate, and embed Director movies in HTML documents for use on the Internet. Also used to refer to the plug-in necessary to view Shockwave movies in Microsoft Internet Explorer and Netscape Navigator browsers.

Shortcut

1. A quick method for accessing a menu item or command, usually through a series of keystrokes. 2. The icon that can be created in Windows to open an application without having to penetrate layers of various folders.

Silhouette

To remove part of the background of a photograph or illustration, leaving only the desired portion.

Skew

A transformation command that slants an object at an angle to the side from its initial fixed base.

Snap-To

An optional feature in graphics applications that drives objects to line up with guides, margins, or other objects if they are within a preset pixel range. This eliminates the need for very precise manual placement of an object with the mouse.

Soft Return

A return command that ends a line but does not apply a paragraph mark that would end the continuity of the style for that paragraph.

Sprite

An individual instance of a cast member on the Stage, placed in the Score. Individual sprites can be edited as necessary. Changes to the source cast member are immediately reflected in all sprites derived from that cast member.

Stage

The window in Director that represents the action transpiring during playback. When a Shockwave file or Projector is created from a movie, the Stage window becomes the only visible window.

Startup Disk

The disk from which the computer is set to start.

Stock Shot

A shot of a common occurrence: clouds, crowds, or cars. They are usually available for rent or purchase from agencies.

Storyboard

A series of sketches of the key visualization points of an event along with audio information. Often includes camera angles, any camera movement, and key phrases from script.

Streaming

The act of sending audio or video from the server to the browser in such a way that the browser (or plug-in) can play the audio or video as it arrives, rather than downloading it first.

Streaming Audio/Video

Technology that allows you to play audio or video while it is still downloading.

Stroke

The width and color attributes of a line.

Style

A defined set of formatting instructions for font and paragraph attributes, tabs, and other properties of text.

Surfing

Browsing the Web.

T-1

High-speed, high-bandwidth, leased-line connection to the Internet. A T-1 line can theoretically deliver information at 1.544 Mbps. Usually used at the corporate level, rather than for home use.

Target Audience

The audience selected or desired to receive a specific message.

Template

A document file containing layout, styles, and repeating elements (such as logos) by which a series of documents can maintain the same look and feel. A model publication you can use as the basis for creating a new publication.

Text Attribute

A characteristic applied directly to a letter or letters in text, such as bold, italic, or underline.

Text Box

A box into which users can type a single line of text. Also called a "text frame," or "text area."

Texture

1. A property of the surface of the substrate, such as the smoothness of paper. 2. Graphically, variation in tonal values to form image detail. 3. A class of fills in a graphics application that create various appearances, such as bricks, grass, tiles.

Theme

1. What the story is all about; its essential idea. 2. The opening and closing music in a show.

Thumbnails

1. The preliminary sketches of a design. 2. Small images used to indicate the content of a computer file.

Timeline

An object on the Director workspace that contains the sequence of frames, layers, and scenes composing an animation.

Toggle

A command that switches between either of two states at each application. Switching between Hide and Show is a toggle.

Tool Tip

Small text explaining the item to which the mouse is pointing.

Tracking

Adjusting the spacing of letters in a line of text to achieve proper justification or general appearance.

Transition

The change from one frame to another, including cuts, dissolves, blurs, blends, wipes, zooms, and many more.

Transparency

1. A full-color photographically-produced image on transparent film. 2. The quality of an image element that allows background elements to partially or entirely show through.

Trash

An icon on the desktop you use to discard programs, documents and folders. Also called trash can.

Tweening

A process by which the in-between frames of an animation are automatically generated by the developing application.

Up State

Normally a button's default state, which occurs when the user has not clicked or passed over the button with his mouse.

URL

Uniform Resource Locator. Address of any resource on the Web.

Variable

A unit of information that can be referred to by name.

Vector Graphics

Graphics defined using coordinate points and mathematically drawn lines and curves, which may be freely scaled and rotated without image degradation in the final output.

Video

1. Picture portion of a television program. 2. Non-broadcast production activities.

Video Card

The graphics card that ships with your computer. The graphics card is responsible for enabling the display or monitor in your computer setup. You can upgrade to a more powerful video card based on the configuration of your computer.

Vignette

An illustration in which the background gradually fades into the paper; that is, without a definite edge or border.

Web Designer

An individual who is the aesthetic and navigational architect of a Web site, determining how the site looks, how it is designed, and what components it contains.

Weight

1. The thickness of the strokes of a typeface. The weight of a typeface is usually denoted in the name of the font; for example, light, book, or ultra (thin, medium, and thick strokes, respectively). 2. The thickness of a line or rule.

White Space

Areas on the page that contain no images or type. Proper use of white space is critical to a well-balanced design.

Zooming

The process of electronically enlarging or reducing an image on a monitor to facilitate detailed design or editing and navigation.

Academic and
Information Services
Library